INDIANA
BIOGRAPHICAL
DICTIONARY

INDIANA
BIOGRAPHICAL
DICTIONARY

PEOPLE OF ALL TIMES AND ALL PLACES
WHO HAVE BEEN IMPORTANT TO THE HISTORY
AND LIFE OF THE STATE

SOMERSET PUBLISHERS, INC.
521 Fifth Ave., 17th Floor
New York, N.Y. 10175

I.S.B.N. No. 0-403-09967-6

Library of Congress Cataloging-in-Publication Data

Indiana biographical dictionary : people of all times and all places
who have been important to the history and life of the state.
      p.   cm.
   ISBN 0-403-09967-6 :
   1. Indiana--Biography--Dictionaries. 2. Indiana--History.
CT233.I53 1993
   920.0772--dc20
                                                        93-32276
                                                            CIP

LIST OF PERSONS

DUNBAR
  JAMES WHITSON,
DUNHAM
  CYRUS LIVINGSTON,
DUNN
  GEORGE GRUNDY,
  GEORGE HEDFORD,
DUNNING
  PARIS C.,
DURBIN
  WINFIELD,
EDGERTON
  JOSEPH KETCHUM,
ELLIOTT
  RICHARD NASH,
EMBREE
  ELISHA,
EVANS
  DAVID WALTER,
  JAMES LA FAYETTE,
EWING
  JOHN,
FAIRBANKS
  CHARLES WARREN,
FAIRFIELD
  LOUIS WILLIAM,
FARIS
  GEORGE WASHINGTON,
FARLEY
  JAMES INDUS,
FARQUHAR
  JOHN HANSON,
FISHER
  CARL GRAHAM,
FITCH
  GRAHAM NEWELL,
FOLEY
  JAMES BRADFORD,
FORD
  GEORGE,
FOSTER
  JOHN HOPKINS,
  NORMAN,

FRICK
  FORD CHRISTOPHER,
FULLER
  BENONI STINSON,
GARDNER
  FRANK,
GARRIGUE
  JEAN,
GATES
  RALPH F.,
GEER
  WILL AUGHE,
GERARD
  DAVE,
GILBERT
  NEWTON WHITING,
GILHAMS
  CLARENCE CHAUNCEY,
GILLEN
  COURTLAND CRAIG,
GILLIE
  GEORGE W.,
GIMBEL
  BERNARD FEUSTMAN,
GIRDLER
  TOM MERCER,
GOODRICH
  JAMES P.,
GORMAN
  WILLIS ARNOLD,
GRAHAM
  WILLIAM,
GRANT
  ROBERT ALLEN,
GRAY
  FINLY HUTCHINSON,
  ISAAC P.,
GREENWOOD
  ARTHUR HERBERT,
GREGG
  JAMES MADISON,
GRIFFITH
  FRANCIS MARION,

vi

LIST OF PERSONS

GRISSOM
  VIRGIL IVAN "GUS",
GRISWOLD
  GLENN HASENFRATZ,
GUTHRIE
  ALFRED BERTRAM, JR,
HALL
  KATIE BEATRICE,
HALLECK
  CHARLES,
HAMILTON
  ANDREW HOLMAN,
  LEE HERBERT,
HAMMOND
  ABRAM A.,
  THOMAS,
HANDLEY
  HAROLD W.,
HANLY
  JAMES FRANKLIN,
HANNAGAN
  STEVE JEROME,
HARDEN
  CECIL MURRAY,
HARDY
  ALEXANDER MERRILL,
HARLAN
  ANDREW JACKSON,
HARNESS
  FOREST ARTHUR,
HARRISON
  BENJAMIN,
  WILLIAM HENRY,
HARTKE
  RUPERT VANCE,
HARVEY
  RALPH,
HATCH
  JETHRO AYERS,
HATCHER
  RICHARD GORDON,
HAYES
  PHILIP HAROLD,

HAYMOND
  WILLIAM SUMMER
  VILLE,
HAYNES
  ELWOOD,
HEILMAN
  WILLIAM,
HENDRICKS
  THOMAS,
  WILLIAM,
HEROD
  WILLIAM,
HICKEY
  ANDREW JAMES,
HILER
  JOHN PATRICK,
HILL
  RALPH,
HILLIS
  ELWOOD HAYNES,
HOGAN
  EARL LEE,
HOGG
  DAVID,
HOLLIDAY
  ELIAS SELAH,
HOLLOWAY
  DAVID PIERSON,
HOLMAN
  WILLIAM STEELE,
HOVEY
  ALVIN P.,
HOWARD
  JONAS GEORGE,
  TILGHMAN ASHURST,
HUDNUT
  WILLIAM HERBERT,
HUGHES
  JAMES,
HUMPHREYS
  ANDREW,
HUNTER
  MORTON CRAIG,

LIST OF PERSONS

PEELLE
STANTON JUDKINS,
PESHEWAH
PETTIT
JOHN UPFOLD,
PHILLIPS
DAVID GRAHAM,
PORTER
ALBERT G.,
COLE,
GENE (VA) STRATTON,
POSEY
FRANCIS BLACKBURN,
PRATT
(DANIE) DARWIN,
PRICE
BYRON,
PRINCE
WILLIAM,
PROFFIT
GEORGE H.,
PURNELL
FRED SAMPSON,
QUAYLE
J. DANFORTH (DAN),
RALSTON
SAMUEL,
RANDALL
JAMES GARFIELD,
RARIDEN
JAMES,
RAUCH
GEORGE WASHINGTON,
RAY
JAMES BROWN,
REXROTH
KENNETH,
RICKEY
GEORGE WARREN,
RILEY
JAMES WHITCOMB,
ROBINSON
ARTHUR RAYMOND,

JAMES MCCLELLAN,
JOHN LARNE,
MILTON STAPP,
ROCKHILL
WILLIAM,
ROCKNE
KNUTE KENNETH,
ROEMER
TIM,
ROREM
NED,
ROUDEBUSH
RICHARD LOWELL,
ROUSH
JOHN EDWARD,
ROYSE
LEMUEL WILLARD,
SAMPLE
SAMUEL CALDWELL,
SANDERS
EVERETT,
SAYLER
HENRY BENTON,
SCHRICKER
HENRY F.,
SCHULTE
WILLIAM THEODORE,
SCOTT
HARVEY DAVID,
SEXTON
LEONIDAS,
SHAFER
PAUL WERNTZ,
SHANKS
JOHN PETER CLEAVER,
SHARP
PHILIP RILEY,
SHIVELY
BENJAMIN FRANKLIN,
SISSLE
NOBLE,

x

LIST OF PERSONS

SKELTON
  RICHARD BERNARD,
  "RED",
SKIDMORE
  LOUIS,
SMITH
  CALEB BLOOD,
  THOMAS,
  WALTER BEDELL,
SPRINGER
  RAYMOND SMILEY,
STEELE
  GEORGE WASHINGTON,
  THEODORE CLEMENT,
STILWELL
  THOMAS NEEL,
STOCKSLAGER
  STROTHER MADISON,
TAGGART
  THOMAS,
TAYLOR
  ARTHUR HERBERT,
  WALLER,
TECUMSEH
TEST
  JOHN,
THOMAS
  JESSE BURGESS,
TIPTON
  JOHN,
TOWNSEND
  M. CLIFFORD,
TRACEWELL
  ROBERT JOHN,
TUCKER
  FORREST,
TYNER
  JAMES NOBLE,
UPDIKE
  RALPH EUGENE,
UREY
  HAROLD CLAYTON,

VAN NUYS
  FREDERICK,
VESTAL
  ALBERT HENRY,
VISCLOSKY
  PETER,
VON ZELL
  HARRY,
VONNEGUT
  KURT, JR.,
VOORHEES
  DANIEL WOLSEY,
WAKEFIELD
  DAN,
WALLACE
  DAVID,
  LEWIS,
WALSH
  JOHN RICHARD,
WAMPLER
  FRED,
WARD
  MARY JANE,
  THOMAS BAYLESS,
WAUGH
  DANIEL WEBSTER,
WAYNE
  ANTHONY,
WEBB
  CLIFTON,
WEBER
  DICK,
WELSH
  MATTHEW E.,
WEST
  JESSAMYN,
WHITCOMB
  EDGAR D.,
  JAMES,
WHITE
  MICHAEL DOHERTY,
WICK
  WILLIAM WATSON,

A

ADAIR, EDWIN ROSS, (1907-   ) - a U. S. Representative from Indiana; born in Albion, Noble County, Indiana, December 14, 1907; attended grade and high schools in Albion, Indiana; was graduated from Hillsdale (Michigan) College, A.B., 1928, and from George Washington University Law School, Washington, D.C., LL. B., 1933; was admitted to the Indiana bar in 1933 and commenced the practice of law in Fort Wayne, Indiana; probate commissioner of Allen County, Indiana, 1940-1950; during World War II was called to active duty as a second lieutenant in the Quartermaster Corps Reserve in September 1941 and served until October 1945; awarded battle stars for the Normandy, Northern France, Ardennes, Rhine, and Central European campaigns; delegate or official at all Indiana State Republican Conventions since 1945; elected as a Republican to the Eighty-second and to the nine succeeding Congresses (January 3, 1951-January 3, 1971); unsuccessful candidate for reelection in 1970 to the Ninety-second Congress; is a resident of Fort Wayne, Indiana.

ADAIR, JOHN ALFRED MCDOWELL, (1864-1938) - a U. S. Representative from Indiana; born near Portland, Jay County, Indiana, December 22, 1864; attended the public schools and Portland High School; engaged in mercantile pursuits; clerk of the city of Portland 1888-1890; clerk of Jay County 1890-1895; studied law; was admitted to the bar in 1895 and commenced practice in Portland, Indiana; member of the State house of representatives in 1902 and 1903; engaged in banking, being elected president of the First National Bank of Portland in 1904; elected as a Democrat to the Sixtieth and to the four succeeding Congresses (March 4, 1907-March 3, 1917); did not seek renomination in 1916, having become a gubernatorial candidate; unsuccessful Democratic nominee for Governor of Indiana in 1916; resumed the banking business in Portland, Indiana; moved to Washington, D.C., in 1924 and served as vice president of Southern Dairies (Inc.) until 1931; chairman of the board of the Finance Service Co., in Baltimore, Maryland, 1933-1935; vice president of the Atlas Tack Corporation, Fairhaven, Massachusetts, 1935-1937; director of the Artloom Corporation, Philadelphia, Pennsylvania, in 1937; died in Portland, Indiana, October 5, 1938.

ADE, GEORGE, (1866-1944) - humorist and playwright, was born in Kentland, Indiana on February 9, 1866. He attended Purdue University, earning a B.S. degree in 1887. After his graduation, Ade worked for two Lafayette newspapers, then moved to Chicago in 1890 where he became a reporter for the Chicago *Morning News*, (later the *Record*). During his years with that paper, he published books that included *Artie*, 1896, *Pink Marsh*, 1897, and *Doc' Horne*. According to one source, "In 1898, Ade wrote his first "fable in slang," *The Blond Girl Who Married a Bucket Shop*. This fable established the formula for Ade: colloquial expressions, irregular capitalizations, characters out of everyday life, a moral frequently seasoned with impertinence.

In 1900, Ade left newspaper work and toured such countries as Japan, China, and the Philippines. For a period of ten years, he continued to write stories and later compiled a number of them into the book *Fables in Slang*, (1900). That same year, he published a second compilation, *More Fables*, and the following year, a third, entitled *Forty Modern Fables*. Ade's unique way with language, noted by one writer as "a picturesque prose with numerous racy colloquialisms and many luxuriant figures of speech," garnered him the description "the Shakespeare of slang" by the British.

Later books by Ade included: *The Girl Proposition*, 1902; *People You Know*, 1903; *In Babel*, 1903; *Breaking into Society*, 1903; *True Bills*, 1904; *In Pastures New*, 1906; *The Slim Princess*, 1907; *Knocking the Neighbors*, 1912; *Ade's Fables*, 1914; *Hand-Made Fables*, 1920; *Single Blessedness*, 1922; *Bang! Bang!*, 1928; *The Old-Time Saloon*, 1931; and *Thirty Fables*, 1933.

Ade began writing plays in 1920 starting with *The Sultan of Sulu*. Others included *The County Chairman*, 1903; *The College Widow*, 1904; *The Sho-Gun*, 1904; *The Bad Samaritan*, 1905; *The Fair Co-ed*, 1908; and *Father and the*

Boys, 1908. *The College Widow* was later made into the musical comedy, *Leave It to Jane*, with famed composer Jerome Kern providing the music.

Ade died on May 16, 1944 in Brook, Indiana.

AKINS, CLAUDE, (1918-   ) - actor, was born in Bedford, Indiana Akins built a solid career as a character actor in such prominent movies as *From Here To Eternity* in 1953, *The Caine Mutiny* in 1954, *The Defiant Ones* and *Onionhead* in 1958, *Rio Bravo* in 1959, *Inherit The Wind* in 1960 and *How The West Was Won* in 1962. After building up numerous movie credits, he found work in television in shows such as the *Night Stalker* and *In Tandem* and eventually starred in three of his own television series, *Movin' On* in 1974, *B.J. and the Bear* in 1979 and *The Misadventures of Sheriff Lobo* in 1979.

ALBERTSON, NATHANIEL, (1800-1863) - a U. S. Representative fron Indiana; born in Fairfax, Fairfax County, Virginia, June 10, 1800; moved to Salem, Washington County, Indiana, and engaged in agricultural pursuits; member of the State house of representatives 1838-1840; moved to Floyd County in 1835 and settled in Greenville, near New Albany, and resumed agricultural pursuits; elected as a Democrat to the Thirty-first Congress (March 4, 1849-March 3, 1851); unsuccessful candidate for reelection in 1850 to the Thirty-second Congress; resumed agricultural pursuits in Floyd County; moved to Boonville, Missouri, in 1856 and continued mercantile pursuits; settled in Central City, Gilpin County, Colorado, in 1860 and engaged in the hotel business; also became interested in mining; died in Central City, Colorado, December 16, 1863.

AMES, LEON, (1903-) - actor, was born Leon Wycoff, in Portland, Indiana on January 20, 1903, to Charles and Cora Wycoff. He attended the University of Indiana, and before he started acting, he worked at such diverse jobs as shoe salesman and as a barnstorming flyer.

Leon Ames worked extensively in the theater at the beginning of his career, starting in 1925 with a stock company in Pennsylvania called the Charles K. Champlin players. He worked in touring companies in various U.S. cities and performed numerous plays in New York, starting with his first role as Gordon Reese in *Bright Honor*, in 1936. Interspersed between his theater jobs was his work in movies, beginning with the 1932 film *Murders in the Rue Morgue*. After he made a handful of films, Leon changed his last name to Ames.

In his films, Ames was equally adept at drama (*Thirty Seconds Over Tokyo*, in 1944; *The Postman Always Rings Twice*, in 1956; *Tora, Tora, Tora*, in 1970), or lighthearted comedies and musicals (*Meet Me in St. Louis*, in 1944; *Yolanda and the Thief* and *Anchors Aweigh*, in 1945; *On a Clear Day You Can See Forever*, 1960).

Ames also found work on television, beginning with his role as Father Day in the series *Life With Father*, in 1953. He was also in the series *Father of the Bride*, and appeared on several programs, including *Beverly Hillbillies*, *The Andy Griffith Show*, *Mr. Ed*, *Bewitched* and *Name of the Game*.

He served as the president of the Screen Actors Guild in 1957, and as Director of the Motion Picture Relief Fund.

He married former actress Christine Gossett in 1938, and they had two children, Shelley and Leon Jr.

ANDERSON, MARGARET, (1893?-1973) - editor. Born in Indianapolis, Indiana, she left home at a very young age, deciding that a bourgeois existence was not her style. Trusting her gut instincts, she set out to find her happiness in the artistic community. She decided to provide an open forum for writers of all kinds and in 1914, she published a magazine called *Little Review*, which according to her, espoused "Life For Art's Sake."
On a nearly non-existent budget, Margaret and close friend Jane Heap provided an opportunity for writers to state their views on subjects that were considered ahead of their time. Some of the most brilliant minds of the day, such as radical feminist Emma Goldman and Frederick Neitzsche contributed their work without any monetary compensation. The scope of good writers widened after Ezra Pound became the foreign editor in 1917. Legendary writers such as T.S. Eliot and William Yeats added their considerable contributions to an already impressive publication.

Immediately after moving the magazine from Chicago to New York in 1918, Anderson decided to publish a serialization of James Joyce's *Ulysses* and the fallout from that decision was significant. The New York postal authorities confiscated four issues and burned them and the magazine had to fight an obscenity charge in court.

Anderson made Paris her final home in 1924, where the *Little Review* continued to flourish. She also published a series of three autobiographies, *My Thirty Years' War*, in 1930, *The Fiery Fountains*, in 1950 and *The Strange Necessity* in 1969.

She died in France on October 18, 1973.

B

BAKER, CONRAD, (1817-1885) - governor of Indiana (1867- 1873), was born on February 12, 1817 in Franklin County, Pennsylvania, the son of Conrad and Catherine (Winterheimer) Baker. He attended Pennsylvania College in Gettysburg, then studied law and was admitted to the bar. After practicing for two years, he moved to Evansville, Indiana. He served a term in the Indiana House of Representatives from 1845 to 1846. Active in Republican politics, he won the Republican nomination for lieutenant governor in 1856, but was defeated in the general election.

When the Civil War began in 1861, Baker joined the Union forces as colonel of the First Cavalry, 28th Regiment of Indiana Volunteers. He served until 1864 when he once again received the Republican nomination for lieutenant governor. Campaigning on a ticket with Oliver P. Morton, Baker won the lieutenant governorship and took office in January, 1865. Later that year when Governor Morton suffered a stroke, Baker carried out the executive duties until the Governor regained his health. In January, 1867, Morton resigned to take a seat in the U.S. Senate and Baker was sworn in to serve out the remainder of his gubernatorial term. Baker was elected to a full term as governor in 1868. His administration was marked by the establishment of various institutions: a normal school in Terre Haute, a women's prison, a refuge house for juvenile offenders, and a retirement home for soldiers.

After leaving office in 1873, Baker practiced law in Indianapolis. He died on April 28, 1885. Conrad Baker was married twice: 1) to Matilda Sommers in 1838, who died in 1855, and 2) to Charlotte Chute in 1858. He had two children by his first marriage, and four children by his second.

BAKER, JOHN HARRIS, (1832-1915) - a U. S. Representative from Indiana; born in Parma Township, Monroe County, New York, February 28, 1832; moved with his parents to the present county of Fulton, Ohio; attended the public schools; taught school; attended the Wesleyan University in Delaware, Ohio, two years; studied law in Adrian, Michigan; was admitted to the bar in 1857 and commenced practice in Goshen, Indiana; member of the State senate in 1962, but, being a notary public at the time, was unseated because the State constitution forbid the simultaneous holding of two lucrative offices; elected as a Republican to the Forty-fourth, Forty-fifth, and Forty-sixth Congresses (March 4, 1875-March 3, 1881); declined to be a candidate for renomination in 1880; resumed the practice of law in Goshen, Indiana; delegate to the Republican National Convention at Chicago in 1888 that nominated Harrison and Morton; appointed judge of the United States District Court for Indiana by President Harrison in 1892 and served until his retirement in 1904; resided in Goshen, Elkhart County, Indiana, until his death on October 21, 1915.

BARBOUR, LUCIEN, (1811-1880) - a U. S. Representative from Indiana; born in Canton, Hartford County, Conneticut, March 4, 1811; was graduated from Amherst (Massachusetts) College in 1837; moved to Indiana the same year and settled in Madison, Jefferson County; studied law; was admitted to the bar and commenced practice in Indianapolis, Indiana, in 1839; acted a nmuber of times as arbitraytor between the State of Indiana and private corporations; appointed United States district attorney for the district attorney for the district of Indiana by President Polk; member of the commission to codify the laws of Indiana in 1852; elected by a combination of the Free Soil,

Temperance, and Know Nothing Parties to the Thirty-fourth Congress (March 4, 1855- March 3;, 1857); was not a candidate for renomination in 1856; affiliated with the Republican Party in 1860; practiced law in Indianapolis, Indiana, until his death in that city on July 19, 1880.

BARNARD, WILLIAM OSCAR, (1852-1939) - a U. S. Representative from Indiana; born near Liberty, Union County, Indiana, October 25, 1852; moved with his parents to Dublin, Wayne County, Indiana, in 1854, to Fayette County in 1856, and to Henry County in 1866; attended the common schools and Spiceland Academy, Spiceland, Indiana; taught school for five years in Henry and Wayne Counties; studied law; was admitted to the bar in 1876 and commenced practice in Newcastle, Indiana; prosecuting attorney of the eighteenth and fifty-third judicial circuits 1887-1893; judge of the fifty-third judicial circuit court of Indiana 1896-1902; resumed the practice of law in Newcastle; elected as a Republican to the Sixty-first Congress (March 4, 1909-March 3, 1911); unsuccessful candidate for reelection in 1910 to the Sixty-second Congress; resumed the practice of law in Newcaslte, Indiana, until his death there on April 8, 1939.

BARNHART, HENRY A., (1858-1934) - a U. S. Representative from Indiana; born near Twelve Mile, Cass County, Indiana, September 11, 1858; attended the common schools, Amboy Academy, and Wabash Normal Training School; taught school; moved to Liberty Township, Fulton County, in 1881 and engaged in agricultural pursuits until 1884; moved to Rochester, Indiana, in 1885 and served as surveyor of Fulton County 1885-1887; owner and editor of the Rochester Sentinel 1886-1924; president and manager of the Rochester Telephone Co. 1895-1934; president of the Indiana Telephone Association; president of the National Telephone Association; director of the United States Bank & Trust Co.; appointed a director of the Indiana State Prison in 1893 and a trustee of the State hospital for the insane in 1903; elected as a Democrat to the Sixtieth Congress to fill the vacancy caused by the death of Abram L. Brick, reelected to the Sixty-first and to the four succeeding Congresses and served from November 3, 1908, to

March 3, 1919; unsuccessful candidate for reelection in 1918 to the Sixty-sixth Congress; resumed his activities in the newspaper publishing business and in the telephone business; also engaged as a lecturer and in agricultural pursuitrs; died in Rochester, Indiana, March 26, 1934.

BARR, JOSEPH WALKER, (1918-1969) - a U. S. Representative from Indiana; born in Bicknell, Knox County, Indiana, January 17, 1918; graduated from DePauw University in 1939 and from Harvard University in 1941; during World War II served in the United States Navy 1942-1945 with subchaser duty in the Mediterranean and Atlantic; rode assault wave in invasion of Sicily, Salerno, Anzio, and South France; received Bronze Star for sinking submarine off Anzio Beach; engaged in the operation of grain elevators, theaters, real-estate, and publishing business; member of the Juvenile Court Advisory Board and Central Indiana Boy Scouts of America Board; elected as a Democrat to the Eighty- sixth Congress (January 3, 1959-January 3, 1961); unsuccessful candidate for reelection in 1960 to the Eighty-seventh Congress; appointed assistant for congressional relations to the Secretary of the Treasury, 1961; appointed Chairman, Federal Deposit Insurance Corporation, 1963; Under Secretary of the Treasury, 1965-1968; appointed by President Johnson as Secretary of the Treasury, December 21, 1968, to January 20, 1969; vice chairman of American Security and Trust Company from February to October 1969.

BASS, SAM, (1851-1878) - outlaw. Bass was born on July 21, 1851, near Mitchell, Indiana. He lost both of his parents by the time he was thirteen and his education was almost negligible. When he turned 18, he left Indiana and moved around until he finally settled in Denton, Texas. After trying a few jobs, he became a deputy sheriff, but somehow along the way, he ended up on the other side of the law.

His infamous outlaw career began with horse-stealing from Indian herds. By the time he moved to the mining town of Deadwood, South Dakota, he was a member of a gang that made raids on stagecoaches. In Big Springs, Nebraska, in September of 1877, they robbed a Union Pacific train of $65,000 in gold and other valuables. The gang attemped to escape the law by fleeing through Kansas and Missouri, but many lost their lives. Bass was able to escape that fate and he returned to Denton in 1878 and created a new gang of outlaws. They continued their train-robbing spree throughout the Dallas area. One of the outlaws who had been captured, turned informant and he helped the Texas Rangers set a trap at a bank the gang had earmarked as their next target. In the inevitable gunfight that followed, Sam Bass was shot, and died two days later on his twenty-seventh birthday, July 21, 1878.

BAXTER, ANNE, (1923-1985) - actress, was born on May 7, 1923 in Michigan City, Indiana, the daughter of Kenneth and Catherine Baxter, and granddaughter of famed architect Frank Lloyd Wright. She attended a variety of schools whose curriculums were based on the dramatic arts, including Theodora Irvine's School of the Theater and The 20th Century Fox Studio School.

In 1936, she made her theater debut in New York as Elizabeth Winthrop in the Henry Miller play, *Seen But Not Heard*, and appeared in numerous plays in the years following. However, film was where she made her mark. She spent her first few years in movies as the wholesome, girl-next-door type. That situation was to change drastically, when in 1946, she played the role of Sophie MacDonald in Somerset Maugham's, *The Razor's Edge*. The character was a tragic one which allowed Baxter to display a full range of emotions. She won an Academy Award for best supporting actress of that year. But her most famous role was yet to come. In 1950, Baxter was cast as Eve Harrington, opposite the formidable Bette Davis as Margo Channing in *All About Eve*. The role won her more critical praise and another Oscar nomination. In 1971 she did a turnabout and played the Margo Channing role in the stage production, *Applause*, which was the musical version of "Eve."

Through the years, she has also made appearances in television dramas such as *Mannix*, *Marcus Welby* and *Columbo*.

She succeeded Bette Davis as grande dame Victoria Cabot in prime- time telivision soap opera *Hotel* in 1983 and remained in that role until her death on Dec. 12, 1985.

She was married to the late actor John Hodiak for seven years with whom she had one daughter. They divorced in 1953, and a few years later she married rancher Randolph Galt, with whom she had two more daughters. They divorced in 1970.

BAYH, BIRCH EVANS JR., (1928-   ) - U.S. Senator and politician, was born on Jan. 22 in Terre Haute, Indiana.

Bayh still owns and manages the Shirkieville, Indiana farm where he once lived with his grandfather. Bayh temporarily abandoned his rural environment in 1946 to serve a two year term in the U.S. Army, and later to spend four years at Purdue University where he earned a B.S. degree in Agriculture in 1951. Soon after graduating, he married the former Marvella Hern and returned to his first interest of farming. Bayh gradually became involved in politics and in 1954 he began an eight-year stay in the Indiana House of Representatives where he served as the Democratic Minority Leader in 1957 and 1961 and as Speaker of the House in 1959. During this time, he also attended law school at Indiana University. In 1962, two years after he received his law degree, he ran a successful race against Homer Capehart for the U.S. Senate. Bayh was able to maintain his seat in the two successive elections, defeating William Ruckelshaus in 1968 and Richard Lugar in 1974.

Following the assassination of President Kennedy, Bayh as chairman (1963) of the U.S. Senate Judicary Subcommittee, introduced the amendment on presidential disability. this legislation, which became the 25th Amendment in 1967, allowed for the filling of a Vice-Presidential vacancy through the approval of a presidential choice by a majority vote in both houses of Congress.

Bayh was also influential in the writing and passage of the 26th Amendment which gave the vote to 18-year olds. His strong support of civil rights was also instrumental in winning Senate approval of the Equal Rights Amendment which, if ratified, will prohibit discrimination based on sex.

Bayh is also known for his opposition to two Nixon Supreme Court nominees. Bayh's successful campaign against the two would be appointees - W. Clement Haynsworth and G. Harrold Carswell was a result of a thorough screening of the men's ethical conduct, which Bayh felt did not live up to the needed standards.

In 1972, Bayh ran a well-supported campaign for the Democratic presidential nomination, but withdrew when his wife became ill.

BEAMER, JOHN VALENTINE, (1896-1911) - a U. S. Representative from Indiana; born on a farm in Wabash County, Indiana, November 17, 1896; attended the public schools of Roann, Indiana; was graduated from Wabash College, Crawfordville, Indiana, in 1918; during the First World War served in the Field Artillery; employed with Service Motor Truck Co., Wabash, Indiana, 1919-1921; representative for the Century Co., school textbook publisher, New York and Chicago, 1921-1928; vice president and general manager, Wabash (Indiana) Baking Powder & Chemical Co., 1928-1941; vice president and sales manager, Union Rock Wool Corp., Wabash, Indiana, 1935-1942; owner and operator of a farm near Wabash, Indiana; served in the State house of representatives in 1949 and 1950.

BEARD, MARY, (1876-1958) - author, was born in Indianapolis on August 5, 1876. Mary Beard (nee Ritter) married Charles Beard in 1900 and co-wrote several books with him including *American Citizenship*, in 1913, *History of the United States*, in 1921 and *America in Mid-Passage*, in 1939. Her solo writing efforts included *A Short History of the American Labor Movement*, in 1920 (revised 1925), *America Through Women's Eyes*, in 1934 and *Women As a Force In History*, in 1946. She also collaborated on an anthology with Martha Bensley Bruere called *Laughing Their Way: Women's Humor In America*, in 1934.

Mary Beard died on August 14, 1958.

BENHAM, JOHN SAMUEL, (1863-1935) - a U. S. Representative from Indiana; born on a farm near Benham, Ripley County, Indiana, October 24, 1863; attended the public schools, a business college in Delaware, Ohio, and a normal school in Brookville, Indiana; taught school in the winter and attended college in the summer, being engaged as a teacher in various places in Indiana from 1882 to 1907; was graduated from Indiana State Normal School at Terre Haute,

Indiana, in 1893 and from Indiana University at Blooming-ton, Indiana, in 1903; specialized in history at the University of Chicago for several terms; superintendent of schools for Ripley County for fourteen years; returned to Benham, Indiana, in 1907 and engaged in the timber, milling, and contracting business; also followed agricultural pursuits; served as chairman of the Republican county committee in 1916; delegate to the Republican National Convention at Chicago in 1916 that nominated Hughes and Fairbanks; elected as a Republican to the Sixty-sixth and Sixty-seventh Congresses (March 4, 1919-March 3, 1923); unsuccessful candidate for reelection in 1922 to the Sixty-eighth Congress; moved to Batesville, Ripley County, Indiana, in 1923 and engaged as a building contractor; again superintendent of schools for Ripley County, Indiana, 1924-1929; retired from active business pursuits in 1931 and resided in Batesville, Indiana, until his death there on December 11, 1935.

BEVERIDGE, ALBERT JEREMIAH, (1862-1927) - a U. S. Senator from Indiana; born near Sugar Tree Ridge, Concord Township, Highland County, Ohio, October 6, 1862; attended the common schools; was graduated from Indiana Asbury (now De Pauw) University, Greencastle, Indiana, in 1885; studied law; was admitted to the bar in 1887 and commenced practice in Indianapolis, Indiana; elected as a Republican to the United States Senate on January 17, 1899, reelected in 1905, and served from March 4, 1899, until March 3, 1911; unsuccessful candidate for reelection in 1910; returned to Indianapolis and engaged in literary pursuits; unsuccessful Progressive candidate for Governor of Indiana in 1912; chairman of the National Progressive Convention at Chicago in 1912; unsuccessful candidate as a Progressive in 1914 and as a Republican in 1922 for election to the United States Senate; died in Indianapolis, Indiana, April 27, 1927.

BICKNELL, GEORGE AUGUSTUS, (1815-1891) - a U. S. Representative from Indiana; born in Philadelphia, Pennsylvania, February 6, 1815; was graduated from the University of Pennsylvania at Philadelphia in 1831; attended Yale Law School one year; completed the study of law; was admitted to the bar in 1836 and commenced practice in New

York City; moved to Lexington, Scott County, Indiana, in 1846; elected prosecuting attorney of Scott County in 1848; circuit prosecutor in 1850; moved to New Albany in 1851; judge of the second judicial circuit of Indiana 1852-1876; professor of law at the University of Indiana 1861- 1870; elected as a Democrat to the Forty-fifth and Forty-sixth Congresses (March 4, 1877-March 3, 1881); unsuccessful candidate for renomination in 1880; appointed commissioner of appeals in the supreme court of Indiana in 1881, which office he held until the completion of its work in 1885; resumed the practice of law; elected judge of the circuit court of Indiana in 1889 and held that office until his death, April 11, 1891.

BIGGER, SAMUEL, (1802-1846) - governor of Indiana (1840- 1843), was born on March 20, 1802 in Warren County, Ohio, the son of John Bigger. He received his A.B. and A.M. degrees at Ohio University, then studied law. In 1829 he moved to Indiana, settling first in Liberty and later in Rushville. He ran for the Indiana House of Representatives in 1833 and 1834 and was elected both times. In 1836, the State Legislature named him presiding judge of the Sixth Judicial Court, a position he held until 1840 when he was nominated for governor by the Whigs.

Bigger won the gubernatorial election and took office in December of 1840. During his term, Indiana suffered under an enormous debt due mainly to a breakdown in the internal improvements program. Bigger took few steps to alleviate these financial problems. As governor, he supported the revision of state's laws and opposed, on religious grounds, the establishment of Methodist Ashbury College. It was believed due to this opposition that he was defeated in his campaign for reelection.

Bigger left office in 1843 and moved to Fort Wayne to practice law. He died there on September 9, 1846. Samuel Bigger was married in 1830 to Ellen Williamson.

BIRD, LARRY JOE, (1956-   ) - Basketball star, was born in French Lick, Indiana on Dec. 7. Larry was College player of the year at Indiana State University before joining the Boston Celtics in 1979 of the National Basketball Association. The 6-ft 9-inch forward became Rookie of the Year in 1980 and then the NBA's Most Valuable Player from 1984 through 1986, and a perennial first-team all NBA selection. He averaged 24.2 points, 10 rebounds, and 6 assists per game over 13 years with the Celtics and led them to 3 championships in 1981, 1984, and in 1986. He retired after playing in the 1992 Olympics.

BLAKE, THOMAS HOLDSWORTH, (1792-1849) - a U. S. Representative from Indiana; born in Calvert County, Md., June 14, 1792; attended the public schools; studied law in Washington, D.C.; member of the militia of the District of Columbia which took part in the Battle of Bladensburg in 1814; moved to Kentucky and thence to Indiana; was admitted to the bar and commenced practice in Terre Haute, Indiana; prosecuting attorney and judge of the circuit court; abandoned the practice of law to engage in business; member of the State house of representatives; elected as an Adams Republican to the Twentieth Congress (March 4, 1827-March 3, 1829); was an unsuccessful candidate for reelection in 1828 to the Twenty-first Congress; declined to be a candidate for the Twenty-second Congress; was appointed Commissioner of the General Land Office by President Tyler on May 19, 1842, and served until April 1845; chosen president of the Erie & Wabash Canal Co.; visited England as financial agent of the State of Indiana and while returning, died in Cincinnati, Ohio, November 28, 1849.

BLAND, OSCAR EDWARD, (1877-1951) - a U.S. Representative from Indiana; born near Bloomfield, Green County, Ind., November 21, 1877; attended the public schools, Valparaiso University, Valparaiso, Ind., and the University of Indiana at Bloomington; taught school for three years; studied law; was admitted to the bar in 1901 and commenced practice in Linton, Ind.; member of the State senate 1907-1909; unsuccessful Republican candidate for election to Congress in 1910, 1912, and 1914; elected as a Republican to the Sixty-fifth, Sixty-sixth, and Sixty-seventh Congresses (March 4, 1917-March 3, 1923); chairman, Committee on Industrial Arts and Expositions (Sixty-sixth and Sixty-seventh Congresses); unsuccessful candidate for reelection in 1922 to the Sixty-eighth Congress; appointed by President Warren G. Harding as associate judge of the United States Court of Customs Appeals (now the United States Court of Customs and Patent Appeals) on March 4, 1923, and served until his resignation on December 1, 1949; resumed the private practice of law in Washington, D.C., where he died August 3, 1951; interment in Fort Lincoln Cemetery.

BOEHNE, JOHN WILLIAM, (1856-1946) - a U. S. Representative from Indiana; born in Scott Township, Vanderburgh County, Indiana, October 28, 1856; attended the district schools, the German parochial school of the Lutheran Church, and Evansville Business College; moved to Evansville, Indiana, in 1872, becoming an accountant; engaged in the manufacture of stoves and ranges and was interested in other manufacturing enterprises; elected councilman at large in 1897 and reelected in 1899; unsuccessful Democratic candidate for mayor of Evansville in 1901; mayor 1905- 1908; delegate to the Democratic National Convention at Denver in 1908; elected as a Democrat to the Sixty-first and Sixty-second Congresses (March 4, 1909- March 3, 1913); was not a candidate for renomination in 1912; director of the Federal Reserve Bank at St. Louis, Missouri; retired from active business pursuits; died in Evansville, Indiana, December 27, 1946.

BOEHNE, JOHN WILLIAM, JR., (1895-) - (son of the preceding), a U. S. Representative from Indiana; born in Evansville, Vanderburgh County, Indiana, March 2, 1895; attended the public and parochial schools; was graduated from the University of Wisconsin at Madison in 1918; during the First World War served as a private and sergeant in the Detached Service, Ordnance, United States Army, from January 9, 1918, to April 8, 1919; secretary and treasurer of the Indiana Stove Works at Evansville, Indiana;, 1920-1931; elected as a Democrat to the Seventy-second and to the five succeeding Congresses (March 4, 1931- January 3, 1943); unsuccessful candidate for reelection in 1942 to the Seventy-eighth Congress; corporation tax counselor in Washington, D.C., 1943-1957; retired; is a resident of Kensington, Md.

BOHN, FRANK PROBASCO, (1866-1944) - a U. S. Representative from Michigan; born in Charlottesville, Hancock County, Indiana, July 14, 1866; attended the common and high schools and the Danville Indiana Normal College; was graduated from the Medical College of Indiana, Indianapolis, Indiana, in 1890; moved to Seney, Michigan, in 1890 and engaged in the practice of medicine; moved to Newberry, Luce County, Michigan, in 1898 and practiced his profession until 1923; also engaged in banking in 1905; served as village president of Newberry 1904 to 1919; member of the Newberry School Board 1908-1914; member of the State senate 1923-1926; elected as a Republican to the Seventieth, Seventy- first, and Seventy-second Congresses (March 4, 1927-March 3, 1933); unsuccessful candidate for reelection in 1932 to the Seventy-third Congress; resumed banking activities in Newberry, Michigan; member of the Michigan State Hospital Commission 1935- 1937; died in Newberry, Michigan, June 1, 1944; interment in Forest Home Cemetery.

BOON, RATLIFF, (1781-1844) - a U. S. Representative from Indiana; born in Franklin County, North Carolina, January 18, 1781; moved with his parents to Warren County, Kentucky; attended the public schools; moved to Danville, Kentucky, and learned the gunsmith's trade; moved to what in now Boon Township, Warrick County, Indiana, in 1809; on the organization of Warrick County was appointed its first treasurer in 1813; member of the State house of representatives in 1816 and 1817; served in the State senate in 1818; elected Lieutenant Governor of Indiana in 1819; upon the resignation of Jonathan Jennings became Governor and served from September 12 to December 5, 1822; reelected Lieutenant Governor in August 1822 and served until January 30, 1824, when he resigned to become a candidate for Congress; elected as a Jacksonian Democrat to the Nineteenth Congress (March 4, 1825-March 3, 1827); unsuccessful candidate for reelection in 1826 to the Twentieth Congress; elected to the Twenty-first and to the four succeeding Congresses (March 4, 1829-March 3, 1839); unsuccessful candidate for election to the United States Senate in 1836; moved to Pike County, Missouri, in 1839; died in Louisana, Missouri, on Nomvember 20, 1844.

BOONE, SQUIRE, (1744 - 1815) - was born on Oct. 5 and was an early explorer of what are now the states of Indiana, Kentucky, and Virginia.

Squire Boone was the tenth of eleven children and the brother of the famous explorer and frontiersman, Daniel Boone. Born near Reading, Pennsylvania, he received little formal education, and was trained at the age of 16 to be a gunsmith. Most of his life, however, was spent investigating unexplored territory and fighting Indians in the process.

The first of a series of exploratory trips began in the mid- 1760s, when Boone accompanied his brother, Daniel, to central Kentucky and Florida. In 1775, he helped to carve out the Wilderness Road to Richmond, Kentucky, and assisted Daniel in building fort Boonesborough near the Kentucky River in the central part of the future state. The following year, Squire Boone moved his family to Boonesborough, where they remained until he established Squire Boone's Station near the present city of Shelbyville, Kentucky, in 1779. When Kentucky Territory became a county of Virginia, Boone undertook a brief political career, and was elected to the Virginia House of Delegates as the Jefferson County representative in 1781.

From 1787 to 1791, Boone explored land in Louisiana and Florida, and made an unsuccessful attempt to start another settlement in Mississippi. Upon returning to Kentucky, he discovered the fraudulent claims had resulted in the loss of most of his land in that state. This, in addition to a brief imprisonment for unpaid debts, caused him to migrate to Harrison County, Indiana, in the early 1800s. There he built Boone Mill on Buck Creek near the famous Squire Boone Caverns that he had discovered in 1790. About 1813, Boone was instrumental in the building of the first Baptist church in Indiana, Old Goshen Church of Laconia.

Boone died at the age of 71 and was buried near the site of his mill. His remains were later moved to Kentucky.

BORMAN, FRANK, (1928-   ) - was a U.S. astronaut, born on March 14, who made two flights of major importance into outer space.

Born into a well-known family of Gary, Indiana, Borman was taken to Arizona for his health when he was six years old of age. He graduated from the U.S. Military

Academy at West Point, ranking in the first ten of his class, in 1950. Choosing the Air Force as his career, he underwent pilot training and served in the Philippines (1951-56). He earned a master's degree in aeronautical engineering in 1957 and subsequently was an instructor at West Point and the Aero-Space Research Pilot School at Edward Air Force Base, California.

Borman joined the astronaut team of the U.S. space program in 1962. He was the command pilot of the 14-day Gemini 7 flight of December 1965 which orbited the Earth long enough to prove that a flight to the Moon was possible. Gemini 7 also made the first rendezvous in space with another craft, Gemini 6.

In December 1968 Borman again commanded a space flight. He and two colleagues in the Apollo spacecraft left the Earth's orbit and became the first men to travel to the Moon. Orbiting 70 miles from the Moon, they took photographs and transmitted television pictures of the lunar space.

Borman became the deputy director of flight-crew operations for the National Aeronautics and Space Administration (NASA) after the Apollo 8 flight. Leaving the space program, he joined Eastern Airlines in 1970. In 1974 he was promoted to vice-president and general operations manager and elected to the company's board of directors. In 1975 he was elected president and chief operating officer. Borman emgineered Eastern's expansion of service to the sunbelt cities.

Borman is the recipient of NASA'S Distinguished Service Medal, the National Geographic Society's Hubbsard Medal, and the Congressional Space Medal of Honor.

BOWEN, OTIS R., (1918-   ) - is a physician and state political leader, born on Feb. 2, who was elected governor of Indiana in 1973. During his long career in the state legislature, he was credited with helping to give the House of Representatives a more buisness-like tone and a higher place in public esteem.

Born on a farm near Rochester, Indiana, Bowen was graduated from Indiana University in 1939 and its school of medicine in 1942. He served in the Army Medical Corps in the South Pacific (1943-46), returning to practice at Bremen.

Bowen exhibits a liberal attitude toward humanitarian issues. He was active in the community - Boy Scouts, medical groups, recreation, the Farm Bureau, the American Legion - while practicing medicine at Bremen. He began his political career as a Republican township chairman. He served as the coroner of Marshall County (1952-56) and as a member of the Indiana House of Representatives (1957-58, 1961-72). Bowen was the minority leader (1965-66) and the speaker (1967-72) of the House before his election as governor in 1973.

Bowen's most cherished accomplishment as governor was a restructuring of the tax system that lowered property taxes, although sales, individual income, and business income taxes rose.

While Governor he was appointed to three presidental committes by President Gerald R. Ford. He was unopposed in seeking renomination as the Republican candidate in the 1976 gubernatorial election. After his wife, Beth, was diagnosed in with cancer he announced that he would not seek a third term and return to medical practice.

In 1985 Predident Ronald Regan nominated Bowen as secretary of health and human services.

Bowen has attributed his political success in part to the fact he had long practiced small-town medicine. "You are closer to people than an ordinary friend."

BRADEMAS, JOHN, (1927-   ) - a U. S. Representative from Indiana; born in Mishawaka, Saint Joseph County, Indiana, March 2, 1927; graduate of Central High School, South Bend, Indiana; during World War II served in the United States Navy in 1945 and 1946; graduated from Harvard University in 1949 anf from Oxford University (Rhodes Scholar for Indiana) in 1954; legislative assistant to United States Senator Pat McNamara of Michigan in 1955; administrative assistant to Representative Thomas L. Ashley of Ohio in 1955; executive assistant to Adlai E. Stevenson in 1955 and 1956; assistant professor of political science, Saint Mary's College, Notre Dame, Indiana, in 1957 and 1958; member of congressional delegation to First Inter-American Conference, Lima, Peru, in 1959; unsuccessful Democratic candidate for election to the Eighty-fourth Congress in 1954 and to the Eighty- fifth Congress in 1956; elected as a Democrat to the Eighty-sixth and to the five succeeding Congresses (January 3, 1959-January 3, 1971). *Reelected to the Ninety-second Congress.*

BRANCH, EMMETT, (1874-1932), governor of Indiana (1924-25) - was born in Martinsville, Indiana on May 16, 1874, the son of Elliott and Alice (Parks) Branch. He attended the local public schools, and after graduation from high school, enrolled at Indiana University to study law. Following graduation from the University in 1896, he decided to study law. Two years later, however, the Spanish-American War broke out and he enlisted in the Army. Although he achieved the rank of first lieutenant by the time of his discharge a year later, Branch saw no action in that conflict.

He resumed his studies and passed the Indiana bar in 1899. Four years later with a successful legal practice underway, Branch decided to enter politics. He ran for and was elected to the Indiana House of Representatives in 1903, and was reelected in 1905 and 1907. In 1909 he resumed his law practice and remained a private citizen until 1916 when he served as a lieutenant colonel on the Mexican Border campaign. This service continued as American participation in World War I broke out, and he was promoted to colonel during this time.

Returning home Branch reentered politics and was elected lieutenant governor on the Republican ticket with Warren McCray. McCray's resignation in 1924 elevated him to the governor's office for a period of eight months. During his short tenure, Governor Branch urged a comprehensive program to improve the public road system and the schools. Emmett Branch died in his hometown on February 23, 1932. He was married to Katherine Bain in 1905 and had one son.

BRANIGIN, ROGER D., (1902-1975) - governor of Indiana (1965-1969), was born in Franklin, Indiana on July 26, 1902, the son of Elba and Zula (Francis) Branigin. After graduation from the local high school, he enrolled at Franklin College, and attained his A.B. degree in 1923. He immediately went to Harvard University and acquired an LL.B. degree in 1926.

His formal education now over, Branigin returned to Franklin and practiced law for the next three years. In 1930 he moved to Louisville, Kentucky to serve as counsel for the Federal Land Bank and Farm Credit Administration. That job ended in 1938 and he returned to Indiana and set up his practice in Lafayette. During World War II Branigin held the office of chief of the Legal Division, Army Transport Corps, with the rank of lieutenant colonel. With the war over, he resumed his practice in Lafayette, and became a trustee of both Franklin College and Purdue University. In 1964 he ran for governor on the Democratic ticket, and beat his Republican challenger. Branigin's administration abolished the poll tax, and began the state's first taxpayer-supported college scholarship program. He terminated the "right to work" law, expanded the powers of the Civil Rights Commission. and set up the Department of Natural Resources. Finishing his term at the age of 67, he went back to Lafayette and practiced law, once again. Roger Branigin died on November 19, 1975. He was married to Josephine Mardis in 1929, and had two children.

BRAY, WILLIAM GILMER, (1903-   ) - a U. S. Representative from Indiana; born on a farm near Mooresville, Morgan County, Indiana, June 17, 1903; attended the public schools of Mooresville, Indiana; was graduated from Indiana University Law School at Bloomington in 1927 and was admitted to the bar the same year; prosecuting attorney of the fifteenth judicial district of Indiana, Martinsville, Indiana, 1926-1930; commenced the private practice of law in Martinsville Indiana in 1930; during World War II was called from the Army Reserve June 21, 1941, with the rank of captain and served with a tank company throughout the Pacific campaign, receiving the Silver Star; after the war was transferred to Military Government and served nine months in Korea as deputy property custodian; released from active duty in November 1946 with the rank of colonel; returned to private law practice in Martinsville, Indiana; elected as a Republican to the Eighty-second and to the nine succeeding Congresses (January 3, 1951-January 3, 1971). *Reelected to the Ninety-second Congress.*

BRENTON, SAMUEL, (1810-1857) - a U. S. Representative from Indiana; born in Gallatin County, Kentucky, November 22, 1810; attended the public schools; was ordained to the Methodist ministry in 1830 and served as a minister; located at Danville, Indiana, in 1834 because of ill health, and studied law; member of the State house of representatives 1838-1841; in 1841, upon the restoration of his health, returned to the ministry and served at Crawfordsville, Perryville, Lafayette, and finally at Fort Wayne, where he suffered a paralytic stroke in 1848 and was compelled to abandon his ministerial duties; appointed register of the land office at Fort Wayne, Indiana, on May 2, 1849, and served until July 31, 1851, when he resigned; elected as a Whig to the Thirty-second Congress (March 4, 1851-March 3, 1853); unsuccessful candidate for reelection in 1852 to the Thirty-third Congress; elected as a Republican to the Thirty-fourth and Thirty-fifth Congresses and served from 4, 1855, until his death in Fort Wayne, Indiana, March 29, 1857.

BRETZ, JOHN LEWIS, (1852-1920) - a U. S. Representative from Indiana; born near Huntingburg, Dubois County, Indiana, September 21, 1852; attended the country schools and Huntingburg High School; taught school 1876-1880; studied law, and was graduated from the Cincinnati Law School in 1880; was admitted to the bar and commenced practice in Jasper, Indiana; prosecuting attorney of the eleventh judicial circuit 1884-1890; elected as a Democrat to the Fifty-second and Fifty-third Congresses (March 4, 1891-March 3, 1895);; unsuccessful candidate for reelection in 1894 to the Fifty-fourth Congress; judge of the circuit court of Pike and Dubois Counties from 1895 until his death; delegate to the Democratic National Convention at Kansas City in 1900; died in Jasper, Dubois County, Indiana, December 25, 1920.

BRICK, ABRAHAM LINCOLN, (1860-1908) - a U. S. Representative from Indiana; born on his father's farm, near South Bend, St. Joseph County, Indiana, May 27, 1860; attended the common schools and was graduated from the South Bend High School; later attended Cornell and Yale Colleges, and was graduated from the law department of the

University of Michigan at Ann Arbor in 1883; was admitted to the bar the same year and commenced practice in South Bend, St. Jospeh County, Indiana; prosecuting attorney for the counties of St. Joseph and La Porte in 1886; delegate to the Republican National Convention at St. Louis in 1896; elected as a Republican to the Fifty-sixth and to the four succeeding Congresses and served from March 4, 1899, until his death; died in Indianapolis, Indiana, April 7, 1908.

BRIGHT, JESSE DAVID, (1812-1875) - a U. S. Senator from Indiana; born in Norwich, Chenango County, New York, December 18, 1812; moved with his parents to Madison, Indiana, in 1820; attended the public schools; studied law; was admitted to the bar in 1831 and commenced practice in Madison, Jefferson County, Indiana; elected judge of the probate court of Jefferson County in 1834; United States marshal for the district of Indiana from January 9, 1840, until December 6, 1841, when he became a member of the State senate, in which he served until 1843; Lieutenant Governor of Indiana 1843-1845; elected as a Democrat to the United States Senate in 1845; reelected in 1850 and 1856, and served from March 4, 1845, to February 5, 1862, when he was expelled for having (in a letter to him) recognized Jefferson Davis as "President of the Confederate States"; was elected President pro tempore of the Senate December 5, 1854, June 11, 1856, and June 12, 1860; unsuccessful candidate for election in 1863 to the United States Senate to fill the vacancy caused by his expulsion; moved to Carrollton, Kentucky, in 1863 and then to Covington, Kentucky; member of the State house of representatives in 1866; president of the Raymond City Coal Co., in 1871; moved to Baltimore in 1874, still retaining his connection with the coal company; died in Baltimore, Maryland, May 20, 1875.

BROOKSHIRE, ELIJAH VOORHEES, (1856-1936) - a U. S. Representative from Indiana; born near Ladoga, Montgomery County, Indiana, August 15, 1856; attended the common schools, and was graduated from Central Indiana Normal College at Ladoga in August 1878; taught in the common schools of Montgomery County, Indiana 1879-1882; also engaged in agricultural pursuits; studied law;

was admitted to the bar in 1883 and commenced practice in Crawfordsville the same year; elected as a Democrat to the Fifty- first, Fifty-second, and Fifty-third Congresses (March 4, 1889- March 3, 1895); unsuccessful candidate for reelection in 1894 to the Fifty-fourth Congress; resumed the practice of law in Washington, D.C., and was admitted to practice before the United States Supreme Court in 1894; moved to Los Angeles, California, in 1925, and to Seattle, Washington, in 1935, having retired from active law practice in 1925; died in Seattle, Washington, April 14, 1936.

BROWN, JASON BREVOORT, (1839-1898) - a U. S. Representative from Indiana; born in Dillsboro, Dearborn County, Indiana, February 26, 1839; attended the common schools and Wilmington Academy, Dearborn County, Indiana; studied law; was admitted to the bar in 1860 and commenced practice in Brownstown, Indiana; member of the State house of representatives 1862-1866; presidential election on the Democratic ticket of Seymour and Blair in 1868; member of the State senate in 1870; secretary of the Territory of Wyoming 1873-1875; moved to Seymour, Indiana, in 1875; again a member of the State senate 1880-1883; elected as a Democrat to the Fifty-first, Fifty-second, and Fifty-third Congresses (March 4, 1889-March 3, 1895); unsuccessful candidate for renomination in 1894; resumed the practice of law in Seymour, Jackson County, Indiana, and died there March 10, 1898.

BROWN, WILLIAM JOHN, (1805-1857) - a U. S. Representative from Indiana; born near Washington, Mason County, Kentucky, August 15; 1805; moved to Clermont County, Ohio, in 1808 with his parents, who settled near New Richmond; attended the common schools and Franklin Academy; in Clermont County; moved to Rushville, Rush County, Indiana, in 1821; studied law; was admitted to the bar in 1826 and commenced practice in Rushville; member of the State house of representatives 1829-1832; prosecuting attorney 1831-1835; secretary of state of Indiana 1836-1840; moved to Indianapolis, Indiana, in 1837; again a member of the State house of representatives 1841-1843; elected as a Democrat to the Twenty-eighth Congress (March 4, 1843-March 3, 1845); appointed Second Assistant

Postmaster General by President Polk and served from 1845 until 1849; elected to the Thirty-first Congress (March 4, 1849-March 3, 1851); unsuccessful candidate for renomination in 1850; chief editor of the Indianapolis Sentinel 1850-1855; many times chairman of the Democratic State central committee of Indiana; appointed by President Pierce as special agent of the Post Office Department for Indiana and Illinois, which position he held from 1853 until his death near Indianapolis, Indiana, March 18, 1857.

BROWNE, THOMAS MCLELLAND, (1829-1891) - a U. S. Representative from Indiana; born in New Paris, Preble County, Ohio, April 19, 1829; moved to Indiana in January 1844; attended the common schools; moved to Winchester, Indiana, in 1848; studied law; was admitted to the bar in 1849 and commenced practice in Winchester; elected prosecuting attorney for the thirteenth judicial circuit in 1855; reelected in 1857 and 1859; secretary of the State senate in 1863; assisted in organizing the Seventh Regiment, Indiana Volunteer Cavalry of the Union Army, and went to the field with that regiment as captain of Company B, August 28, 1863; commissioned lieutenant colonel October 1, 1863; promoted to colonel October 10, 1865, and subsequently commissioned by President Lincoln as brigadier general by brevet March 13, 1865, "for gallant and meritorious services during the war"; mustered out February 18, 1866; appointed United States attorney for the district of Indiana in April 1869 and served until his resignation August 1, 1872; unsuccessful candidate for Governor in 1872; delegate to the Republican National Convention at Cincinnati in 1876; elected as a Republican to the Forty-fifth and to the six succeeding Congresses (March 4, 1877-March 3, 1891); was not a candidate for renomination in 1890; died in Winchester, Randolph County, Indiana, July 17, 1891.

BROWNSON, CHARLES BRUCE, (1914-   ) - a U. S. Representative from Indiana; born in Jackson, Michigan, February 5, 1914; moved with his parents to Flint, Michigan, in 1916; attended the public schools and Flint Central High School; was graduated from the University of Michigan at Ann Arbor in 1935; entered Thomasson Act training as second lieutenant, Infantry Reserve, Fort Sheridan, Illinois, August 1, 1935; moved to Indianapolis, Indiana, October 1936 and established the Central Wallpaper & Paint Corp.; during World War II entered on active duty as first lieutenant, Infantry Reserve, Chanute Field, Illinois, February 10, 1941; served as Assistant Chief of Staff, G-1, Eighty-third Infantry Division, Camp Atterbury, Indiana, in 1943; executive officer to Assistant Chief of Staff, G-1, First Army, during invasion planning in England and combat in Europe until V-E Day; transferred with First Army Planning Headquarters to Canlubang, Philippine Islands, August 5, 1945; released from active duty February 27, 1946, as lieutenant colonel, Army Reserve, and promoted to colonel in 1960; awarded five battle stars and invasion arrowhead on European Theater Ribbon, Legion of Merit, Bronze Star, and French Medaille de Reconnaissance; chairman Marion County Juvenile Court Advisory Council in 1948 and 1949; elected as a Republican to the Eighty-second and to the three succeeding Congresses (January 3, 1951-January 3, 1959); unsuccessful candidate for reelection in 1958 to the Eighty-sixth Congress; assistant administrator for public affairs and congressional liaison, Housing and Home Finance Agency, Washington, D.C., from August 12, 1959, to January 20, 1961; editor and publisher of Congressional Staff Directory; engaged in public relations in Washington, D.C.; is a resident of Alexandria, Virginia.

BRUCE, DONALD COGLEY, (1921-1969) - a U. S. Representative from Indiana; born in Troutville, Clearfield County, Pennsylvania, April 27, 1921; graduated from high school in Allentown, Pennsylvania; and attended Muskingum College in New Concord, Ohio; engaged in the radio broadcasting industry, serving as program director, business manager, and general manager, 1941-1960; elected as a Republican to the Eighty-seventh and Eighty-eighth Congresses (January 3, 1961-January 3, 1965); was not a candidate in 1964 for renomination to the Eighty-ninth Congress, but was an unsuccessful candidate for nomination for United States Senator in primary election; on leaving Congress, he helped form the American Conservative Union, a political action group; created a management and political consulting firm, Bruce Enterprises in Round Hill, Virginia; died in Round Hill, Virginia, August 31, 1969.

BURTON, DAN, (1938-   ) - Republican, of Indianapolis,; born in Indianapolis, on June 21, 1938; attended Indianapolis public schools; graduated, Shortridge High School, 1956, Indiana University, 1956-57; Cincinnati Bible Seminary, 1958-60, served in the U.S. Army Reserves, 1957-62; businessman, insurance and real estate firm owner since 1968; elected to Indiana House of Representatives, 1967-68 and 1977-80; elected to Indiana State Senate, 1969-70 and 1981-82; president : volunteers of America, Indiana Support Center; member, Jaycees; married to the former Barbara Jean Logan, 1959; three children: Kelly, Danielle Lee, and Danny Lee II; elected on November 2, 1982, to the 98th Congress; reelected to each succeeding Congress.

C

CALKINS, WILLIAM HENRY, (1842-1894) - a U. S. Representative from Indiana; born in Pike County, Ohio, February 18, 1842; studied law; was admitted to the bar and practiced; during the Civil War served in the Union Army from May 1861 to December 1865, except three months in 1863, attached to the Fourteenth Iowa Infantry and the Twwelfth Indiana Cavalry; took up his residence in La Porte, Indiana; State's attorney for the ninth Indiana judicial circuit 1866-1870; member of the State house of representatives in 1871; elected as a Republican to the Forty-fifth and to the three succeeding Congresses and served from March 4, 1877, to October 20, 1884, when he resigned; moved to Tacoma, Washington, and resumed the practice of law; appointed United States associate justice of the Territory of Washington in April 1889 and served until November 11, 1889, when the Territory was admitted as a State into the Union; died in Tacoma, Washington, on January 29, 1894.

CALL, JACOB, (? -1826) - a U. S. Representative from Indiana; born in Kentucky; was graduated from an academy in Kentucky; studied law; was admitted to the bar and practiced in Vineennes and Princeton, Indiana; judge of the

Knox County Circuit Court in 1817, 1818, and 1822-1824; elected to the Eighteenth Congress to fill the vacancy caused by the death of William Prince and served from December 23, 1824, to March 3, 1825; died in Frankfort, Kentucky, April 20, 1826.

CANFIELD, HARRY CLIFFORD, (1875-1945) - a U.S. Representative from Indiana; born near Moores Hill, Dearborn County, Ind., November 22, 1875; attended the public schools, Moores Hill College, Central Normal College, Danville, Ind., and Vorhies Business College, Indianapolis, Ind.; taught school in Dearborn County 1896-1898; moved to Batesville, Ripley County, in 1899 and engaged in the manufacture of furniture; also interested in the jobbing of furniture, and in farming and banking; elected as a Democrat to the Sixty-eighth and to the four succeeding Congresses (March 4, 1923-March 3, 1933); unsuccessful candidate for renomination in 1932; restuned the furniture manufacturing business in Batesville, Ind., where he died February 9, 1945; interment in the First Methodist Episcopal Cemetery.

CAPEHART, HOMER EARL, (1897-   ) - a U. S. Senator from Indiana; born in Algiers, Pike County, Indiana, June 6, 1897; attended the public schools; was graduated from the high school at Polo, Illinois, in 1916; interested in agricultural pursuits since 1916; during the First World War enlisted as a private in the United States Army; promoted to sergeant and served in the Twelfth Infantry 1917-1919; engaged in the radio, phonograph, and television manufacturing business; delegate to six Republican National conventions; elected as a Republican to the United States Senate in 1944 for the term commencing January 3, 1945; reelected in 1950 and again in 1956 for the term ending January 3, 1963; unsuccessful candidate for reelection in 1962 to the Eighty-eighth Congress; engaged in farming, manufacturing and investment pursuits; is a resident of Indianapolis, Indiana.

CARMICHAEL, HOAGY, (1899-1981) - composer of the classic ballad "Stardust," along with several other popular songs, was born Hoagland Howard Carmichael on November 22, 1899 in Bloomington, Indiana. Initially deciding to become a lawyer, he attended the University of Indiana, earning an LL.B. degree in 1926.

Carmichael pursued his law career for a time, but having become enamored of jazz while in college, and having performed with his own band, he gave up law, moved to New York, and began working in a music publishing house as an arranger. Carmichael's first major composition was "Stardust," a song he wrote in 1929 with Mitchell Parish, who wrote the lyrics. Recalling how he came up with the name of the song, Carmichael later said: "I had no idea what 'Stardust' meant, but I thought it would make a gorgeous title." The song was not only a popular standard in its day, but is now considered a classic.

Other songs that he wrote during that period included "Rockin' Chair," "Georgia on My Mind," "Two Sleepy People," "Heart and Soul," "The Nearness of You," "Skylark," "I Get Along Without You Very Well," and "Lazy River." For the recording of the latter song, Carmichael put together what was, to some observers, the ultimate jazz band--including Bix Beiderbecke, Tommy and Jimmy Dorsey, Jack Teagarden, Benny Goodman, and Gene Krupa, among others. In 1951, Carmichael, along with co-writer Johnny Mercer, won an Academy Award for the song "In the Cool, Cool, Cool of the Evening."

Beginning in 1944, Carmichael embarked on a second career when he appeared in the film *To Have and Have Not*. Other movies included: *Topper*; *Johnny Angel*, *The Best Years of Our Lives*; *Night Song*; *Young Man with a Horn*; *Johnny Holiday*; *The Las Vegas Story*; and *Timberjack*; among others.

Carmichael hosted a radio show in the 1940's, and in later years, also appeared on several television shows including the series *Laramie*, in which he had a recurring role from 1959 to 1962. In 1970 he taped 15 episodes of *Hoagy Carmichael's Music Shop*, a musical series for children that appeared on PBS, which contained several of his original compositions.

Carmichael wrote two autobiographies: *The Stardust Road*, 1946, and *Sometimes I Wonder: The Story of Hoagy Carmichael*, 1965 (the latter written with Stephen Longstreet). In the early 1970's, when the Songwriters' Hall of

Fame was established, Carmichael was one of the first ten contemporary songwriters to be inducted.

Carmichael was married twice and had two sons. He died on December 27, 1981.

CARR, JOHN, (1793-1845) - a U. S. Representative from Indiana; born in Uniontown, Perry County, Indiana, April 9, 1793; moved with his parents to Clark County, Indiana, in 1806; attended the public schools; fought in the Battle of Tippecanoe; appointed lieutenant in a company of United States Rangers, authorized by an act of Congress for defense of western frontiers, in 1812; brigadier general and major general of the Indiana Militia until his death; county clerk 1824-1830; presidential elector on the Democratic ticket of Jackson and Calhoun in 1824; elected as a Democrat to the Twenty-second, Twenty-third, and Twenty-fourth Congresses (March 4, 1831-March 3, 1837); unsuccessful candidate in 1836 for reelection to the Twenty-fifth Congress; elected to the Twenty-sixth Congress (March 4, 1839-March 3, 1841); died in Charlestown, Clark County, Indiana, January 20, 1845.

CARR, NATHAN TRACY, (1833-1885) - a U. S. Representative from Indiana; born in Corning, Steuben County, New York, December 25, 1833; attended the common schools, and was graduated from Starkey Academy in 1851; moved to Midland County, Michigan; studied law; was admitted to the Midland County bar in 1858 and commenced practice at Vassar, Michigan; member of the State house of representatives 1858-1860; recorder of Midland County in 1861 and 1862; during the Civil War served as a lieutenant in the Second Regiment, Michigan Volunteer Infantry, in 1862; moved to Columbus, Indiana, in 1867; prosecuting attorney for Bartholomew, Shelby, Jackson, and Brown Counties in 1870; elected as a Democrat to the Forty-fourth Congress to fill the vacancy caused by the death of Michael C. Kerr and served from December 5, 1876, to March 3, 1877; unsuccessful candidate for renomination in 1876; resumed the practice of law in Columbus, Bartholomew County, Indiana; appointed judge of the ninth judicial circuit court of Indiana in 1878; died in Columbe, Indiana, May 28, 1885.

CASE, CHARLES, (1817-1883) - a U. S. Representative from Indiana; born in Austinburg, Ohio, December 21, 1817; studied law; was admitted to the bar and commenced practice in Fort Wayne, Indiana; elected as a Democrat to the Thirty-fifth Congress to fill the vacancy caused by the death of Samuel Brenton; reelected to the Thirty-sixth Congress and served from December 7, 1857, to March 3, 1861; unsuccessful candidate for reelection in 1860 to the Thirty-seventh Congress; during the Civil War served as first lieutenant and adjutant of the Forty- fourth Regiment, Indiana Volunteer Infantry; subsequently became a major in the Third Regiment, Indiana Volunteer Cavalry, and served from November 26, 1861, to August 15;, 1862; resumed the practice of his profession in Washington, D.C.; died in Brighton, Washington County, Iowa, June 30, 1883.

CATHCART, CHARLES WILLIAM, (1809-1888) - a U. S. Representative and a U. S. Senator from Indiana; born July 24, 1809, in Funchal, Island of Madeira, where his father was the United States consul; came to the United States with his parents in 1815; sailed with his parents to Cadiz, Spain, in 1817; attended private schools; returned to the United States in 1819; bacame a sailor before the mast; moved to Washington, D.C., in 1830, and was a clerk in the General Land Office; went with the ammunition team to Fort Dearborn (now Chicago), Illinois, in 1832; joined a military company under the command of Captain Finch; justice of the peace at New Durham Township, Indiana, in 1833; engaged in agricultural pursuits near La Porte, Indiana, in 1837; United States land surveyor; member of the State senate 1837-1840; presidential elector on the Democratic ticket of Polk and Dallas in 1844; elected as a Democrat to the Twenty-ninth and Thirtieth Congresses (March 4, 1845-March 3, 1849); appointed to the United States Senate to fill the vacancy caused by the death of James Whitcomb and served from December 6, 1852, to March 3, 1853; unsuccessful candidate for election in 1860 to the Thirty- seventh Congress; engaged in agricultural pursuits; died on his farm near La Porte, La Porte County, Indiana, August 22, 1888.

CHAMBERLAIN, EBENEZER MATTOON, (1805-1861) - a U. S. Representative from Indiana; born in Orrington, Maine, August 20, 1805; attended the public schools; employed in his father's shipyard; studied law; moved to Connersville, Indiana, where he completed his studies; was admitted to the bar in 1832 and commenced practice in Elkhart County in 1833; member of the State house of representatives 1835-1837; served in the State senate 1839-1842; elected prosecuting attorney of the ninth judicial circuit in 1842; elected president judge of the ninth judicial district in 1843, reelected in 1851 and served until he resigned, having been elected to Congress; delegate to the Democratic National Convention at Baltimore in 1844; elected as a Democrat to the Thirty-third Congress (March 4, 1853-March 3, 1855); engaged in the practice of law in Goshen, Elkhart County, Indiana, until his death there March 14, 1861.

CHAPMAN, JOHN, (1775 -1847) - Pioneer; popularly known as Johnny Appleseed.   Chapman is believed to have been born either in Boston or Springfield, Massachusetts. His first recorded appearance in the Midwest was in the early 1800s near Steubenville. Chapman was reportedly transporting a cargo of decaying apples from Pennsylvania down the Ohio River. About 1810, Chapman took up residence in the area of Ashland County, Ohio which he apparently used as a base to tend his widely scattered apple orchards.

Chapman has also been described as a religious man who would read the Bible to anyone who would listen as a medicine man who spread the seeds of such "healing" herbs as catnip and hoarhound. Chapman's concern for his fellow settlers is evidenced by a hasty night trip about 1812 to Mt. Vernon, Ohio to summon troops to protect Mansfield from British-instigated Indian attacks.

Chapman moved to northern Indiana about 1838 where he continued planting apple orchards. During a trip to one of his orchards, Chapman contacted the pneumonia that led to his death in a cabin in Allen County, Indiana.

CHASE, IRA, (1834-1895) - governor of Indiana (1891-1893), was born in Monroe County, New York on December 7, 1834, the son of Benjamin and Lorinda (Mix) Chase. His family moved to Milan, Ohio when he was twelve years old and Chase studied at the Milan Seminary. As a young man, he returned to New York to attend Medina Academy. After graduation he settled in Barrington, Illinois where his family was then living, and worked as a school teacher. In 1861, at the outbreak of the Civil War, Chase signed up for military service in the 19th Illinois Regiment. After a year in the regiment, however, he had to be discharged due to poor health.

Back in Barrington, he tried his luck in the hardware business, but his store failed after a short time. He then turned to the Christian Church and became a minister, preaching over the next several years to congregations in Danville, Wabash, Mishawaka, and LaPorte, Indiana, Peoria, Illinois, and Pittsburgh, Pennsylvania. In 1886, Chase served as chaplain for the Indiana G.A.R. The following year, he became department commander.

During his time in the ministry Chase was vocal in political matters and strong in his support of the Republican Party. In 1888, the Republicans made him their nominee for lieutenant governor, and later that year Chase won over Democrat, William R. Myers. Chase served under Governor Alvin P. Hovey, and when Hovey died on November 23, 1891 Chase was sworn in to complete the Governor's unexpired term. As Indiana governor, Chase supported appropriations for public works, particularly for the construction of new roads. He ran for a term of his own as governor in 1892, but lost to the Democratic candidate, Claude Matthews.

Chase left office in 1893 and returned to the ministry and the lecture circuit. Two years later, in Maine, he died on May 11. Chase was married to Rhoda Castle in 1859. They had four children.

CHEADLE, JOSEPH BONAPARTE, (1842-1904) - a U. S. Representative from Indiana; born in Perrysville, Vermillion County, Indiana, August 14, 1842; attended the common schools; entered Asbury (now De Pauw) University, Greencastle, Indiana, but upon the organization of the Seventy-first Regiment, Indiana Volunteer Infantry, during the Civil War enlisted as a private in Company K and served until the close of the war; returned home and entered upon the study of law; was graduated from the Indianapolis Law College in 1867; was admitted to the bar and commenced practice in Newport, Indiana; continued in practice until 1873, when he entered upon newspaper work; elected as a Republican to the Fiftieth and Fifty-first Congresses (March 4, 1887-March 3, 1891); unsuccessful candidate for renomination in 1890, 1892, and 1894; affiliated with the Democratic Party in 1896; unsuccessful candidate for election in 1896 and 1898 on the Democratic and Populist tickets; editor of the American Standard in 1896; died in Frankfort, Clinton County, Indiana, May 28, 1904.

CLARK, GEORGE ROGERS, (1752 - 1818) - was a U.S. military leader famous for capture of British territory in what is now Illinois and Indiana during the American Revolution.

Clark was born in Charlottesville, Virginia. He received some formal education during his youth, but his first occupation as a surveyor was largely self-taught. His initial military experience was as a militia captain in Lord Dunmore's War against the Shawnee Indians in 1774. Early the next year, he went to Kentucy as a surveyor for the Ohio Company and became the leader of the settlers' defense against the British and the Indians. Clark's strategy was to conquer the British forts in Illinois territory from which the Indians received supplies. Kaskaskia and Cahokia were captured by Clark and his men in 1778. Envoys sent to the settlement of Fort Sackville (Vincennes, Indiana) on the Wabash River persuaded the French inhabitants to switch their allegiance from Britain to Virginia. Fort Sackville returned into British hands the following December, but was recaptured by Clark in February 1779. A lack of supplies and reinforcements prevented Clark from carrying out a planned march against the British headquarters in Fort Detroit.

From 1780, when Clark established Fort Jefferson, until the end of the war, Clark was active in a series of campaigns to protect the land he had won from attempted takeovers by the British and the Indians. Because of his efforts, most of the territory of what was known as the Old Northwest was awarded to the United States in the Treaty of Paris of 1783. As a reward for their services, in 1781 the state of Virginia awarded Clark and his men a 150,000-acre tract of land known as Clark's Grant.

In 1784 Clark accepted a position as an Indian commissioner of the Northwest Territory. This led him to establish a garrison at Vincennes to combat Indians. In order to maintain his army, he impressed privately-owned merchandise. Unfortunately, both the state of Virginia and the U.S. government refused to pay for the goods, resulting in legal judgements against Clark which were used by his enemies to prevent him from obtaining further goverment appointments. Desperate and deeply in debt, he sold a large part of the land he was entitled to under Clark's Grant and accepted commissions in the French army in 1793 and 1798. He resigned the last commission at the insistance of the U.S. government and took refuge in St. Louis, returning to Louisville in 1799.

In 1803 Clark settled in Clarksville, Indiana, the town that was founded on Clark's Grant. There he ran a grist mill and served on the commission to appropriate land on Clark's Grant to veterans of his Illinois regiment. Ill health and the amputation of his right leg forced him in 1809 to move to his sister's home near Louisville, where he remained until his death.

CLINE, CYRUS, (1856-1923) - a U. S. Representative from Indiana; born near Mansfield, Richland County, Ohio, July 12, 1856; moved to Steuben County, Indiana, in 1858 with his parents, who settled near Angola; attended the Angola High School, and was graduated from Hillsdale College, Michigan, in 1876; superintendent of the schools of Steuben County 1877-1883; studied law; was admitted to the bar and began practice in Angola, Steuben county, Indiana, in 1884; elected as a Democrat to the Sixty-first and to the three succeeding Congresses (March 4, 1909-March 3, 1917); unsuccessful candidate for reelection in 1916; resumed the practice of law in Angola, Indiana, and died there on October 5, 1923.

COATS, DANIEL RAY, (1943-   ) - a U.S. Representative from Indiana; born in Jackson, Jackson County, Mich., May 16, 1943; attended the public schools; graduated from Jackson High School, 1961; B.A., Wheaton College, Wheaton, Ill., 1965; J.D., Indiana University School of Law, Indianapolis, 1971; admitted to the Indiana bar in 1972 and commenced practice in Fort Wayne; served in the United States Army, 1966-1968; district representative, United States Congressman Dan Quayle, 1976-1980; elected as a Republican to the Ninetyseventh and to the three succeeding Congresses (January 3, 1981-January 3, 1989); appointed by the Governor, January 3, 1990 to the U.S. Senate seat vacated by Vice President-elect Dan Quale; elected November 6, 1990 to complete the term ending January 3, 1993; member, Senate Committe of Armed Services and ranking member on the Subcommitte on Industry and Technology; member, Labor and Human Recources Committe and ranking member on the Subcommittee on Children, Families, Drugs, And Alcoholism; is a resident of Fort Wayne, Ind.

COBB, THOMAS REED, (1828-1892) - a U.S. Representative from Indiana; born in Springville, Lawrence County, Ind., July 2, 1828; attended Indiana University, Bloomington, Ind.; studied law; was admitted to the bar in 1851 and commenced practice in Bedford, Ind.; commissioned major of Indiana Militia in 1852; moved to Vincennes, Ind., in 1867; member of the State senate 1858-1866; president of the Democratic State convention in 1876; delegate to the Democratic National Convention in 1876; elected as a Democrat to the Forty-fifth and to the four succeeding Congresses (March 4, 1877-March 3, 1887); chairman, Committee on Mileage (Forty-fifth and Forty-sixth Congresses), Committee on Public Lands (Fortyeighth and Forty-ninth Congresses); was not a candidate for renomination in 1886; resumed the practice of law and also engaged in agricultural pursuits; died in Vincennes, Knox County, Ind., June 23, 1892; interment in Old Vincennes Cemetery.

COBURN, JOHN, (1825-1908) - a U. S. Representative from Indiana; born in Indianapolis, Indiana, October 27, 1825; attended the public schools, and was graduated from Wabash College, Crawfordsville, Indiana, in 1846; studied law; was admitted to the bar in 1849 and commenced practice in Indianapolis; member of the State house of representatives in 1850; judge of the court of common pleas from 1859 to 1861, when he resigned to enter the Union Army; during the Civil War became colonel of the Thirty-third Regiment, Indiana Volunteer Infantry, September 16, 1861, and was mustered out September 20, 1864; brevetted brigadier general of Volunteers March 13, 1865, "for gallant and meritorious services during the war"; appointed as the first secretary of the Territory of Montana in March 1865 but resigned at once; elected judge of the fifth judicial circuit of Indiana in October 1865 and resigned in July 1866; elected as a Republican to the Fortieth and to the three succeeding Congresses (March 4, 1867-March 3, 1875); was an unsuccessful candidate for reelection in 1874 to the Forty-fourth Congress; was appointed a justice of the supreme court of the Territory of Montana on February 19, 1884, and served until December 1885; returned to Indianapolis, and resumed the practice of law; died in Indianapolis, Indiana, on January 28, 1908.

COLERICK, WALPOLE GILLESPIE, (1845-1911) - a U. S. Representative from Indiana; born in Fort Wayne, Indiana, August 1, 1845; attended the public schools; studied law; was admitted to the bar in 1872 and commenced practice at Fort Wayne, Indiana; elected as a Democrat to the Forty-sixth and Forty-seventh Congresses (March 4, 1879-March 3, 1883); supreme court commissioner from 1883 to 1885; again engaged in the practice of law at Fort Wayne, Indiana, until his death there on January 11, 1911.

COLFAX, SCHUYLER, (1823-1885) - a U. S. Representative from Indiana and a Vice President of the United States; born in New York City, March 23, 1823; attended the common schools; in 1836 moved with his parents to New Carlisle, Indiana, where he was appointed deputy auditor of St. Joseph County in 1841 by his stepfather, George W. Mathews, with office in South Bend; became a legislative correspondent in Indianapolis; purchased an interest in the South Bend Free Press and changed its name in 1845 to the St. Jospeh Valley Register, the Whig organ of northern Indiana; delegate to the Whig National Conventions in 1848 and 1852; member of the State constitutional convention in 1850; unsuccessful Whig candidate for election to the

Thirty- second Congress; elected as a Republican to the Thirty-fourth and to the six succeeding Congresses (March 4, 1855-March 3, 1869); wsa not a candidate for renomination in 1868, having become the Republican nominee for Vice President; served as Speaker of the House of Representatives in the Thirty-eighth, Thirty-ninth, and Fortieth Congresses; elected Vice President of the United States on the Republican ticket headed by General U.S. Grant in 1868, was inaugurated March 4, 1869, and served until March 3, 1873; unsuccessful candidate for renomination in 1872; declined the chief editorship of the New York Tribune the same year; fully exonerated from charges of corruption brought against Members of Congress in 1873 in connection with the Credit Mobilier of America; devoted his time to lecturing; died in Mankato, Blue Earth County, Minnesota, January 13, 1885.

COMSTOCK, DANIEL WEBSTER, (1840-1917) - a U. S. Representative from Indiana; born in Germantown, Montgomery County, Ohio, December 16, 1840; attended the common schools, and was graduated from the Ohio Wesleyan University, Delaware, Ohio, in 1860; studied law; was admitted to the bar in 1861 and commenced practice in New Castle, Indiana; district attorney in 1862; during the Civil War enlisted in the Ninth Indiana Cavalry and was successively promoted to regimental sergeant major, first lieutenant, captain, and acting assistant adjutant general in the military division of Mississippi; settled in Richmond, Indiana, in 1866; city attorney in 1866; prosecuting attorney of the Wayne circuit court 1872-1874; member of the State Senate in 1878; judge of the appelate court 1896-1911; resumed the practice of law; elected as a Republican to the Sixty-fifth Congress and served from March 4, 1917,until his death in Washington, D.C., May 19, 1917.

CONDON, EDDIE, (1905-1973) - musician (born Albert Edwin), was born in Goodland, Indiana on November 16, 1905. His family moved to Chicago Heights, Illinois, where he began his first year at Bloom Township High School. But formal education immediately took a backseat when his music beckoned. He left school at 15 when he got his musician's card, joined Homer Peavey's Jazz Bandits, and began what became a highly respected career as a jazz guitarist.

From the very beginning, his passion was for free-form jazz. "I'm a free soul," he once said. "Guys like me want to play hot jazz, the stuff you make up as you go along."

At the young age of nineteen, he was the leader of his own band which included the even younger (seventeen) Gene Krupa, as well as, Jimmy McPartland and Bud Freeman. Calling themselves the Chicago Rhythm Kings, they took off for New York and got a job at the Chateau Madrid, which they soon lost, as the New York audiences weren't ready for their rougher style of music. The other band members left for home, but Eddie stuck it out in New York. He formed another band for awhile, then went solo. He had a hard time finding places to play the kind of music he loved, especially when the swing era hit in the 1930's. However, in 1937, a club in Greenwich Village called Nick's, hired musicians who enjoyed playing hot jazz, such as Bobby Hackett, George Brunis, and Pee Wee Russell -- and Eddie found his niche.

He and his band were some of the first musicians ever recorded on the Commodore label, which was run by Milt Gabler. Condon also got work playing guitar in Artie Shaw's orchestra, and in 1939, he formed the Summa Cum Laude Orchestra, who played Chicago's Sherman Hotel for a couple of years.

Condon was then pegged to help out with a series of jazz concerts to be presented at New York Town Hall. He had free reign in choosing the musicians and the material, and after a slow start, the concerts became extremely popular. During that time, he was also involved in what was to be the first televised jazz concert.

In October of 1944, Condon's Jazz Concerts, as they were called, moved from Town Hall to Carnegie Hall. Even in such a prestigious setting, the atmosphere was informal. Condon was a witty and gracious host, casually guiding the musicians, yet allowing them to go in any musical direction they wished. He considered that kind of playing, the purest jazz there was. Ironically, Condon never took any solos for himself. He held the rhythm in place on every song, knowing the importance of that task. His talent wasn't over looked by the music world, as he won musician's polls two years in a row for his guitar work.

Condon wrote music, sometimes collaborating with other musicians and he also wrote his autobiography in 1948, entitled, "We Called It Music." He was knowledgable and articulate about his craft. When he was first starting out, he was immediately tagged as a "Chicago-style" musician, but he disdainfully shook off the label, saying, "There are two kinds of music, good and bad--and if you're in Fairbanks, Alaska, and you can play the piano good, you can play the piano."

Eddie Condon married Phyllis Smith Reay on November 16, 1942, and they had one daughter. He died on August 4, 1973, and was cremated.

CONN, CHARLES GERARD, (1844-1931) - a U.S. Representative from Indiana; born in Phelps, Ontario County, N.Y., January 29, 1844; moved with his parents to Elkhart, Ind., in 1851; attended the common schools; enlisted in the Union Army May 18, 1861, and served as a private in the band of Company B, Fifteenth Regiment, Indiana Volunteer Infantry; discharged September 10, 1862; reenlisted in Company G, First Michigan Sharpshooters, November 18, 1862; was wounded and taken prisoner, being released from Columbia (S.C.) prison camp at the close of hostilities; awarded the Congressional Medal of Honor; engaged in the grocery and bakery business and, in 1877, in the manufacture of band instruments at Elkhart, Ind.; mayor of Elkhart 1880-1883; member of the State house of representatives in 1889; established the Elkhart Daily Truth in 1890; was owner of the Washington (D.C.) Times during part of his congressional term; elected as a Democrat to the Fifty-third Congress (March 4, 1893-March 3, 1895); was not a candidate for renomination in 1894; resumed the manufacture of band instruments at Elkhart, Ind.; in 1916 retired and moved to Los Angeles, Calif., where he died on January 5, 1931; interment in Grace Lawn Cemetery, Elkhart, Ind.

COOK, JOE, (1890-1959) - actor (ne Joseph Lopez), was born in Evansville, Indiana.

Cook was twelve when he joined a traveling show, and then began working in vaudeville in 1907. He eventually became a Broadway star, starting with the Earl Carroll Vanities for three years and achieving success in *Rain or Shine* and *Fine and Dandy*. His stage persona was once described as "contagious good-naturedness." He created a popular character named "Rube Goldberg" and had a routine called The Four Hawaiians.

Cook also did some film work, both in short films and regular features such as *Arizona Mahoney* and *Rain or Shine*.

Joe Cook died in Clinton Hollow, New York on May 16, 1959.

COOK, SAMUEL ELLIS, (1860-1946) - a U.S. Representative from Indiana; born on a farm in Huntington County, Ind., September 30, 1860; attended the common schools in Whitley County and the normal schools at Columbia City, Ind., and Ada, Ohio; taught school and engaged in agricultural pursuits; studied law; was graduated from the law department of Valparaiso University, Indiana, in 1888; was admitted to the bar the same year and commenced practice in Huntington, Ind.; prosecuting attorney for Huntington County 1892-1894; delegate to the Democratic National Convention in 1896; editorial writer for the Huntington News- Democrat 1896-1900; judge of the Huntington circuit court for the fifty-sixth judicial district 1906-1918; elected as a Democrat to the Sixtyeighth Congress (March 4, 1923-March 3, 1925); unsuccessful candidate for reelection in 1924 to the Sixty-ninth Congress; resumed the practice of law in Huntington, Ind., where he died February 22, 1946; interment in Mount Hope Cemetery.

COOPER, GEORGE WILLIAM, (1851-1899) - a U. S. Representative from Indiana; born near Columbus, Bartholomew County, Indiana, May 21, 1851; attended the country schools, and was graduated in the academic and law courses from the Indiana University at Bloomington in 1872; was admitted to the bar and commenced practice in Columbus, Indiana; prosecuting attorney of Columbus in 1872; mayor of Columbus in 1877; city attorney of Columbus 1879-1883; elected as a Democrat to the Fifty-first, Fifty-second, and Fifty-third Congresses (March 4, 1889-March 3, 1895); unsuccessful candidate for reelection in

1894 to the Fifty-fourth Congress; resumed the practice of law in Columbus, Indiana; died in Chicago, Illinois, November 27, 1899.

CORNWELL, DAVID LANCE, (1945-   ) - a U.S. Representative from Indiana; born in Paoli, Orange County, Ind., June 14, 1945; attended Paoli public schools, Culver (Ind.) Military Academy, Phillips Andover (Mass.) Academy; graduated from Park High School, Indianapolis, Ind., 1964; attended Hillsdale College, 1964; American College of Monaco, 1969; Indiana University, 1974; secretary, Board of Directors, Cornwell Co., Inc., Paoli; served in the United States Army in Vietnam 1966-1968; unsuccessful candidate for nomination in 1974 to the Ninety-fourth Congress; elected as a Democrat to the Ninety-fifth Congress (January 3, 1977-January 3, 1979); unsuccessful candidate for reelection in 1978 to the Ninetysixth Congress; works in governmental and international relations; is a resident of Falls Church, Va.

COWGILL, CALVIN, (1819-1903) - a U.S. Representative from Indiana; born in Clinton County, Ohio, January 7, 1819; attended the common schools; moved with his parents to Indiana in 1836; studied law in Winchester, Randolph County; moved to Wabash County, Ind., in 1846; was admitted to the bar and commenced practice in Wabash; member of the State house of representatives in 1851 and again during the special session of 1865; treasurer of Wabash County 1855-1859; provost marshal of the eleventh district of Indiana 1862-1865; elected as a Republican to the Forty-sixth Congress (March 4, 1879-March 3, 1881); was not a candidate for renomination in 1880 to the Forty-seventh Congress; resumed the practice of his profession in Wabash, Wabash County, Ind., where he died February 10, 1903; interment in Falls Cemetery.

COX, WILLIAM ELIJAH, (1861-1942) - a U.S. Representative from Indiana; born on a farm near Birdseye, Dubois County, Ind., September 6, 1861; attended the common and high schools of Huntingburg and Jasper, Ind.; was graduated from Lebanon University, Tenn., in 1888 and from the law department of the University of Michigan at

Ann Arbor in 1889; was admitted to the bar July 10, 1889, and commenced practice at Rockport, Spencer County, Ind., moving to Jasper, Ind., later in the same year; prosecuting attorney for the eleventh judicial district of Indiana 1892-1898; elected as a Democrat to the sixtieth and to the five succeeding Congresses (March 4, 1907-March 3, 1919); chairman, Committee on Expenditures in the Department of the Treasury (Sixty-second Congress); unsuccessful candidate for reelection in 1918 to the Sixtysixth Congress; resumed the practice of law and also was engaged with a desk-manufacturing company, serving as president at the time of his death; died in Jasper, Ind., March 11, 1942; interment in Fairmount Cemetery, Huntingburg, Ind.

CRAIG, GEORGE N., (1909-   ) - governor of Indiana (1953-1957), was born in Brazil, Indiana on August 6, 1909, the son of Bernard and Clo (Branson) Craig. As a young man, he enrolled at Culver Military Academy, then went on to the University of Indiana where he received his LL.B. degree in 1932. He returned home to Brazil and practiced law with his father's firm. He also worked as an attorney in Indianapolis up until 1942. When the United States entered World War II, Craig began military service and was sent to Europe. During his four years in the armed forces he rose to the rank of lieutenant colonel. He was discharged in 1946. In the years after the war, he was an active member of the American Legion in Indiana and served as national commander of the Legion from 1949 to 1950. He also participated in Republican politics and practiced law until 1953 when he became governor of Indiana.

Serving during the post-war boom, Craig supported plans for various public works, including the creation of an Indiana port on Lake Michigan, the construction of the Indiana Toll Road, and the implementation of such ay safety features as widened bridges and roads. Several state offices were reorganized within the Department of Health, and the Department of Corrections was established to manage the state prison system.

Craig completed his term in 1957 and went to Washington, D.C. where he practiced law. He later moved his law practice to California and then back to his hometown of

Brazil, Indiana. He was married in 1931 to Kathryn Heiliger and had two children.

D

DEBS, EUGENE VICTOR, (1855 - 1926) was a labor leader; born Nov. 5, who ran for the U.S. presidency on the Socialist Party ticket five times between 1900 and 1920.

Debs was one of a large family born to immigrant parents in Terre Haute, Indiana. His world was peopled with workers who labored long grinding hours for little pay. Mostly self-educated after grammar school, Debs' heores were Thomas Paine, Patrick Henry, and John Brown. The book that most impressed him in boyhood was Victor Hugo's *Les Miserables*.

At the age of 14, Debs worked in the railway yards, scraping paint off old railway cars. He soon became a locomotive fireman, earning $1 a day. After studying bookkeeping, he obtained a job as a ledger clerk in a wholesale grocery establishment.

Debs helped to organize a lodge of the Brotherhood of Locomotive Firemen in 1875, and became the organization's secretary-treasurer in 1880. He put the union on a sound financial basis while simultaneously holding the positions of city clerk of Terre Haute (1879-83) and representative in the Indiana Legislature (1885).

Although Debs initially opposed labor strikes, he soon decided that they were a necessary weapon. It was his belief that the only hope of the working man was in the organization of labor by industry, rather than by craft or trade.

Debs helped to organize the American Railway Union and became its president in 1893. The following year the union conducted a successful strike against the Great Northern Railroad for higher wages. Debs helped to direct the bitter Chicago Pullman Car Company strike that same year. As a result of the strike, he and other union leaders were jailed for six months on a contempt of court conviction. A later federal investigation could find no evidence that Debs or the other union leaders had participated in or advised intimidation or violence. After his release from the Illinois jail in 1895, he was greeted by 100,000 persons at Chicago as he went through that city on his way home to Terre Haute.

A confirmed socialist thereafter, Debs was a founder of the Socialist Party in the United States. As the party's presidential candidate in the election of 1900 he won 96,000 votes, and in 1904 he received 402,000 votes.

While working as an editor for a Socialist weekly and as a lecturer, Debs helped found the Industrial Workers of the World (IWW) in 1905. As the Socialist Party presidential candidate, he polled 402,000 votes in 1908, 901,000 (amounting to almost six percent of the total) in 1912, and 900,000 votes in 1920.

Debs' final candidacy for the presidency occurred while the Socialist leader was in prison. He had been convicted of sedition under the provisions of the 1917 Espionage Act because of his views against World War I. President Harding released Debs from jail in 1921, but did not restore his U.S. citizenship, which had been revoked because of his conviction.

Debs hailed the Russian October Revolution, but soon condemned the resulting Communist Party because it did not adhere to his belief that socialism should be achieved through the democratic methods of debate and consent. Debs continued to lecture and work as a contributor and editor of periodicals until his death in Elmhurst, Illinois on Oct. 20. His writings include *Unionism and Socialism* (1904) and *Walls and Bars* (1927).

DENBY, EDWIN, (1870-1929) - a U. S. Representative from Michigan; born in Evansville, Vanderburg County, Indiana, February 18, 1870; attended the public schools; went to China in 1885 with his father, who was United States Minister; employed in the Chinese imperial maritime customs service 1887-1894; returned to the United States in 1894; was graduated from the law department of the University of Michigan at Ann Arbor in 1896; moved to Detroit, Michigan; was admitted to the bar and commenced practice in 1896; during the war with Spain served as a gunner's mate, third class, United States Navy, on the *Yosemite*; member of the State house of representatives in 1903; elected as a Republican to the Fifty-ninth, Sixtieth, and Sixty-first Congresses (March 4, 1905-March 3, 1911); unsuccessful candidate for reelection in 1910 to the Sixty-second Congress; resumed the practice of law in Detroit; also engaged in banking and various other business enterprises; president of the Detroit Charter Commission in 1913 and 1914; president of the Detroit Board of Commerce in 1916 and 1917; during the First World War enlisted as a private in the United States Marine Corps in 1917; retired as major in the United States Marine Corps Reserve in 1919; appointed chief probation officer in the recorder's court of the city of Detroit and in the circuit of Wayne County in 1920; appointed Secretary of the Navy by President Harding and served from March 4, 1921, until March 10, 1924, when he resigned; again resumed the practice of law and various business enterprises; died in Detroit, Michigan, February 8, 1929; interment in Elmwood Cemetery.

DENTON, WINFIELD KIRKPATRICK, (1896-1971) - (son of George Kirkpatrick Denton), a U.S. Representative from Indiana; born in Evansville, Vanderburgh County, Ind., October 28, 1896; attended the public schools and De Pauw University, Greencastle, Ind., until the beginning of the First World War, when he enlisted as a private; later commissioned a second lieutenant as an aviator in the United States Army Air Corps and served until discharged in 1919 with overseas service; A.B., De Pauw University, 1919; J.D., Harvard Law School, 1922; was admitted to the bar in 1920 and commenced the practice of law in Evansville, Ind., in 1922; prosecuting attorney of Vanderburgh County, Ind., 1932-1936; member of the Indiana State Legislature 1937-1942, serving as caucus chairman in 1939 and as minority leader in 1941; member of the State budget committee 1940-1942; entered the service as a major in 1942; served in the Judge Advocate General's Depart ment, Wright Field, Ohio, and was discharged as a lieutenant colonel in 1945; elected as a Democrat to the Eighty-first and Eighty-second Congresses (January 3, 1949-January 3, 1953); unsuccessful candidate for reelection in 1952 to the Eighty-third Congress; delegate to each Democratic

National Convention from 1952 to 1964; elected to the Eighty-fourth and to the five succeeding Congresses (January 3, 1955- January 3, 1967); unsuccessful candidate for reelection in 1966 to the Ninetieth Congress; resumed the practice of law; died in Evansville, Ind., November 2, 1971; interment in Oak Hill Cemetery.

DOUGLAS, LLOYD CASSEL, (1877 - 1951) was a clergyman and author of several popular religious novels; born August 27, including *The Robe* and *The Big Fisherman.*

Douglas was born in Columbia City, Indiana. He earned his bachelor of arts degree from Wittenberg College in 1900. Three years later, he received a master's degree from his alma mater and a bachelor of divinity degree from Hamma Divinity School in Springfield, Ohio. Also in the same year, he was ordained in the Lutheran ministry and assigned to the pastorship of Zion Church in North Manchester, Indiana, where he remained until 1905. Between 1905 and 1911 he held the ministry of a church in Lanchester, Ohio, and another in Washington, D.C. He returned to the Midwest in 1911 and became director of religious work at the University of Illinois. A series of pastorships in Michigan, Ohio, Los Angeles, and Montreal, Canada, ended when he retired in the late 1920s to devote more time to lecturing and writing.

In all, Douglas wrote more than ten novels. A few were derived from his religious essays, while others were written to dramatize Christian faith and morals. His first novel, *The Magnificent Obsession* (1929), was written when Douglas was more than 50 years old. The book became a huge success and was followed by two other equally popular novels - *The Robe* (1942) and *The Big Fisherman* (1948). Other works include *Precious Jeopardy* (1933), *Green Light* (1935), *White Banners* (1936), *Disputed Passage* (1939), and *Invitation to Live* (1940). His autobiography, *Time to Remember*, was published in 1951, the year of his death in Los Angeles, California, on Feb. 13, 1951. A sequel *The Shape of Sunday*, was written by his daughter and published in 1952.

DOXEY, CHARLES TAYLOR, (1841-1897) - a U.S. Representative from Indiana; born in Tippecanoe County, Ind.,

July 13, 1841; moved with his mother to Minnesota in 1855 and worked on a farm; later moved to Fairbury, Ill., where he attended the public schools; moved to Anderson, Ind.; entered the service as first sergeant of Company A, Nineteenth Regiment, Indiana Volunteer Infantry, in July 1861; promoted to second lieutenant, subsequently resigned, and then became captain of Company K, Sixteenth Indiana Infantry; engaged in the manufacture of staves and headings; member of the State senate in 1876; member of the board of directors in the first natural-gas companies of Anderson; elected as a Republican to the Forty-seventh Congress to fill the vacancy caused by the death of Godlove S. Orth and served from January 17 to March 3, 1883; unsuccessful candidate for election in 1884 to the Forty-ninth Congress; resumed former business activities; died in Anderson, Ind., April 30, 1898; interment in Maplewood Cemetery.

DRESSER, PAUL, (1857 - 1906) - was an actor and composer of popular songs; born on April 21, he wrote the music for the Indiana state song, "On the Banks of the Wabash," for which his brother, Theodore Dreiser, wrote the words.

Dresser was born in Terre Haute. He left home at the age of 16 to join a medicine show. Shortly afterward, he changed his last name and toured in vaudeville as a singer, monologist, and comedian. He also toured with the Billy Rice Minstrels as an end man.

Dresser wrote his first song, "Wide Wings," around 1875. After becoming established as a songwriter, he helped orgize the music publishing firm of Howley, Haviland, and Dresser in 1901. He started his own publishing company a few years before his death on Jan. 30, in New York City in 1906. He compositions include "The Letter that Never Came" (1886), "The Blue and the Gray" (1890), "Just Tell Them That You Saw Me" (1903), and "My Gal Sal" (1903).

DUMONT, EBENEZER, (1814-1897) - a U.S. Representative from Indiana; born in Vevay, Ind., November 23, 1814; pursued classical studies; studied law; was admitted to the bar and commenced practice in Vevay; member of the State house of representatives in 1838; treasurer of Vevay 1839-

1845; lieutenant colonel of Volunteers in the Mexican War; member of the State house of representatives in 1850 and 1853; colonel of the Seventh Regiment, Indiana Volunteer Infantry, during the Civil War; promoted to brigadier general of Volunteers September 3, 1861, and served until February 28, 1863, when he resigned; elected as a Unionist to the Thirty-eighth Congress and reelected as a Republican to the Thirty-ninth Congress (March 4, 1863-March 3, 1867); chairman, Committee on District of Columbia (Thirty-eighth Congress), Committee on Expenditures in the Department of the Interior (Thirty-ninth Congress); was not a candidate for renomination in 1866; appointed by President Grant Governor of Idaho Territory, but died in Indianapolis, Ind., April 16, 1871, before taking the oath of office; interment in Crown Hill Cemetery.

DUNBAR, JAMES WHITSON, (1860-1943) - a U.S. Representative from Indiana; born in New Albany, Floyd County, Ind., October 17, 1860; attended the public schools and was graduated from New Albany High School in 1878; engaged in mercantile pursuits; manager of public utilities in New Albany and Jeffersonville; secretary-treasurer of the Western Gas Association 1894-1906; secretary of the American Gas Institute 1906-1909; president of the Indiana Gas Association 1908-1910 and secretary 1914-1919; elected as a Republican to the Sixty-sixth and Sixty-seventh Congresses (March 4, 1919-March 3, 1923); was not a candidate for reelection in 1922; elected to the Seventy-first Congress (March 4, 1929-March 3, 1931); unsuccessful candidate for reelection in 1930 to the Seventy-second Congress; resumed his former business pursuits; died in New Albany, Ind., May 19, 1943; interment in Fairview Cemetery.

DUNHAM, CYRUS LIVINGSTON, (1817-1877) - a U.S. Representative from Indiana; born in Dryden, Tompkins County, N.Y., January 16, 1817; attended the common schools; taught school; studied law and was admitted to the bar; moved to Salem, Washington County, Ind., in 1841 and commenced practice; elected prosecuting attorney of Washington County in 1845; member of the State house of representatives in 1846 and 1847; elected as a Democrat to the

Thirty-first, Thirty-second, and Thirty-third Congresses (March 4, 1849-March 3, 1855); chairman, Committee on Roads and Canals (Thirty-third Congress); unsuccessful candidate for reelection in 1854 to the Thirty-fourth Congress; appointed by Governor Willard secretary of state and served in 1859 and 1860; served in the Union Army as colonel of the Fiftieth Regiment, Indiana Volunteer Infantry, 1861-1863; resumed the practice of law in New Albany, Floyd County, Ind.; elected a member of the State house of representatives in 1864 and 1865; moved to Jeffersonville, Ind., in 1871; judge of Clark County Criminal Court 1871-1874; resumed the practice of law; died in Jeffersonville, Clark County, Ind., November 21, 1877; interment in Walnut Ridge Cemetery.

DUNN, GEORGE GRUNDY, (1812-1857) - a U.S. Representative from Indiana; born in Washington County, Ky., December 20, 1812; moved to Monroe County, Ind.; completed preparatory studies and attended the Indiana University at Bloomington; moved to Bedford, Lawrence County, Ind., in 1833, where he taught school; studied law; was admitted to the bar in 1835 and commenced practice in Bedford, Ind.; prosecuting attorney of Lawrence County in 1842; elected as a Whig to the Thirtieth Congress (March 4, 1847-March 3, 1849); unsuccessful candidate for reelection in 1848; served in the State senate from 1850 until 1852, when he resigned; elected as a Republican to the Thirty-fourth Congress (March 4, 1855-March 3, 1857); was not a candidate for renomination in 1856; died in Bedford, Ind., September 4, 1857; interment in Green Hill Cemetery.

DUNN, GEORGE HEDFORD, (1794-1854) - a U.S. Representative from Indiana; born in New York City, November 15, 1794; moved to Lawrenceburg, Dearborn County, Ind., in 1817; studied law; was admitted to the bar in 1822 and commenced practice in Lawrenceburg; member of the State house of representatives in 1828, 1832, and 1833; promoter of the first railway in Indiana; unsuccessful candidate for election to the Twentyfourth Congress; elected as a Whig to the Twenty-fifth Congress (March 4, 1837- March 3, 1839); unsuccessful candidate for reelection; resumed the practice of law; State treasurer 1841-1844; judge of Dearborn

County, Ind.; president of the Cincinnati & Indianapolis Railroad at the time of his death in Lawrenceburg, Ind., January 12, 1854; interment in New Town Cemetery.

DUNNING, PARIS C., (1806-1884) - governor of Indiana (1848- 1849), was born near Greensboro, North Carolina on March 15, 1806, the son of James and Rachel (North) Dunning. He attended school in Greensboro, and after the death of his father, in 1823, moved to Indiana with his family. As a young man, he attended medical school in Louisville, Kentucky, then switched to law and returned to Bloomington, Indiana and studied in the office of Governor Whitcomb. He soon entered politics, winning a seat in the State House of Representatives in 1833 and again in 1834 and 1835. In 1836, he was elected to the Indiana Senate and served for four years. He was a member of the Board of Trustees of Indiana State College from 1838 to 1841.

Dunning was the Democrat's nominee for lieutenant governor in 1846 and won by a margin of about 3,000 votes. He remained in that office until 1848 when he became governor upon James Whitcomb's resignation to take a U.S. Senate seat. Dunning served out the remainder of Whitcomb's term and left office in 1849. He continued to play an active role in state politics. In 1863 he was elected to the Indiana Senate and served for one term.

Paris Dunning died on May 9, 1884 in Bloomington. He was married twice: 1) to Sarah Alexander in 1826, who died in 1863, and 2) to Ellen Lane Ashford in 1865. He had five children.

DURBIN, WINFIELD, (1847-1928) - governor of Indiana (1901- 1905), was born on May 4, 1847 in Lawrenceburg, Indiana, the son of William and Eliza (Sparks) Durbin. His father owned a tannery. When Winfield Durbin was young, his family moved to New Philadelphia, Indiana and he attended public schools. During the Civil War, he served for five months in the 139th Regiment. He moved to St. Louis shortly after the war and pursued studies at a commercial college. Following college, he taught school and worked during the summers at his father's tannery.

Over the next several years, Durbin participated in various business ventures: a dry goods company in Indianapolis; the Citizens' Bank in Anderson; and a paper mill in Anderson. He returned to military duty in 1898 during the Spanish-American War and served for ten months as a colonel in the 161st Indiana Regiment. In 1900, he was nominated for governor by the Republican Party and won easily over his Democratic opponent, John Worth Kern in the general election. While in office, Durbin worked to defeat legislation he saw as benefiting the few rather than the many, and ruffled some Republican supporters as a consequence. He was in favor of luring industry to Indiana and advocated highway improvements as a means to that end. Durbin left office in 1905. He ran for governor a second time in 1912 on the Republican ticket, but lost to Democrat, Samuel M. Ralston.

Durbin returned to live and work in Anderson, Indiana, and died there on December 18, 1928. He was married in 1875 to Bertha McCullough and had a son and a daughter.

E

EDGERTON, JOSEPH KETCHUM, (1818-1893) - (brother of Alfred Peck Edgerton), a U.S. Representative from Indiana; born in Ver gennes, Addison County, Vt., February 16, 1818; attended the public schools of Clinton County, N.Y.; studied law in Plattsburg (N.Y.) Academy; was admitted to the bar and commenced practice in New York City in 1839; moved to Fort Wayne, Ind., in 1844 and continued the practice of law; director of the Fort Wayne & Chicago Railroad Co. in 1854 and later its president; president of the Grand Rapids & Indiana Railroad Co. in 1855; director of the Ohio & Indiana Railroad Co. in 1856; elected as a Democrat to the Thirtyeighth Congress (March 4, 1863-March 3, 1865); unsuccessful candidate for reelection in 1864 to the Thirty-ninth Congress; died in Boston, Mass., August 25, 1893; interment in Lindenwood Cemetery, Fort Wayne, Ind.

ELLIOT, RICHARD NASH, (1897-1948) - a U.S. Representative from Indiana; born near Connersville, Fayette County, Ind., April 25, 1873; attended the common schools; taught school three years; studied law; was admitted to the bar in 1896 and commenced practice in Connersville, Ind.; county attorney of Fayette County 1897-1906; member of the State house of representatives tives1905- 1909; city attorney of Connersville 1905-1909; delegate to the Republican National Convention in 1916; chairman of the Republican State convention in 1930; elected as a Republican to the Sixty-fifth Congress to fill the vacancy caused by the death of Daniel W. Comstock; re-elected to the Sixty-sixth and to the five succeeding Congresses and served from June 26, 1917, to March 3, 1931; chairman, Committee on Expenditures in the Department of State (Sixty-sixth and Sixty-seventh Congresses), Committee on Elections No. 3 (Sixty-eighth Congress), Committee on Public Buildings and Grounds (Sixty-ninth through Seventy- first Congresses); unsuccessful candidate for reelection in 1930 to the Seventysecond Congress; served as assistant comptroller general of the United States from March 6, 1931, to April 30, 1943, when he retired; resided in Washington, D.C., until his death on March 21, 1948; interment in Dale Cemetery, Connersville, Ind.

EMBREE, ELISHA, (1801-1863) - a U.S. Representative from Indiana; born in Lincoln County, Ky., September 28, 1801; moved to Indiana in 1811 with his father, who settled in Knox (now Gibson) County, near where Princeton was subsequently located; received limited schooling; engaged in agricultural pursuits; studied law; was admitted to the bar in 1836 and commenced practice in Princeton, Gibson County, Ind.; circuit judge for the fourth circuit of Indiana 1835-1845; was nominated as the Whig candidate for Governor of Indiana in 1849, but declined, preferring to run for Congress; elected as a Whig to the Thirtieth Congress (March 4, 1847-March 3, 1849); unsuccessful candidate for reelection in 1848 to the Thirty-first Congress; resumed the practice of law and also interested in farming; died in Princeton, Ind., February 28, 1863; interment in Warnock Cemetery.

EVANS, DAVID WALTER, (1946-   ) - a U.S. Representative from Indiana; born in Lafayette, Tippecanoe County, Ind., August 17, 1946; attended public schools in Shoals, Ind.; A.B., Indiana University, 1967; postgraduate work at Indiana University, 1967- 1969, Butler University, 1969-1971; teacher of social studies and science, 1968-1974; delegate to Democratic National Mid-term Convention, 1974; elected as a Democrat to the Ninety-fourth and to the three succeeding Congresses (January 3, 1975-January 3, 1983); unsuccessful candidate for nomination in 1982 to the Ninety-eighth Congress from the tenth congressional district of Indiana; legislative consultant in Washington, D.C.; is a resident of McLean, Va.

EVANS, JAMES LA FAYETTE, (1825-1903) - a U.S. Representative from Indiana; born in Clayville, Harrison County, Ky., March 27, 1825; attended the public schools; moved to Indiana, with his parents, who settled in Hancock County in 1837; moved to Marion, Ind., in 1845 and engaged in mercantile pursuits; moved to Hamilton County, Ind.; settled in Noblesville in 1850 and continued mercantile pursuits; also engaged in the grain-elevator business and in the pork-packing business; elected as a Republican to the Forty-fourth and Forty-fifth Congresses (March 4, 1875-March 3, 1879); was not a candidate for renomination in 1878; resumed the grain-elevator business; died in Noblesville, Ind., May 28, 1903; interment in Crownland Cemetery.

EWING, JOHN, (1789-1858) - a U.S. Representative from Indiana; born in Cork, Ireland, May 19, 1789; immigrated to the United States with his parents, who settled in Baltimore, Md.; attended the public schools; moved to Vincennes, Ind., in 1813 and engaged in commercial pursuits; established the Wabash Telegraph; associate judge of the circuit court of Knox County from 1816 to 1820, when he resigned; unsuccessful candidate for the State senate in 1816 and 1821; appointed lieutenant colonel of the State militia in 1825; member of the State senate 1825- 1833; elected to the Twenty-third Congress (March 4, 1833-March 3, 1835); elected as a Whig to the Twenty-fifth Congress (March 4, 1837-March 3, 1839); unsuccessful candidate for reelection in 1838 to the Twentysixth Congress; again a member of the State senate 1842- 1844; retired from public life and active business pursuits; died in Vincennes, Ind., April 6, 1858; interment in the City Cemetery.

FAIRBANKS, CHARLES WARREN, (1852-1918) - a U.S. Senator from Indiana and a Vice President of the United States; born near Unionville Center, Union County, Ohio, May 11, 1852; attended the common schools and graduated from Ohio Wesleyan University, Delaware, Ohio, in 1872; agent of the Associated Press in Pittsburgh, Pa., and in Cleveland, Ohio; studied law; was admitted to the Ohio bar in 1874; moved to Indianapolis, Ind., the same year and commenced practice; unsuccessful candidate for election to the United States Senate in 1893; appointed a member of the United States and British Joint High Commission which met in Quebec in 1898 for the adjustment of Canadian questions; elected as a Republican to the United States Senate in 1896; reelected in 1902 and served from March 4, 1897, until his resignation March 3, 1905, having been elected Vice President of the United States; chairman, Committee on Immigration (Fifty- fifth Congress), Committee on Public Buildings and Grounds (Fifty-sixth through Fifty-eighth Congresses); elected Vice President of the United States in 1904 on the Republican ticket with Theodore Roosevelt and served from March 4, 1905, to March 3, 1909; unsuccessful candidate for Vice President of the United States on the Republican ticket with Charles E. Hughes for President in 1916; resumed the practice of law in Indianapolis, Ind., where he died June 4, 1918; interment in Crown Hill Cemetery.

F

FAIRFIELD, LOUIS WILLIAM, (1858-1930) - a U.S. Representative from Indiana; born in a log cabin near Wapakoneta, Auglaize County, Ohio, October 15, 1858; moved to Allen County, Ohio, in 1866 and resided on a farm near Lima; attended the public schools; moved to

Middle Point, Van Wert County, Ohio, in 1872; taught school for six months, and then attended the Ohio Northern University at Ada in 1876; continued teaching and attending school until 1888; editor of the Hardin County Republican at Kenton, Ohio, in 1881 and 1882; taught school in Middle Point in 1883 and 1884; moved to Angola, Steuben County, Ind., in 1885, being selected to assist in the building of Tri-State College, Angola, Ind.; vice president of and teacher at Tri-State College 1885-1917; unsuccessful candidate for the State senate in 1912; elected as a Republican to the Sixty-fifth and to the three succeeding Congresses (March 4, 1917-March 3, 1925); chairman, Committee on Insular Affairs (Sixty-eighth Congress); unsuccessful candidate for renomination in 1924; occasionally engaged as a lecturer and resided in Angola, Ind.; died in Joilet, Ill., while on a visit, February 20, 1930; interment in Circle Hill Cemetery.

FARIS, GEORGE WASHINGTON, (1854-1914) - a U. S. Representative from Indiana;born near Renssolaer, Jasper County, Indiana, June 9, 1854; attended the public schools; was graduated from Asbury (now De Pauw) University, Greencastle, Indiana, in 1877; studied law; was admitted to the bar in 1877 and commenced practice in Indianapolis, Indiana; resided in Colorado for the benefit of his health in 1879; returned to Terre Haute, Indiana, in 1880 and continued the practice of law; unsuccessful Republican candidate for judge of the circuit court in 1884; elected as a Republican to the Fifty-fourth, Fifty-fifth, and Fifty-sixth Congresses (March 4, 1895-March 3, 1901); declined to be a candidate for renomination in 1900; resumed the practice of law in Terre Haute, Indiana, and shortly thereafter moved to Washington, D.C., and continued the practice of law until his death in that city on April 17, 1914.

FARLEY, JAMES INDUS, (1871-1948) - a U. S. Representative from Indiana; born on a farm near Hamilton, Steuben County, Indiana, on February 24, 1871; attended the public schools and Tri-State College, Angola, Indiana, and Simpson College, Indianola, Iowa; taught in the public schools of Steuben and De Kalb Counties, Indiana, 1890-1894; engaged as a salesman for the Auburn Automobile Co. in 1906, later becoming sales manager, vice president, and president of the company, retiring in 1926; delegate to the Democratic National Convention at Houston in 1928; elected as a Democrat to the Seventy-third, Seventy-fourth, and Seventy-fifth Congresses (March 4, 1933-January 3, 1939); unsuccessful candidate for reelection in 1938 to the Seventy- sixth Congress; engaged in agricultural pursuits; died in a hospital at Bryn Mawr, Pennsylvania, on June 16, 1948.

FARQUHAR, JOHN HANSON, (1818-1873) - a U. S. Representative from Indiana; born in Union Bridge, Carroll County, Md., December 20, 1818; attended the public schools; moved to Indiana with his parents, who settled in Richmond in 1833; employed as an assistant engineer on the White River Canal until 1840; studied law; was admitted to the bar and commenced practice in Brookville, Indiana; secretary of the State senate in 1842 and 1843; chief clerk of the State house of representatives in 1844; unsuccessful candidate for election in 1852 to the Thirty-third Congress; presidential elector on the Republican ticket of Lincoln and Hamlin in 1860; served as captain in the Nineteenth Infantry of the Regular Army in the Civil War; elected as a Republican to the Thirty-ninth Congress (March 4, 1865-March 3, 1867); was not a candidate for renomination in 1866; moved to Indianapolis in 1870 and engaged in banking; appointed secretary of state by Governor Conrad Baker; died in Indianapolis, Indiana, October 1, 1873.

FISHER, CARL GRAHAM, (1874 - 1939) - Promoter and developer of Miami Beach, the Indianapolis Speedway, and Lincoln Highway, the country's first coast to caost motoway; born on Jan. 12, in Greensburg Indiana. Fisher spent part of his youth as a bicycle and automobile racing star. In 1904 he organized the Prest-O-Lite Company to supply carbide gas headlights for the late model automobiles.

The idea of the "Indy 500" originated during a trip to Europe in 1905 when Fisher witnessed the defeat of the U.S. entry to the James Gordon Bennet Cup Races. The need for a place for U.S. car drivers to test drive racing cars was immediately apparent to Fisher who successfully completed the track in 1909.

Fisher is best known as the promoter who developed Miami Beach. He acquired a large part of the land in 1912 and preceded to build the hotels, boulevards, recreation areas, and stores that helped to make Miami Beach one of the world's leading resort areas.

Fisher was also a major promoter of the Lincoln Highway, the first motorway from New York to California and thus indirectly influenced the trend to long-distance automobile travel in the United States. Fisher took his crusade for marked and paved roads to the masses using the slogan "See America First." To accomplish his goal, Fisher organized the Lincoln Highway Association which eventually raised ten million dollars to build the highway which was not completed until the government took over the task in the early 1920s.

A more successful undertaking for Fisher was the Dixie Highway, which was the country's first north/south motor road.

Fisher died July 15, 1939 in Miami, Florida.

FITCH, GRAHAM NEWELL, (1809-1892) - (grandfather of Edwin Denby), a U. S. Representative and a U. S. Senator from Indiana; born in Le Roy, Genesee County, New York, December 5, 1809; attended Middlebury Academy and Geneva (New York) College; studied medicine and completed his medical course at the College of Physicians and Surgeons; commenced practice in Logansport, Indiana, in 1834; member of the State house of representatives in 1836 and 1839; professor of anatomy at the Rush Medical College, Chicago, Illinois, 1844-1848 and at the Indianapolis (Indiana) Medical College in 1878; Democratic presidential elector in 1844, 1848, and 1856; elected as a Democrat to the Thirty-first and Thirty-second Congresses (March 4, 1849-March 3, 1853); was not a candidate for renomination in 1852; resumed the practice of medicine; elected to the United States Senate to fill a vacancy in the term beginning March 4, 1855, and served from February 4, 1857, to March 3, 1861; was not a candidate for reelection in 1860; raised the Forty-sixth Regiment, Indiana Volunteer Infantry, during the Civil War and served as its colonel from November 1, 1861, to August 2, 1862, when he resigned because of injuries received in action; commanded a brigade at the capture of Fort Thompson, Missouri, and Island No. 10; also participated in the capture of Forts Pillow and Charles; resumed the practice of medicine in Logansport, Indiana; delegate to the Democratic National Convention at New York City in 1868, which nominated the presidential ticket of Seymour and Blair; died in Logansport, Indiana, November 29, 1892.

FOLEY, JAMES BRADFORD, (1807-1886) - a U. S. Representative from Indiana; born near Dover, Mason County, Kentucky, October 18, 1807; received a limited schooling; employed on a flatboat on the Mississippi River in 1823; moved to Greensburg, Indiana, in 1834; engaged in mercantile pursuits 1834-1837, and afterwards in farming; treasurer of Decatur County 1841-1843; member of the State constitution convention in 1850; appointed commander of the Fourth Brigade of State militia in 1852; elected as a Democrat to the Thirty-fifth Congress (March 4, 1857-March 3, 1859); resumed agricultural pursuits in Decatur County; died in Greensburg, Indiana, December 5, 1886.

FORD, GEORGE, (1846-1917) - a U. S. Representative from Indiana; born in South Bend, St. Jospeh County, Indiana, January 11, 1846; attended the common schools; engaged in the cooper's trade in early youth; entered the law department of the University of Michigan at Ann Arbor, and was graduated from that institution in 1869; was immediately admitted to the bar and commenced practice in South Bend, Indiana; prosecuting attorney of St. Joseph County in 1873 and 1875-1884, when he retired, having been elected to Congress; elected as a Democrat to the Forty-ninth Congress (March 4, 1885-March 3, 1887); declined to be a candidate for reelection in 1866 to the Fiftieth Congress; became the head of the legal department of implement concern, but subsequently resumed the private practice of his profession in South Bend, Indiana; elected judge of the superior court of St. Joseph County in 1914 and served until failing health compelled him to retire; died in South Bend, Indiana, on August 30, 1917.

FOSTER, JOHN HOPKINS, (1862-1917) - a U. S. Representative from Indiana; born in Evansville, Vanderburg

County, Indiana, January 31, 1862; attended the common schools of his native city and was graduated from Indiana University at Bloomington in 1882 and from the law department of Columbian University (now George Washington University), Washington, D.C., in 1884; was admitted to the bar in 1885 and commenced the practice of his profession in Evansville, Indiana; member of the State house of representatives in 1893; judge of the superior court of Vanderburg County 1896-1905; elected as a Republican to the Fifty-ninth Congress to fill the vacancy caused by the resignation of James A. Hemenway; reelected to the Sixtieth Congress and served from May 16, 1905, to March 3, 1909; unsuccessful candidate for reelection in 1908 to the Sixty-first Congress; resumed the practice of law in Evansville, Indiana, where he died September 5, 1917.

FOSTER, NORMAN, (1903-1976) - actor, producer, writer, was born in Richmond, Indiana on December 13, 1903. He became a film star of the 1930's who quit acting for a period of over 30 years in order to direct. He directed most of the "Mr. Moto" films, as well as *Rachel and the Stranger*, *Woman On The Run*, and a number of Disney movies, including *Davy Crockett, King of the Wild Frontier*, for which he won a Christopher award.

He was married to Claudette Colbert from 1928 to 1935. After their divorce, he married Sally Blane, sister of Loretta Young, and they had two children. In the 1970's, he resumed his acting career, with a role in the television series *Cannon*.

Norman Foster died on July 7, 1976.

FRICK, FORD CHRISTOPHER, (1894-) - baseball executive, journalist, was born in Wawaka, Indiana on December 19, 1894. He graduated from Consolidated High School in 1910. In 1911, he enrolled at De Pauw Univeristy, where he was a member of both the baseball and track teams. After graduation in 1915, he became an assistant professor of English at Colorado College. In 1917, he got a job as a reporter for the Colorado Springs *Telegraph*, which he left after a year to help in the war effort during World War I, where he supervised the training of rehabilitation workers in four states.

When the war ended, Frick wrote for a variety of newspapers, and finally settled in at the New York *Evening Journal* for eleven years. Every year, he traveled with the New
York Yankees, writing not only his own column, but ghost-
writing articles for Babe Ruth, Lou Gehrig and manager
Miller Huggins.

In 1930, after successfully filling in as a sports broad-
caster for someone, he was offered a twice-daily sportscast
which he did for four years, along with his newspaper writing. He then became the publicity director of the National
League. In less than a year, he was unanimously voted in
as president. Being one month shy of his 40th birthday, he
was the youngest person to hold the position.

When his tenure began in 1934, he had his hands full
with eccentric, opinionated players, such as Leo Durocher
and Dizzy Dean, and it seemed to his colleagues that he
was not forceful enough for the job. However, as the years
went by, he proved his mettle, not only with the players,
but as an administrator who took three teams that were failing financially and turned them into strong, viable members
of the league. He also slowly integrated night baseball into
the game, and was one of the founders of the National
Baseball Museum in Cooperstown, New York.

In 1941, when the United States was involved in World
War II, Frick once again lent his support, managing the
Baseball Equipment Fund and supervising the distribution
of playing equipment to the Armed Forces.

He remained president of the National League until
1951. He was then named National Commissioner of Baseball, a position he held until 1965. In 1970, he was inducted into the National Baseball Hall of Fame.

He married Eleanor Cowing in 1916 and they had one
son.

FULLER, BENONI STINSON, (1825-1903) - a U. S. Representative from Indiana; born near Boonville, Warrick
County, Indiana, November 13, 1825; attended the common
schools; taught school in Warrick County; sheriff of Warrick County in 1856 and 1858; served in the State senate in
1862, 1870, and 1872; member of the State house of representatives 1866-1868; elected as a Democrat to the Forty-
fourth and Forty-fifth Congresses (March 4, 1875-March 3,

1879); was not a candidate for renomination in 1878; engaged in agricultural pursuits in Warrick County; died in Boonville, Indiana, April 14, 1903.

G

GARDNER, FRANK, (1872-1937) - a U. S. Representative from Indiana; born on a farm in finley Township, near Scottsburg, Scott County, Indiana, May 8, 1872; attended the rural schools; was graduated from Borden Institute, Clark County, Indiana, in 1896 and from the law department of the University of Indiana at Bloomington in 1900; was admitted to the bar in 1900 and commenced the practice of law in Scottsburg, Indiana; auditor of Scott County 1903-1911; county attorney 1911-1917; member of the Democratic county committee and served as chairman 1912-1922; served as field examiner for the State board of accounts 1911- 1920; elected as a Democrat to the Sixty-eighth, Sixty-ninth, and Seventieth Congresses (March 4, 1923-March 3, 1929); unsuccessful candidate for reelection in 1928 to the Seventy-first Congress; resumed the practice of law in Scottsburg, Indiana; elected judge of the sixth judicial circuit of Indiana in 1930; reelected in 1936 and served until his death in Scottsburg, Indiana, February 1, 1937.

GARRIGUE, JEAN, (1914-1972) - poet, was born in Evansville, Indiana on December 8, 1914. She received a B.A. from the University of Chicago in 1937 and an M.A. from the University of Iowa in 1943.

In the late 1930's, she made a living by editing a weekly newspaper. Through the years she taught English literature at different schools including The University of Iowa, Bard College, Queens College, The New School for Social Research, The University of Connecticut, Storrs, and Smith College.

The first work she had published was "Thirty Six Poems and a Few Songs," which was included in the book, *Five*

Young Poets of 1944. Some of her other books were, *The Ego and The Centaur*, *The Monument Rose* and *Country Without Maps.* She also contributed short stories and novellas to different publications such as *Cross Sections*, *Saturday Review* and *New Republic.*

Her poetry was praised by critics as having a "noble style" and the Saturday Review said that she was "undeniably original and individual as an artist, and a craftsman in complete command of her medium."

Jean Garrigue died on December 27, 1972.

GATES, RALPH F., (1893-   ) - governor of Indiana (1945- 1949), was born on February 24, 1893 in Columbia City, Indiana, the son of Benton and Alice (Fessler) Gates. He attended the University of Michigan and received his A.B. degree in 1915 and his LL.B. in 1917. During World War I, he served as an ensign in the Pay Corps of the Naval Reserves.   He was assigned to the War Risk Insurance Bureau as a lieutenant, junior grade, and was sent overseas from December 1917 to April 1919.

Gates returned home to Columbia City after the war and worked as an attorney with his father's law firm. He became interested in politics, aligned himself with the Republicans, and from 1941 to 1944 was chairman of the Republican Party. In 1944, he ran for governor of Indiana and won over his Democratic rival, Samuel D. Jackson by more than 45,000 votes. Gates took office just as World War II came to a close. His administration was concerned with the reorganization of state government. A number of new public offices were established, including the Department of Veteran Affairs, the Department of Revenue, the Flood Control Commission, and the Traffic Safety Commission. During his term a retirement pension plan for public employees was also begun.

Gates left office in 1949 and returned to Columbia City where he practiced law and remained   active in Republican politics. He was married in 1919 to Helene Edwards and had two children.

GEER, WILL AUGHE, (ne Ghere), (1902-1978) - actor, was born in Frankfort, Indiana on March 9, 1902. He attended the University of Chicago, graduating in 1924 with a Ph.B. He continued his education at Columbia University and Oxford University in England.

He began his professional stage career doing walk-ons in plays done by the Southern and Marlowe Shakespearean Repertory Company. He spent years performing in various stock companies throughout the United States, and did theater work from the 1920's until the early 1970's.

His first appearance in film was in *The Misleading Lady*, in 1930. Some of his other movies were *Winchester 73*, *Broken Arrow*, *Advise and Consent*, *In Cold Blood* and *Jeremiah Johnson*.

Geer added television to his already massive body of work by doing roles on such prominent shows as, *Bonanza*, *Gunsmoke*, *Mission Impossible* and *Hawaii Five-O*. His most famous role as an actor was as Grandpa Walton in the hit series, *The Waltons*, which ran from 1972 to 1978.

He was married to Herta Ware in 1936 and they had one son and two daughters. He died in 1978.

GERARD, DAVE, (1909-) - cartoonist, was born in Crawfordsville, Indiana on June 18, 1909. He attended the University of Arizona for one year and then went to Wabash College where he received an A.B. in 1931.

He began his career as a cartoonist for the National Newspaper Syndicate in Chicago, from 1949 to 1967. He was the creator of the "Will-Yum" cartoon and the "Will-Yum" comic books for Dell Publishing. In 1967, he created the syndicated cartoon strip "Citizen Smith."

Gerard was a member of the Crawfordsville City Council from 1948 to 1955 and in 1972, he became the mayor of that city. Also, during that year, he published a book based on his cartoon character, "Citizen Smith," entitled, "Citizen Smith Fights Pollution."

He married Sarah Hunt in 1934 and they had two daughters.

GILBERT, NEWTON WHITING, (1862-1939) - a U.S. Representative from Indiana; born in Worthington, Franklin County, Ohio, May 24, 1862; moved with his parents to Steuben County, Ind., in 1875; attended the common schools of Ohio and Indiana and Ohio State University at

Columbus; studied law; was admitted to the bar in 1885 and commenced practice in Angola, Ind.; appointed surveyor of Steuben County, Ind., in 1886 and elected to the office in 1888; member of the State senate 1896- 1900; Lieutenant Governor of Indiana 1900-1904; captain of Company H, One Hundred and Fifty-seventh Indiana Volunteer Infantry, during the war with Spain; elected as a Republican to the Fifty-ninth Congress and served from March 4, 1905, to November 6, 1906, when he resigned; judge of the court of first instance at Manila, Philippine Islands, 1906-1908, by appointment of President Roosevelt; member of the Philippine Commission in 1908 and 1909; president of the board of regents, Philippine University, in 1908 and 1909; served as secretary of public instruction of the Philippine Islands in 1909; Vice Governor of the Philippine Islands 1909-1913; moved to New York City in 1916 and resumed the practice of law; delegate to the Republican National Convention in 1916; retired in 1937 and moved to Santa Ana, Calif. where he died on July 5, 1939; interment in Circle Hill Cemetery, Angola, Ind.

GILHAMS, CLARENCE CHAUNCEY, (1860-1912) - a U. S. Representative from Indiana; born in Brighton, Lagrange County, Indiana, April 11, 1860; attended the common schools and the State norman school at Terre Haute, Indiana; taught school; was employed as a salesman; auditor of Lagrange County 1894-1902; engaged in the life insurance business; elected as a Republican to the Fifty-ninth Congress to fill the vacancy caused by the resignation of Newton W. Gilbert; reelected to the Sixtieth Congress and served from November 6, 1906, to March 3, 1909; unsuccessful candidate for reelection in 1908 to the Sixty-first Congress; studied law; was admitted to the bar in 1910; resumed the life insurance business; died in Lagrange, Indiana, June 5, 1912.

GILLEN, COURTLAND CRAIG, (1880-1954) - a U. S. Representative from Indiana; born in Roachdale, Putnam County, Indiana, July 3, 1880; attended the rural schools; was graduated from Fincastle High School in 1897; taught common and high schools for five years 1897-1904; attended De Pauw University at Greencastle, Indiana, 1901-

1903; was graduated from the law department of the University of Indianapolis (Indiana Law School) in 1905; was admitted to the bar in 1904 and commenced practice in Greencastle, Putnam County, Indiana; served as county attorney 1909-1914 and as prosecuting attorney of the sixty-fourth judicial circuit in 1917 and 1918; delegate to the Democratic State convention in 1924; alternate delegate to the Democratic National Convention at Philadelphia in 1936; elected as a Democrat to the Seventy-second Congress (March 4, 1931-March 3, 1933); unsuccessful candidate for renomination in 1932; elected judge of the sixty-fourth judicial circuit (Putnam Circuit Court) in 1934 and served from January 1, 1935, until his resignation on April 15, 1939; resumed the private practice of law; died in Greencastle, Indiana, September 1, 1954.

GILLIE, GEORGE W., (1880-1963) - a U.S. Representative from Indiana; born in Berwickshire, Scotland, August 15, 1880; moved to the United States with his parents, who settled in Kankakee, Ill., in 1882 and in Fort Wayne, Ind., in 1884; attended the public schools, International Business College, Fort Wayne, Ind., in 1898, and Purdue University, Lafayette, Ind., 1899-1901; was graduated from Ohio State University at Columbus in 1907 as doctor of veterinary surgery; meat and dairy inspector of Allen County, Ind., 1908-1914; began the practice of veterinary medicine in Fort Wayne, Ind., in 1914; sheriff of Allen County 1917-1920, 1929-1930, and 1935-1937; elected as a Republican to the Seventy-sixth and to the four succeeding Congresses (January 3, 1939-January 3, 1949); unsuccessful candidate for reelection in 1948 to the Eightyfirst Congress; engaged in agricultural pursuits; jury commissioner for the Federal courts for the northern district of Indiana; resident of Fort Wayne, Ind., until his death there on July 3, 1963; interment in Lindenwood Cemetery.

GIMBEL, BERNARD FEUSTMAN, (1885-   ) - merchant, was born in Vincennes, Indiana on April 10, 1885. After high school, he enrolled in the Wharton School of Finance and Commerce at the University of Pennsylvania and graduated in 1907 with a B.S. degree.

Gimbel came from a long line of retailers, beginning with his grandfather Adam, who had a retail establishment in Vincennes, in 1842. Adam taught seven of his sons the retail business, "from the ground up." The brothers opened their first store, Gimbel Brothers in Milwaukee, in 1887. The family then moved to Philadelphia where a second store was opened and where Bernard began his first job working on the loading dock. He worked briefly in various departments and then became a vice-president in 1907. In 1927, when his father retired as president, Bernard was elected to the position.

Gimbel Brothers opened another store in New York, ready to take on the already established retail giant, Macy's. It became a famous rivalry that the president of each company reportedly enjoyed.

A series of lucrative business ventures including the financing of Saks Fifth Avenue, and a new Gimbel's in Chicago, led Fortune magazine to note that "Bernard Gimbel has become the top merchant of the United States." By 1950, Gimbel's had fifteen stores, with approximately twenty thousand employees, and the family owned 20 percent of the stock.

His business continued to thrive during World War II when he borrowed twenty million dollars and had his buyers purchase as much merchandise as they could, with the overflow being put in rented warehouses. Customers were able to buy hard-to-find items at his store that were not available elsewhere.

Gimbel served as the director of the 1939 World's Fair and was made chairman of the board of the Madison Square Garden Corporation.

He married Alva Bernheimer in 1912 and they had five children. Bernard Gimbel died on September 29, 1966.

GIRDLER, TOM MERCER, (1877-1965) - steel company executive, was born in Clark County, Indiana on May 19, 1877.

A wealthy aunt paid his way to Lehigh University in 1897, where he decided to become a mechanical engineer. It was the perfect choice for the boy who at sixteen, had built a locomotive from an old vertical-boiler twin engine. He got his degree in mechanical engineering in 1901, ranking second in his class.

His first job at the Buffalo Forge Company sent him to England for a year. He returned home in 1902 and decided to accept a job offer from the Oliver Iron & Steel Company in Pittsburgh, where he worked for three years. He then moved to Pueblo, Colorado to work for the Colorado Fuel & Iron Company. He was supposed to begin working at a better position than his last job, but he asked his new boss if he could work in the rail rolling mill, which meant less pay and harder physical work. However, he fulfilled his objective, which was to learn as much as he could about how steel was made.

He continued to get good positions in steel plants until in 1929, he joined with Cyrus Eaton in forming Republic Steel in Cleveland, Ohio.

The company floundered in the beginning, a situation not helped by the impending stock market crash. But as a manager, Girdler was someone to be reckoned with and although the first years showed heavy financial losses, in 1935 the company was finally out of the red and went on to take its place as one of the "big three," along side U.S. Steel and Bethlehem Steel.

Eventually, Eaton was dropped from the company and Girdler was sole owner. There were years of union fights down the road for him because of his refusal to deal with any of the union leaders. In one particularly violent episode on Memorial Day, 1937, at his South Chicago plant, ten people were killed in a clash between police and the union sympathizers. After four years and eight more deaths in other union-related fights, Republic Steel gave in to the workers' demands for union representation, which included reinstating workers in jobs and paying thousands of dollars in back pay.

In 1937, he joined the board of what was later to become Vultee Aircraft Corporation, and helped create major advances in airplane designing and manufacturing. Under his direction, Vultee grew, and in 1941, the company bought out Consolidated Aircraft Corporation, a company that produced long-range flying boats and four-engine bombers. In 1942, he took over the reins of Consolidated and at the age of 65, made a new career for himself. At that time, he was the chairman of the board and chief executive officer of both Consolidated and Vultee, while still remaining as chairman of Republic. By 1941, the combined assets of his companies totaled almost $600,000,000, and yet he would not accept any compensaton other than the $275,000 a year he received from Republic Steel.

To the end of his life, he never changed his mind about his opposition to unions. In 1943, he collaborated with Boyden Sparkes on an autobiography entitled, "Bootstraps," in which he defended his company's involvement in the Little Steel strike of 1937.

Girdler was married four times and had four children. He died on February 4, 1965.

GOODRICH, JAMES P., (1864-1940) - governor of Indiana (1917-1921), was born on February 18, 1864 in Winchester, Indiana, the son of John and Elizabeth (Edger) Goodrich. He grew up in Winchester, attended the public schools, and after high school, enrolled at DePauw University. By the age of twenty- three he gained admittance to the bar and began a highly successful practice in his home town. Over the next two decades Goodrich amassed a large fortune before moving his office to Indianapolis in 1910.

With wealth had come political connection, and he served as Republican state chairman from 1901 until 1910. From 1912 until 1916 he served as Republican national committeeman, but resigned that year to run for governor. Despite a close race he defeated his Democratic rival, and assumed office just as the United States entered World War I. During his term of office a Department of Conservation was organized, more state parks added to the system, and the highways improved.

After his successor's inauguration, James Goodrich toured Europe as part of the American Relief Administration and served on the commission which brought succor to numerous Russian famine districts. Upon his return home in 1923 he worked on the Indiana Deep Waterway Commission, and in 1924 accepted appointment to the International St. Lawrence Waterways Commission. In the last decade of his life Goodrich became a prominent philanthropist, and donated significant sums to a number of Indiana Colleges.

He died in his home town of Winchester on August 15, 1940. He was married to Cora I. Prist, and had one son.

GORMAN, WILLIS ARNOLD, (1816-1876) - a U. S. Representative from Indiana; born near Flemingsburg, Kentucky, January 12, 1816; pursued an academic course; moved to Bloomington, Indiana, in 1835; was graduated from the law department of the Indiana University at Bloomington in 1845; was admitted to the bar the same year and commenced practice in Bloomington; clerk of the State senate in 1837 and 1838; major and colonel of Indiana Volunteers in the Mexican War; elected as a Democrat to the Thirty-first and Thirty-second Congresses (March 4, 1849-March 3, 1853); was not a candidate for renomination in 1852; moved to Minnesota in 1853; Territorial Governor of Minnesota 1853-1857; delegate to the constitutional convention of Minnesota in 1857; practiced law in St. Paul, Minnesota, 1857-1861; member of the State house of representatives in 1858; during the Civil War entered the Union Army in 1861 and was colonel of the First Regiment, Minnesota Volunteer Infantry; was mustered out as brigadier general in 1864; resumed the practice of law; prosecuting attorney of St. Paul 1869-1875; died in St. Paul, Minnesota, May 20, 1876.

GRAHAM, WILLIAM, (1782-1858) - a U. S. Representative from Indiana; born at sea March 16, 1782; settled with his parents in Harrodsburg, Mercer County, Kentucky; attended the public schools; moved to Vallonia, Indiana, in 1811; engaged in agricultural pursuits; member of the Territorial house of representatives in 1812; delegate to the State constitutional convention in 1816; member of the State house of representatives 1816-1821 and served as speaker; served in the State senate 1821- 1833; elected as a Whig to the Twenty-fifth Congress (March 4, 1837-March 3, 1839); unsuccessful candidate for reelection in 1838 to the Twenty-sixth Congress; resumed agricultural pursuits; died near Vallonia, Indiana, August 17, 1858.

GRANT, ROBERT ALLEN, (1905-   ) - a U. S. Representative from Indiana; born near Bourbon, Marshall County, Indiana, July 31, 1905; moved to Hamlet, Indiana, in 1912 and to South Bend, Indiana, in 1922; attended the public schools; University of Notre Dame at South Bend, Indiana, A. B., 1928 and from its law department, J. D., 1930; was admitted to the bar in 1930 and commenced practice in South Bend; deputy prosecuting attorney of St. Joseph County, Indiana, in 1935 and 1936; elected as a Republican to the Seventy-sixth and to the four succeeding Congresses (January 3, 1939-January 3, 1949); unsuccessful candidate for reelection in 1948 to the Eighty-first Congress; resumed the practice of law in South Bend, Indiana; United States district judge, northern district of Indiana, 1957 and chief judge since 1961; is a resident of South Bend, Indiana.

GRAY, FINLY HUTCHINSON, (1863-1947) - a U. S. Representative from Indiana; born near Orange, Fayette County, Indiana, July 21, 1863; attended the common schools; studied law; was admitted to the bar in 1892 and commenced practice in Connersville, Indiana; mayor of Connersville 1904-1910; elected as a Democrat to the Sixty-second, Sixty-third, and Sixty-fourth Congresses (March 4, 1911-March 3, 1917); unsuccessful candidate for reelection in 1916 to the Sixty-fifth Congress and for election in 1917 to fill the vacancy in the same Congress caused by the death of Daniel W. Comstock; resumed the practice of law and also engaged in lecturing; again elected to the Seventy- third, Seventy-fourth, and Seventy-fifth Congresses (March 4, 1933-January 3, 1939); unsuccessful candidate for reelection in 1938 to the Seventy-sixth Congress; reengaged in the practice of law in Connersville, Indiana; until his death there on May 8, 1947.

GRAY, ISAAC P., (1828-1895) - governor of Indiana (1880- 1881, 1885-1889), was born on October 18, 1828 in Chester County, Pennsylvania, the son of John and Hannah (Worthington) Gray. As a boy, Gray attended common schools. His family moved to Ohio in 1839, and when he was older, Gray went to live in Union City, Indiana. He worked in the dry goods business and then as a banker, and eventually studied law and became an attorney. When the Civil War broke out, Gray entered the military and served as a colonel of the 4th Indiana Cavalry for six months. In

July, 1863 he served for a week as colonel of the 106th Regiment which took part in the Indiana raid against John H. Morgan. The regiment was disbanded on July 17, 1863. Gray later mustered the 147th Regiment in the spring of 1865.

Following the Civil War, in 1866, Gray ran for U.S. Congress and was defeated. Two years later, however, he won a seat in the Indiana Senate and served until 1872. Originally a Republican, Gray's views changed over time and he aligned himself with the Liberal Republicans which later joined with the Democrats. He was nominated for lieutenant governor by the Democratic Party in 1876 and was elected, serving under James D. Williams. On November 20, 1880, Governor Williams died, and Gray became governor for the remaining six weeks of Williams' term. Gray was defeated in a second bid for lieutenant governor in 1880, but returned strong in the 1884 election and won the governorship from his Republican opponent, William Calkins. During Gray's term, appropriations were made for several institutions: a school for the mentally handicapped in Fort Wayne, and the reconstruction of the Soldiers' Orphan Home in Knightstown. Monies were also provided for the Indiana Soldiers and Sailors' Monument in Indianapolis.

Gray left office in 1889 and practiced law in the capital for four years. In 1893, he was sent to Mexico City as U.S. minister. He died there on February 14, 1895. Gray was married to Eliza Jaqua in 1850 and had four sons, two of whom died in childhood.

GREENWOOD, ARTHUR HERBERT, (1880-1963) - a U. S. Representative from Indiana; born near Plainville, Daviess County, Indiana, January 31, 1880; attended the country schools of Daviess County; was graduated from the high school of Washington, Indiana, from the law department of the University of Indiana at Bloomington, Indiana, in 1905, and from George Washington University, Washington, D.C., in 1925; was admitted to the bar in 1905 and commenced practice in Washington, Indiana; member of the board of education 1910-1916; county attorney of Daviess county 1911-1915; prosecuting attorney for the forty- ninth judicial circuit 1916-1918; member of Geroge Rogers Clark Memorial Commission, Vincennes, Indiana; member of the official delegation attending the inauguration of President Manuel Quezon of the Philippine Republic at Manila, P.I., in 1935; elected as a Democrat to the Sixty-eighth and to the seven succeeding Congresses (March 4, 1923-January 3, 1939); unsuccessful candidate for reelection in 1938 to the Seventy-sixth Congress and for election in 1944 to the Seventy-ninth Congress; served as majority whip in the Seventy-second Congress; lawyer, farmer, and banker in Washington, Indiana, until his retirement in 1946; resided in Brandenton, Florida, and Bethesda, Md.; died in Bethesda, Md., April 26, 1963.

GREGG, JAMES MADISON, (1806-1869) - a U. S. Representative from Indiana; born in Patrick County, Virginia, June 26, 1806; attended the public schools; studied law; was admitted to the bar in 1830 and began practice in Danville, Indiana; county surveyor of Hendricks County 1834-1837; clerk of the circuit court 1837- 1845; elected as as Democrat to the Thirty-fifth Congress (March 4, 1857-March 3, 1859); unsuccessful candidate for reelection in 1858 to the Thirty-sixth Congress; resumed the practice of law in Danville, Indiana; member of the State house of representatives in 1862; died in Danville, Indiana, on June 16, 1869.

GRIFFITH, FRANCIS MARION, (1849-1927) - a U. S. Representative from Indiana; born in Moorefield, Switzerland County, Indiana, August 21, 1849; attended the country schools of the county, the high school in Vevay, Indiana, and Franklin College, Franklin, Indiana; taught school; appointed school superintendent of Switzerland County in 1873; studied law; was admitted to the bar in 1875 and commenced practice in Vevay; county treasurer 1875-1877; delegate to the Democratic National Convention at Cincinnati in 1880; member of the State senate 1886-1894 and served as Acting Lieutenant Governor 1891-1894; unsuccessful candidate for attorney general of Indiana in 1894; elected as a Democrat to the Fifty-fifth Congress to fill the vacancy caused by the death of William S. Holman; reelected to the Fifty-sixth, Fifty-seventh, and Fifty-eighth Congresses and served from December 6, 1897, to March 3, 1905; declined to be a candidate for renomination in 1904;

resumed the practice of law in Vevay, Indiana; city attorney 1912-1916; judge of the circuit court of the fifth judicial district 1916-1922; again engaged in the practice of his profession; died in Vevay, Indiana, February 8, 1927.

GRISSOM, VIRGIL IVAN "GUS", (1926 - 1967) was the second American astronaut to enter space and the first to maneuver an in-flight space capsule.

Grissom was born in Mitchell, Indiana on April 3. He earned his nickname "Gus" after joining the U.S. Army Air Corps pilot-training program in 1944. He left the Corps in 1945 and shortly afterward entered Purdue University, from which he received his bachelor of science degree in engineering in 1950. He then reenlisted in the Air Force and flew more than 100 missions in the Korean War. When the war ended, he remained in the Air Force first as an instructor in the pilot-training program, and later as a test pilot. On April 9, 1959, the National Aeronautics and Space Administration (NASA) announced that Grissom was one of seven men chosen to be astronaut trainees for the U.S. space program. On July 17, 1961, NASA disclosed that Grissom was to become the second American to enter space in a flight similar to the one undertaken by Alan B. Shepard, Jr., in May of that year. Grissom's flight took place on July 21, 1961, in the Liberty Bell 7 space capsule. The suborbital flight lasted 16 minutes, covering a distance of 302 miles and reaching an altitude of 118 miles.

Project Mercury was followed by Project Gemini, which was designed to perfect the docking and rendezvous maneuvers essential to the success of the Project Apollo lunar flights. Grissom's contribution to Project Gemini began with the early design and construction stages of the Gemini 3 spacecraft and included a four-hour space journey in the vehicle on March 23, 1965. During the flight, Grissom (accompanied by John W. Young) successfully piloted the first flight maneuvers by a space capsule under human control.

Grissom, together with Edward H. White and Roger B. Chaffe, died on January 27, 1967. The first casualties of the U.S. space program occurred during a simulation of what was to be the first flight of the Apollo mission, when a fire broke out in the test capsule while it was grounded at Cape Canaveral (now Cape Kennedy), Florida.

GRISWOLD, GLENN HASENFRATZ, (1890-1940) - a U. S. Representative from Indiana; born in New Haven, Franklin County, Missouri, January 20, 1890; attended the public schools; moved to Peru, Miami County, Indiana, in 1911; attended Valparaiso (Indiana) Law School; was admitted to the bar in 1917 and commenced practice in Peru, Indiana; during the First World War served in the United States Army as a private in Company B, Fourth Regiment Casual Detachment, at Camp Zachary Taylor, Kentucky; city attorney of Peru, Indiana, 1921-1925; prosecuting attorney of Miami County, Indiana, 1925 and 1926; member of the Indiana Railroad Commission in 1930; elected as a Democrat to the Seventy-second and to the three succeeding Congresses (March 4, 1931-March 3, 1939); unsuccessful candidate for reelection in 1938 to the Seventy-sixth Congress; reengaged in the practice of law in Peru, Indiana, until his death there on December 5, 1940.

GUTHRIE, ALFRED BERTRAM, JR, (1901-   ) - novelist, was born in Bedford, Indiana on January 13, 1901. When he was six months old, his family moved to Choteau, Montana, a small town south of the Blackfoot Reservation.

In 1919, he attended school at the University of Washington in Seattle for one year. He then moved back home to enroll in the University of Montanta, where he received an A.B. in 1923. He did his graduate study at Harvard in 1944.

He began a career as a reporter at the Lexington Leader in Lexington, Kentucky, in 1926. During the next 20 years, he moved up through the ranks to city editor and editorial writer, and finally, to executive editor.

He quit the newspaper business in 1947, because his first novel, *The Big Sky*, had received immediate critical and popular acclaim. His next book, *The Way West*, written in 1949, won Guthrie the Pulitzer Prize for fiction. He wrote other books, including, *These Thousand Hills*, *The Big It* and *The Blue Hen's Chick*.

From 1947 to 1952, he was a teacher of creative writing at the University of Kentucky, and through the years, contributed articles to periodicals such as *Esquire* and *Holiday*.

In 1953, he wrote the screenplay for the film *Shane*, for

which he won an Oscar. He also wrote the screenplay for *The Kentuckian*, in 1955.

Guthrie was married twice, and had two children from his first marriage.

H

HALL, KATIE BEATRICE, (1938-   ) - a U.S. Representative from Indiana; born Katie Beatrice Green in Mound Bayou, Bolivar County, Miss., April 3, 1938; attended public schools of Mound Bayou, Miss.; B.S., Mississippi Valley State University, Itta Bena, Miss., 1960; M.S., Indiana University, Bloomington, Ind., 1968; teacher; served in the Indiana house of representatives,atives 1974-1976; Indiana senate, 1976-1982; delegate, Democratic Mini Convention, Memphis, Tenn., 1978; chairperson, Indiana State Democratic convention, 1980; elected by special election on November 2, 1982, to the Ninetyseventh Congress to fill the vacancy caused by the death of Adam Benjamin; also elected at the same time as a Democrat to the Ninety-eighth Congress (November 2, 1982-January 3, 1985); was an unsuccessful candidate for renomination to the Ninety-ninth Congress; is a resident of Gary, Ind.

HALLECK, CHARLES, (1900 -   ) is a lawyer and politician who served in the U.S. House of Representatives longer than any Hoosier before him.

Halleck was born in DeMotte, Indiana, on August 22 to Abraham (a lawyer) and Lura Luce Halleck. He was a Phi Beta Kappa graduate of Indiana University and its law school. The year he completed his schooling (1924), he was elected county prosecutor, a post that he held until he was first elected to the U.S. Congress in 1932.

An expert at winning elections - his northern Indiana district returned him to Congress from 1932 until he announced in 1968 he would retire at term's end - he could make his magic work for others as well. Serving as Congressional campaign chairman in 1946, he helped the national Republican Party regain control of Congress for the first time in 15 years.

Halleck was believed to have come close to his party's vice- presidential nomination on two occasions, but he never managed to grasp it. He was credited with a key role in obtaining the 1940 Republican presidential nomination for Hoosier Wendell L. Willkie.

As majority leader of the 80th and 83rd Congresses and minority leader of the 86th and 88th Congresses, his legislative prowess was an aid to both Republican and Democratic presidents. He described himself as a political "gut fighter," but the description is belied by his ability to make friends in the opposition party, as well as his own.

In all probability it was his gravelly voice on the "Ev and Charlie" television program with Sen. Everett M. Dirksen of Illinois that drew him the most national attention.

HAMILTON, ANDREW HOLMAN, (1834-1895) - a U. S. Representative from Indiana; born in Fort Wayne, Indiana, June 7, 1834; attended the common schools, and was graduated from Wabash College, Crawfordsville, Indiana, in 1854; studied law at Harvard University; was admitted to the bar in 1859 and commenced practice in Fort Wayne, Indiana; elected as a Democrat to the Forty-fourth and Forty-fifth Congresses (March 4, 1875-March 3, 1879); resumed the practice of law; died in Fort Wayne, Indiana, May 9, 1895.

HAMILTON, LEE HERBERT, (1931-   ) - a U. S. Representative from Indiana; born in Daytona Beach, Volusia County, Florida, April 20, 1931; moved with his parents to Evansville, Indiana, in 1944; attended the public schools of Evansville, Indiana; graduated from Central High School in Evansville in 1948 and from De Pauw University in 1952; studied at Goethe University, Frankfurt on Main, Germany, in 1952 and 1953; graduated from Indiana University School of Law in 1956; was admitted to the bar in 1957 and began the practice of law in 1958 in Columbus, Indiana; treasurer of Bartholomew County Young Democrats, 1960-1963, and served as president in 1963 adn 1964; elected as a Democrat to the Eighty-ninth, Ninetieth, and Ninety- first

Congresses (January 3, 1965-January 3, 1971). *Reelected to the Ninety-second Congress.*

HAMMOND, ABRAM A., (1814-1874) - governor of Indiana (1860- 1861), was born on March 21, 1814 in Brattleboro, Vermont, the son of Nathaniel and Patty (Ball) Hammond. His family moved to Brookville, Indiana when he was six years old. As a young man, Hammond studied law and was admitted to the bar. He practiced his profession in Greenfield, and later in Columbus where he was prosecuting attorney. He subsequently lived and worked in Indianapolis, Cincinnati, San Francisco, and Terre Haute. In 1849, in Indianapolis, he was judge of the Court of Common Pleas.

Hammond was elected lieutenant governor of Indiana in 1856 and served under Governor Ashbel Willard. When Willard died in office on October 3, 1860, Hammond succeeded him as governor and served out the remainder of his term. With a mere three months in office, Hammond had little chance to leave his mark. Appearing before the Legislature, however, he urged the establishment of a refuge house for juvenile offenders, an institution that was eventually founded several years later.

Hammond left office in January of 1861 in poor health. He was never to regain his former stamina. He lived out his final days in Colorado, and died in Denver on August 27, 1874. Hammond was married to Mary Amsden and had one son.

HAMMOND, THOMAS, (1843-1909) - a U. S. Representative from Indiana; born in Fitchburg, Worcester County, Massachusetts, February 27, 1843; attended the common schools; engaged in carpentry and contracting work until twenty-one years of age; moved to Detroit, Michigan, and engaged in the packing-house business; moved to Hammond, Lake County, Indiana, in 1876 and assisted in the establishment of the dressed-beef industry; mayor of Hammond 1888-1893; president of the Commercial Bank of Hammond 1892-1907; elected as a Democrat to the Fifty-third Congress (March 4, 1893-March 3, 1895); was not a candidate for renomination in 1894; resumed his former business pursuits; also engaged in the real estate business and banking; member of the city council; appointed by Governor Hanly a member of the metropolitan police board; died in Hammond, Indiana, September 21, 1909.

HANDLEY, HAROLD W., (1909-1972) - governor of Indiana (1957-1961), was born on November 27, 1909 in LaPorte, Indiana, the son of Harold L. and Lottie (Brackbill) Handley. He attended Indiana University and graduated with an A.B. degree in 1932. After graduation he worked with his father at the Rustic Furniture Company in LaPorte, and then became a sales representative for the Unagusta Furniture Corporation of Hazelwood, North Carolina. In 1941, he entered the State Senate and served for a single session. With the entry of the United States into World War II, he enlisted in the army and served in the 85th Division, attaining the rank of lieutenant colonel. After his return from duty, he was elected a second time to the Indiana Senate and served from 1949 to 1952.

In 1952, Handley was the Republican nominee for lieutenant governor on the ticket with George N. Craig. He was elected, served for four years, and in 1956 ran for governor. Winning easily over his Democratic opponent, Ralph Tucker, Handley entered office in January, 1957. During his administration funding was appropriated for a Lake Michigan port, a new highrise state office building was erected, and the Purdue University Veterinary School was founded. Handley refused to approve controversial "right to work" legislation and it was put into effect without his signature.

After completion of his term in 1961, Handley joined an Indianapolis public relations firm and served in the capacity of president. He later went out to Rawlins, Wyoming, and on August 30, 1972 he died there. Handley was married in 1944 to Barbara Winterble and had a son and a daughter.

HANLY, JAMES FRANKLIN, (1863-1920) - governor of Indiana (1905-1909), was born on April 4, 1863 in Champaign County, Indiana, the son of Elijah and Ann (Calton) Hanly. He grew up on a farm and received an intermittent education at rural schools. In 1879, he moved to Williamsport and worked as a teacher in the common school there. Over the next several years, he taught and did manual labor in the summers. He studied law, passed the Warren County Bar in 1889, and started a law practice in Williamsport.

Through his legal work, Hanly, or J. Frank Hanly, was he came to be known, became involved in Republican politics. He was elected to the State Senate in 1890, and to the U.S. Congress in 1894. In 1904, the Republicans nominated him for governor and he won a wide victory over John Worth Kern, the Democratic contender. Several public structures were built during Hanly's term: the Coliseum at the Indiana State Fairgrounds, a tuberculosis clinic near Rockville, and the Industrial School for Girls in Clermont. A temperance law was passed during his administration and moves were made to curb gambling and vice in Indiana. Ethics was a major issue, and a number of state officials were charged in a financial scandal and forced to give up their jobs.

After Hanly completed his term in 1909, he remained active in the temperance movement. He helped establish what was known as the "Flying Squadron," a group that traveled throughout the United States and gave anti-saloon lectures. In 1916, Hanly ran for president of the U.S. as a Prohibition candidate, but was not elected. He continued active in politics until his death in an accident on August 1, 1920 in Denison, Ohio when his car was hit by a train. Hanly was married to Eva Simmer in 1881 and had one daughter.

HANNAGAN, STEVE JEROME, (1899-1953) - publicity agent, was born in Lafayette, Indiana on April 4, 1899.

Though he graduated high school in 1917, he had already been working as a newspaper reporter from the age of 14. After graduation, he tried college at Purdue University for two years, but quit. He continued to work for the Lafayette *Morning Journal*, where he eventually became the sports editor and then the city editor. He became a sports writer for the Indianapolis *Star* in 1918, and the next year he left to join the Russel advertising agency where he wrote copy for products like automobiles and cough syrups.

He got his first big break in 1919, when Carl G. Fisher asked him to handle the publicity for the Indianapolis Motor Speedway. Hannagan bypassed the technical information usually written about the cars and zeroed in on the drivers and their colorful stories. The different angle achieved the great success that Fisher was hoping for.

In 1920, he went back to newspaper writing for United Press, the NEA Service and United Features Syndicate. However, he always felt that journalism was not his forte and yearned to open his own publicity office. He got his chance after he was offered another big assignment from Carl Fisher. Fisher wanted to turn the very quiet, low-key Miami Beach into a thriving vacation mecca. Hannagan studied the situation and realized that the draw would be the warm weather and ocean swimming in the middle of winter and he decided that pictures of beautiful women in bathing suits would get people's attention. The results were overwhelmingly successful for the city.

Hannagan then opened his own business called the Miami Beach News Bureau, whose employees came up with ways to lure out-of- towners to the new resort. Later on, he also handled the publicity campaigns for Jack Dempsey and Gene Tunney.

In 1933, he gave up his agency to become vice president of the Lord & Thomas advertising agency in Chicago. After two years, he once again opened his own office in New York and also opened a branch in Hollywood. That office handled the entertainment industry for awhile, but Hannagan decided to venture into publicity for corporations, which was a very lucrative field. Some of his clients included the Union Pacific Railroad, the Coca-Cola Company and the Sun Valley, Idaho resort. He later decided to include a couple of entertainment accounts when he took over the publicity for the Jack Benny radio show in 1944, and New York's Stork Club.

Hannagan was married twice, and died on February 3, 1953.

HARDEN, CECIL MURRAY, (1894-   ) - a U. S. Representative from Indiana; born in Covington, Fountain County, Indiana, November 21, 1894; graduated from the public schools of Covington, Indiana, in 1912, and attended the University of Indiana at Bloomington; taught all grades in Troy township schools, Fountain County, Indiana, and Covington (Indiana) public schools 1912-1914; Republican National committeewoman from Indiana 1944-1959, and from 1964 to present; delegate at large to the Republican National Conventions in 1948, 1952, 1956, and 1968; elected as a Republican to the Eighty-first and to the four succeeding Congresses (January 3, 1949-January 3, 1959); unsuccessful candidate for reelection in 1958 to the Eighty-sixth Congress; special assistant for women's affairs to Postmaster General, Washington, D.C., March 1959 to March 1961; appointed August 18, 1970, to the National Advisory Committee for the White House Conference on Aging; is a resident of Covington, Indiana.

HARDY, ALEXANDER MERRILL, (1847-1927) - a U. S. Representative from Indiana; born in Simcoe, Norfolk County, Ontario, Canada, December 16, 1847; pursued a college course and studied law; came to the United States in 1864, taking a commercial course at Eastman College, Poughkeepsie, New York; went to New Orleans in 1869, where he engaged in newspaper work until 1873, when he moved to Natchez, Mississippi; conducted a Republican newspaper until 1877; collector of the port of Natchez under appointment of President Grant; moved to Washington, Daviess County, Indiana, in 1884; was admitted to the bar in 1884 and commenced practice in Terre Haute, Indiana; elected as a Republican to the Fifty-fourth Congress (March 4, 1895-March 3, 1897); unsuccessful candidate for reelection in 1896 to the Fifty-fifth Congress; resumed the practice of law in Washington, Indiana; moved to Los Angeles, California, in 1904 and continued the practice of law; moved to Searchlight, Nevada, thence to Salt Lake City, Utah, and finally settled in Tonopah, Nevada, in 1914 and engaged in the practice of his profession; was also interested in mining; died in Tonopah, Nevada, on August 31, 1927.

HARLAN, ANDREW JACKSON, (1815-1907) - (a cousin of Aaron Harlan), a U. S. Representative from Indiana; born near Wilmington, Clinton County, Ohio, March 29, 1815; attended the public schools; studied law; was admitted to the bar in 1839 and commenced practice in Richmond, Indiana; moved to Marion, Indiana, in 1839; clerk of the State house of representatives in 1842 and a member 1846-1848; presidential elector on the Demcratic ticket of Cass and Butler in 1848; elected as a Democrat to the Thirty-first Congress (March 4, 1849-March 3, 1851); elected to the Thirty-third Congress (March 4, 1853-March 3, 1855); in a Democratic congressional convention at Marion, Indiana, in 1854 he was publicly read out of the Democratic Party for voting against the repeal of the Missouri Compormise; declined the nomination from the People's Party in 1854 for the Thirty-fourth Congress; afterward allied himself with the Republican Party; moved to Dakota Territory in 1861; member of the Territorial house of representatives in 1861 and served as speaker; driven from the Territory by the Indians in September 1862 and settled in Savannah, Missouri, where he resumed the practice of law; member of the State house of representatives 1864-1868, serving as speaker the last two years; moved to Wakeeney, Kansas, in 1885 and practiced law; appointed by President Harrison as postmaster of Wakeeney and served from 1890 to 1894; removed to Savannah, Andrew County, Missouri, in 1894; retired from practice of law; died in Savannah, Missouri, May 19, 1907.

HARNESS, FOREST ARTHUR, (1895-1974) - a U.S. Representative from Indiana; born in Kokomo, Howard County, Ind., June 24, 1895; attended the public schools and was graduated from the law department of Georgetown University, Washington, D.C., in 1917; served overseas as a first lieutenant, Three Hundred and Nineteenth Infantry, 1917-1919; awarded the Purple Heart; captain, Infantry Reserve, United States Army, 1920-1949; admitted to the District of Columbia bar in 1917, to the Indiana bar in 1919, and commenced practice in Kokomo, Ind.; prosecuting attorney of Howard County, Ind., 1920-1924; special assistant to the Attorney General of the United States from 1931 to 1935 when he resigned to resume private practice; elected as a Republican to the Seventy-sixth and to the four succeeding Congresses (January 3, 1939-January 3, 1949); chairman, Select Committee on the Federal Communications Commission (Eightieth Congress); unsuccessful candidate for reelection in 1948 to the Eighty-first Congress; resumed the practice of law; Sergeant at Arms of the United States Senate from January 3, 1953, to January 3, 1955; retired in

1960 and resided in Sarasota, Fla., where he died, July 29, 1974; entombment in the mausoleum at Crown Hill Cemetery.

HARRISON, BENJAMIN, (1833 - 1901) - Indianapolis, Indiana) Twenty-third President of the United States was born on August 20, 1833.

Harrison, the grandson of former U.S. President, William Henry Harrison, graduated from Miami University in Oxford, Ohio in 1852 and read law for two years at a Cincinnati based law office. In 1854, he moved to Indianapolis where he started a law practice and became involved with the Indiana Republican Party. He was subsequently appointed to several governmental offices including city attorney (1857) and reporter of the Indiana Supreme Court (1860 and 1864).

During the Civil War, he organized the 70th Indiana Infantry and was appointed its colonel in 1862. Two years of relatively quiet duty in Kentucky was followed by heated action alongside General Sherman at the Atlanta campaign (1864). The next year, Harrison left the army a breveted brigadier general, whereupon he immediately resumed his law career.

He was thrust into the national spotlight in 1876 when he made an unsuccessful bid for the governorship of Indiana. His prestige and viability mounted with his appointment by President Hayes to the Mississippi River Commission in 1876 and his chairmanship of the Indiana delegation to the Republican National Convention in 1880. The following year, he was elected to represent Indiana in the U.S. Senate, serving in this position until 1887 when his bid for reelection was defeated.

In 1888, Harrison secured the Republican nomination to oppose President Grover Cleveland in the upcoming election. In the November contest, Cleveland won the popular vote by a margin of 100,000 votes; but Harrison received 233 electoral votes, 65 more than his opponent, making Harrison the 23rd President of the United States.

The most notable events of the Harrison administration were the McKinley Tariff Act (1890); the Sherman Silver Purchase Act (1890); and the Sherman Anti-Trust Law

(1890) and the Conference of 1889-90 which formed the Pan-American Union.

Under Harrison, the Union grew by six states - North Dakota, South Dakota, Montana, Washington, Idaho, and Wyoming. In addition, Oklahoma was opened for public settlement. An attempt to annex Hawaii was defeated by the anit-Imperalist. Harrison also gave the country its first "billion dollar Congress."

Public reaction to the higher tariffs enacted by the McKinley Act helped to wipe out the Republican majority in 1890 congressional elections and contributed to Harrison's defeat in the presidential election two years later.

Harrison evenually returned to his home in Indianapolis and resumed a highly successful law practice. In one of his better known cases (1898-99) he served as senior counsel to Venezuela in its arbitration with Great Britain over a boundary dispute. Many of Harrison's articles and speeches were published in *This Country of Ours* (1897) and *Views of an Ex-President* (1901).

Harrison died on March 13, 1901.

HARRISON, WILLIAM HENRY, (1773 - 1841) - was a military hero who became the first territorial governor of Indiana and the ninth president of the United States.

Born on Feb. 9, Harrison was the third son of Benjamin Harrison, a prominent politician and one of the original signers of the Declaration of Independence. He was born at Berkeley Pantation, Charles City County, Virginia, and educated at Hampden-Sydney College in Virginia (1787-90) and the University of Pennsylvania (1790-91) where he studied medicine. Immediately after leaving school, he joined the army and served as an aide- de-camp under General Anthony Wayne in 1783.

Harrison resigned from the army in 1798 and was appointed to the position of secretary of the Northwest Territory. He served in this capacity for one year before he was elected the territory's first delegate to the U.S. Congress. His work on the act which created Indiana Territory led to his appointment on May 12, 1800, the first territorial governor of Indiana, an office he held for 12 years.

During the first four years of Harrison's term, the inhabitants of Indiana Territory were subject to the Ordinance of 1787, which provided for a non-representative type of government. Harrison used this enormous power to alter existing tax laws, change the court system, and permit a form of slavery. In 1805, he allowed the territory to pass into a semi-representative stage of government, which actually did very little to alter his sovereign type of leadership. The creation of Illinois Territory by an Act of Congress on February 3, 1809, greatly reduced the size of Indiana Territory and resulted in an increase of the anti-Harrison representation in the territorial assembly. The 1810 legislature reflected this opposition by repealing the laws permitting slavery, nullifying the requirement of land ownership in order to vote, and persuading the U.S. Congress to strip Harrison of much of his power. This marked the beginnings of a true democracy in Indiana.

As Superintendent of Indian Affairs, Harrison negotiated treaties that turned over millions of acres of land in what is now Indiana and Illinois to the U.S. Opposition to these treaties by the famous Shawnee leader, Tecumseh, and his brother, Tenskwatawa, the Shawnee Prophet, was unsuccessful. Harrison defeated the Indian forces in the Battle of Tippecanoe on November 7, 1811.

With the outbreak of the War of 1812, Harrison was commissioned major general in the Kentucky militia and brigadier general in the regular army. In October 1813, he overwhelmed General Proctor of the British forces and Tecumseh in the Battle of the Thames. His victory broke the British hold on the Northwest Territory and, with the death of Tecumseh in the battle, marked the end of Indian resistance to White settlement in the area. In 1816 and 1825, Harrison was elected to the U.S. Congress by the state of Ohio. He served as the U.S. minister to Colombia in 1828 and, upon returning to the U.S. in 1829, he settled on his farm in North Bend, near Cincinnati, Ohio, where he was active as the clerk of the county court and president of the County Agricultural Society.

Harrison's first attempt to gain the U.S. presidency came with his unsuccessful Whig candidacy in 1836. He was renominated by the party in 1840 and, together with John Tyler, ran against President Van Buren. Harrison ran as a people's candidate and a military hero, incorporating his victory at Tippecanoe into the famous slogan "Tippecanoe and Tyler Too." Harrison won the election, receiving 234 electoral votes to Van Buren's 60. He was inaugurated in Washington, D.C., on March 4, 1841, at the age of 68, making him the oldest president to take office. One month later he developed a fatal case of pheumonia, and became the first president to die in office on April 4, 1841.

HARTKE, RUPERT VANCE, (1910-   ) - a U. S. Senator from Indiana; born in Stendal, Pike County, Indiana, May 31, 1910; attended the public schools of Stendal; graduated from Evansville College in 1940 and Indiana University Law School in 1948; during World War II served in the United States Coast Guard and Navy as a seaman and through the ranks to lieutenant from 1942-1946, including supply and purchasing duties at Underwater Sound Laboratory at New London, Connecticut; was admitted to the Indiana bar in 1948 and commenced the practice of law in Evansville, Indiana; deputy prosecuting attorney of Vandenburgh County, Indiana, in 1950 and 1951; mayor of Evansville, Indiana, from 1956 until his resignation December 5, 1958; elected as a Democrat to the United States Senate for the term commencing January 3, 1959, and ending January 3, 1965; reelected in 1964 for the term ending January 3, 1971. *Reelected in 1970 for the term ending January 3, 1977.*

HARVEY, RALPH, (1901-   ) - a U.S. Representative from Indiana; born on a farm near Mount Summit, Henry County, Ind., August 9, 1901; attended the public schools; was graduated from Purdue University, Lafayette, Ind., in 1923; engaged as an agricultural instructor 1923-1928; also engaged in agricultural pursuits; served as county councilman 1932-1942; member of the State house of representatives 1942-1947; elected as a Republican to the Eightieth Congress to fill the vacancy caused by the death of Raymond S. Springer; reelected to the Eighty-first and to the four succeeding Congresses and served from November 4, 1947, to January 3, 1959; unsuccessful candidate for re-election in 1958 to the Eighty-sixth Congress; elected to the Eighty-seventh and the two succeeding Congresses (January

3, 1961-January 3, 1967); unsuccessful candidate for renomination in 1966 to the Ninetieth Congress; resumed agricultural pursuits; is a resident of New Castle, Ind.

HATCH, JETHRO AYERS, (1837-1912) - A U. S. Representative from Indiana; born in Pitcher, Chenango County, New York, June 18, 1837; settled in Sugar Grove, Kane County, Illinois; attended the common schools and the institute in Batavia, Illinois; was graduated from Rush Medical College, Chicago, Illinois, in February 1860 and commenced practice at Kentland, Indiana, in July 1860; served as city health officer of Kentland and county health officer of Newton County, Indiana, for several years;during the Civil War was commissioned assistant surgeon of the Thirty-sixth Regiment, Illinois Volunteer Infantry, on December 11, 1862, and promoted to surgeon of the same regiment; mustered out of service February 8, 1865, and returned to Kentland, Indiana; secretary and later president of the pension examining board 1865-1907; member of the State house of representatives 1872 and 1873; alternate delegate to the Republican National Convention at Chicago in 1888; elected as a Republican to the Fifty-fourth Congress (March 4, 1895-March 3, 1897); was not a candidate for renomination in 1896; returned to Kentland, Indiana, and resumed the practice of medicine; member of board of the hospital for the insane at Logansport, Indiana; physician and surgeon for the Logansport division of the Pennsylvania Railroad for many years; physician and surgeon for the Chicago and Cairo division of the New York Central Railroad from the time it was built until 1907; moved to Victoria, Texas, in 1907 and engaged in the real estate business; died in Victoria, Texas, August 3, 1912.

HATCHER, RICHARD GORDON, (1933 -   ) - lawyer who became the first black mayor of Gary, Indiana.

Born on July 10, 1933, Hatcher grew up in the slum area of Michigan City known as The Patch. Funds raised through summer employment, his church, and a track scholarship allowed him, in the fall of 1951, to enter Indiana University where he majored in government and economics. The following summer, Hatcher organized Michigan City's first civil rights sit-in against a restaurant that had once employed him as a dishwasher.

Soon after receiving his B.A. in 1956, Hatcher entered Valpariso University Law School from which he obtained his L.L.B. in 1959. Hatcher set up his first law practice in East Chicago Heights, Indiana but was most politically active in Gary where he led civil rights demonstrations and helped to end de facto segregation in the school system. In 1961, he was appointed deputy prosecutor of the Criminal Court of Lake County but resigned two years later to make a successful bid for a seat on the Gary City Council.

At this time, the city of Gary was controlled by a powerful democratic machine that received most of its support from organized crime and corruption and thus did very little to provide the average citizen with a workable, efficient government. It was against this background that Hatcher decided to run for mayor in 1967.

Hatcher won the Democratic primary despite a lack of monetary and moral support. However he was not endorsed by the Democratic machine which had decided to back the Republican candidate, Joseph Radigan. this same group was also responsible for an unsuccessful attempt to sway the election by adding 5,000 ghost voters to the voter registration rolls.

Despite such foul play, Hatcher won the election and became the first black mayor in Gary's history. His popularity carried him through the next mayoral election of November, 1971 at which time he defeated the Republican candidate, Theodore Nering by a margin of three to one. Hatcher's efforts to eliminate government corruption and provide better housing, employment and services to the people of Gary won badly needed federal funds which have been very useful to the city in its battle against urban blight.

HAYES, PHILIP HAROLD, (1940-   ) - a U.S. Representative from Indiana; born in Battle Creek, Calhoun County, Mich., September 1, 1940; attended Rensselaer (Ind.) Elementary School; graduated from Rensselaer High School, 1958; B.A., Indiana University, 1963; J.D., Indiana University Law School, 1967; admitted to the Indiana bar in 1967 and commenced practice in Evansville; served as deputy prosecuting attorney, Vanderburgh County, Ind., 1967-1968;

member, Indiana State senate, 1971-1974; elected as a Democrat to the Ninetyfourth Congress (January 3, 1975-January 3, 1977); was not a candidate in 1976 for reelection but was an unsuccessful candidate for nomination to the United States Senate; resumed the practice of law; is a resident of Evansville, Ind.

HAYMOND, WILLIAM SUMMERVILLE, (1823-1885) - a U.S. Representative from Indiana; born near Clarksburg, Harrison County, Va. (now West Virginia), February 20, 1823; attended the common schools and was graduated from Bellevue Hospital Medical College, New York City; commenced the practice of his profession at Monticello, Ind., in 1852; during the Civil War entered the Union Army as a surgeon in 1862 and served one year; unsuccessful candidate for the State senate in 1866; president of the Indianapolis, Delphi & Chicago Railroad Co. 1872-1874; elected as a Democrat to the Fortyfourth Congress (March 4, 1875-March 3, 1877); unsuccessful candidate for reelection in 1876 to the Forty-fifth Congress; resumed his former professional and business activities; organized the Central Medical College in Indianapolis in 1877 and was dean until his death; published in 1879 a history of Indiana; died in Indianapolis, Ind., December 24, 1885; interment in Crown Hill Cemetery.

HAYNES, ELWOOD, (1857 - 1925) - inventor and metallurgist who designed one of the first successful U.S. automobiles.

Born on Oct 14, 1857 in Portland Indiana, Haynes studied at Worcester Polytechnic Institute (1881) and John Hopkins University before becoming a science teacher in Portland, Indiana. He subsequently became the manager of the Portland Natural Gas and Oil Company (1886-1890) and a field superintendent for the Indiana Oil and Gas Company (1890-1901). During the mid 1890s Haynes (with the help of two machinists - Elmer Edgar Apperson) designed and built one of the first American automobiles. The car was tested near Kokomo, Indiana on July 4, 1894 and is now on exhibit at the Smithsonian Institution in Washington, D.C.

In 1898 Haynes established and became president of the Haynes-Apperson Automobile Company, a position he held until his death in 1925.

Other contributions by Haynes to the U.S. automobile industry include the rotary valve gas engine (1903) and the use of aluminum in the construction of the automobile engine.

Haynes was also a successful metallurgist, discovering tungsten chrome steel in 1881 followed by an alloy of cobalt and chromium in 1900. His greatest contribution to this field came in 1911 for his discovery of Stellite, or "stainless steel" which he patented in 1919.

HEILMAN, WILLIAM, (1824-1890) - (great-grandfather of Charles Marion LaFollette), a U.S. Representative from Indiana; born in Albig, Duchy of Hesse-Darmstadt, Germany, October 11, 1824; immigrated to the United States in 1843 and settled on a farm in Vanderburg County, Ind.; moved to Evansville, Ind.; worked for a manufacturing company and subsequently became president of a cotton mill; founded a machine shop for the manufacture of drills in 1847; member of the city council 1852- 1865; member of the State house of representatives tives1870-1876; delegate to the Republican National Convention in 1876; served in the State senate from 1876 until March 3, 1879; elected as a Republican to the Forty-sixth and Forty-seventh Congresses (March 4, 1879-March 3, 1883); unsuccessful candidate for reelection in 1882 to the Forty-eighth Congress; resumed his former business activities; died in Evansville, Ind., September 22, 1890; interment in Oak Hill Cemetery.

HENDRICKS, THOMAS, (1819-1885) - governor of Indiana (1873- 1877), was born on September 7, 1819 in Zanesville, Ohio, the son of John and Jane (Thompson) Hendricks. He graduated from Hanover College in 1841, then studied law in Chambersburg, Pennsylvania. After completing his studies, he moved to Shelbyville, Indiana, and in 1848 won a seat in the State House of Representatives. Hendricks was a member of the Indiana Constitutional Convention in 1851, and was elected to Congress in 1851 and 1852. From 1855 to 1859 he was commissioner of the General Land Office.

Hendricks served in the U.S. Senate from 1863 to 1869. An active member of the Democratic Party in his state, he received the Democratic nomination for governor three times: first in 1860 when he was defeated by Henry S. Lane; second in 1868 when he lost to Conrad Baker; and third, in 1872 when he won over Republican, Thomas M. Browne. During his term as governor, Hendricks signed the Baxter Prohibition Law, but saw it repealed a just two years later. He also worked to mediate labor disputes in Clay County and Logansport.

While still governor, in 1876, Hendricks ran as the Democratic candidate for vice president with Samuel J. Tilden, but was not elected. He completed his term as governor of Indiana in January, 1877. In 1884, Hendricks ran again as a candidate for vice president, this time with Grover Cleveland, and won. He was sworn in as vice president in 1885, but served only about eight months. On November 25, 1885, he died in Indiana. Hendricks was married in 1845 to Eliza Morgan, and had one son, who died at the age of three.

HENDRICKS, WILLIAM, (1782-1850) - governor of Indiana (1822-1825), was born in Westmoreland County, Pennsylvania on November 12, 1782, the son of Abraham and Ann (Jamison) Hendricks. He attended school in Canonsburg, Pennsylvania, and as a young man, moved to Cincinnati where he studied law and was admitted to the bar. He practiced for a short time, meanwhile moving to Madison, Indiana Territory. There, with partner, Seth M. Levenworth, from 1813 to 1815, he published the newspaper, *Western Eagle*.

In 1814, he was a member of the House of Representatives of Indiana Territory. He became involved in the Territory's bid for statehood, serving in 1816 as secretary of the Indiana Constitutional Convention. Later that year, he was elected to be the new state's first state representative to the U.S. Congress. As congressman, he was a strong proponent of public works, particularly the building of roads and canals.

After three terms in Congress, Hendricks ran for governor of Indiana and was elected on August 5, 1822. As governor he saw an increase in population in his state as settlers moved north from the Ohio River. He also supervised the moving of the state capitol from Corydon to Indianapolis in 1824. Hendricks resigned the governorship in 1825 to take a seat in the U.S. Senate. He served in that body until 1837, then retired to his estate in Jefferson County. He died there on May 16, 1850. Hendricks was married in 1816 to Ann Parker Paul. They had nine children.

HEROD, WILLIAM, (1801-1871) - a U.S. Representative from Indiana; born in Bourbon County, Ky., March 31, 1801; completed preparatory studies; studied law and was admitted to the bar in Bracken County, Ky.; later moved to Columbus, Ind.; was admitted to the bar in Bartholomew County in 1825 and began practice in Columbus, Ind.; member of the State house of representatives in 1829, 1830, and 1844; served in the State senate 1831-1834, 1845, and 1846; elected prosecuting attorney of Bartholomew County and served from 1833 until 1837, when he resigned; elected as a Whig to the Twentyfourth Congress to fill the vacancy caused by the death of George L. Kinnard; reelected to the Twenty-fifth Congress and served from January 25, 1837, to March 3, 1839; unsuccessful candidate for reelection in 1838 to the Twenty-sixth Congress; resumed the practice of his profession in Columbus, Ind.; clerk of the circuit court of Bartholomew County in 1853; became a Republican upon the formation of that party; engaged in the practice of law until his death at Columbus, Ind., October 20, 1871; interment in City Cemetery.

HICKEY, ANDREW JAMES, (1872-1942) - a U.S. Representative from Indiana; born in Albion, Orleans County, N.Y., August 27, 1872; attended the public schools of his native city and Buffalo (N.Y.) Law School; was admitted to the New York bar in 1896 and commenced practice in La Porte, Ind., in 1897; elected as a Republican to the Sixtysixth and to the five succeeding Congresses (March 4, 1919-March 3, 1931); unsuccessful candidate for reelection in 1930 to the Seventy-second Congress, for election in 1934 to the Seventy-fourth Congress, and in 1936 to the Seventy-fifth Congress; resumed the practice of law; died in

Buffalo, Erie County, N.Y., August 20, 1942, while on a motor trip; interment in Pine Lake Cemetery, La Porte, Ind.

HILER, JOHN PATRICK, (1953-   ) - a U.S. Representative from Indiana; born in Chicago, Ill., April 24, 1953; attended public and Catholic schools in Walkerton and La Porte, Ind.; B.A., Williams College, Williamstown, Mass., 1975; M.B.A., University of Chicago School of Business, 1977; marketing director; delegate, White House Conference of Small Business, 1980; delegate, Indiana State Republican conventions, 1978-1980; elected as a Republican to the Ninety-seventh and to the three succeeding Congresses (January 3, 1981-January 3, 1989); is a resident of La Porte, Ind.

HILL, RALPH, (1827-1899) - a U.S. Representative from Indiana; born in Trumbull County, Ohio, October 12, 1827; attended the district school, the Kinsman Academy and the Grand River Institute, Austinburg, Ohio; taught school in 1846, 1847, 1849, and 1850; studied law at the New York State and National Law School, Ballston, N.Y., and was admitted to the bar in Albany, N.Y., in 1851; returned to Jefferson, Ohio, in August 1851 and practiced; established a select school at Austinburg, Ohio, in November 1851; resumed the practice of law in Jefferson, Ohio, in March 1852; moved to Columbus, Ind., in August 1852 and continued the practice of law; elected as a Republican to the Thirty-ninth Congress (March 4, 1865-March 3, 1867); was not a candidate for renomination in 1866; collector of internal revenue for the third district of Indiana 1869-1875; moved to Indianapolis, Ind., in 1879 and resumed the practice of law; died in Indianapolis, Ind., August 20, 1899; interment in Crown Hill Cemetery.

HILLIS, ELWOOD HAYNES, (1926-   ) - a U.S. Representative from Indiana; born in Kokomo, Howard County, Ind., March 6, 1926; attended Kokomo public schools; graduated from Culver Military Academy, 1944; B.S., Indiana University, 1949; J.D., Indiana University School of Law, 1952; served in United States Army in the European Theater with rank of first lieutenant, 1944-1946; retired from the Reserves in 1954 with rank of captain in the infantry; admitted to the Indiana bar in 1952 and commenced practice in Kokomo; member, Indiana house of representatives, Ninety-fifth and Ninety-sixth General Assemblelies; delegate, Indiana State Republican conventions, 1962-197(); elected as a Republican to the Ninety-second and to the seven succeeding Congresses (January 3, 1971-January 3, 1987); was not a candidate for reelection in 1986; resumed the practice of law; is a resident of Kokomo, Ind.

HOGAN, EARL LEE, (1920-   ) - a U.S. Representative from Indiana; born in Hope, Bartholomew County, Ind., March 13, 1920; attended the public schools of Burney; also attended Indiana University and the University of Kentucky; served from 1940 to 1945 in the Air Force as a bombardier on a B-17; awarded the Distinguished Flying Cross, Purple Heart, and Air Medal with three oak leaf clusters; deputy sheriff of Bartholomew County, Ind., 1946-1950 and sheriff 1950-1958; elected as a Democrat to the Eighty-sixth Congress (January 3, 1959-January 3, 1961); unsuccessful candidate for reelection in 1960 to the Eighty-seventh Congress; assistant to administrator, Farmers Home Administration, 1961; assistant to administrator, Rural Electric Administration, 1961-1962; midwest field representative, Office of Rural Areas Development, 1962-1966; rural development specialist, 1966-1970, special projects representative, 1971- 1975, chief of business and industrial loan division, 1975-1980, all in Farmers Home Administration; secretary, Indidana State Rural Development Committee, 1966-1980; chairman, State advisory board, Indiana Green Thumb, Inc., 1975-1982; owns and operates a farm; is a resident of Naples, Fla., and Columbus, Ind.

HOGG, DAVID, (1886-1973) - a U.S. Representative from Indiana; born near Crothersville, Jackson County, Ind., August 21, 1886; attended the common schools; was graduated from Indiana University College of Liberal Arts at Bloomington in 1909 and from the law department of Indiana University in 1912; was ad mitted to the bar in 1913 and commenced practice in Fort Wayne, Ind.; chairman of the Allen County Republican Committee 1922- 1924; elected as a Republican to the Sixty-ninth and to the three succeeding Congresses (March 4, 1925-March 3, 1933); unsuccessful candidate for reelection in 1932 to the Seventy-third Congress and for election in 1934 to the Seventy-fourth Congress and in 1936 to the Seventy-fifth Congress; resumed the practice of law; organized a mutual life insurance company in 1939; president of Goodwill Industries of Fort Wayne 1940-1943; co-publisher of an interdenominational newspaper, 1941-1946; again resumed the practice of law; resided in Fort Wayne, Ind., until his death there October 23, 1973; interment in Lindenwood Cemetery.

HOLLIDAY, ELIAS SELAH, (1842-1936) - a U.S. Representative from Indiana; born in Aurora, Dearborn County, Ind., March 5, 1842; spent the early part of his life on farms in Indiana, Missouri, and Iowa; attended the common schools and taught in the public schools in Iowa; during the Civil War enlisted in the Fifth Kansas Regiment and served until August 12, 1864, when he was mustered out with the rank of first sergeant; attended Hartsville College, Bartholomew County, Ind.; engaged in teaching in Jennings County, Ind.; studied law at Mount Vernon, Ind.; was admitted to the bar in 1873 and commenced practice in Carbon, Clay County, Ind.; moved to Brazil, Ind., in 1874; mayor of Brazil 1877-1880, 1887, and 1888; city attorney in 1884; member of the city council 1892- 1896; elected as a Republican to the Fifty-seventh and to the three succeeding Congresses (March 4, 1901-March 3, 1909); was not a candidate for renomination in 1908; reengaged in the practice of law in Brazil until 1922; died in Brazil, Ind., March 13, 1936; interment in Cottage Hill Cemetery.

HOLLOWAY, DAVID PIERSON, (1809-1883) - a U.S. Representative from Indiana; born in Waynesville, Warren County, Ohio, December 7, 1809; moved with his parents to Cincinnati in 1813; attended the common schools; learned the printing business and served four years in the office of the Cincinnati Gazette; moved to Richmond, Ind., in 1823; purchased the Richmond Palladium in 1832 and was its editor and proprietor until he died; member of the State house of representatives in 1843 and 1844; served in the State senate 1844-1850; appointed in 1849 examiner of land offices; elected as a Republican to the Thirty- fourth Congress (March 4, 1855-March 3, 1857); chairman, Committee on Agriculture (Thirty-fourth Congress); appointed Commissioner of Patents and served from 1861 to 1865; engaged as a patent attorney in Washington, D.C., until his death, September 9, 1883; interment in Maple Grove Cemetery, Richmond, Ind.; reinterment in Earlham Cemetery.

HOLMAN, WILLIAM STEELE, (1822-1897) - a U.S. Representative from Indiana; born near Aurora, Dearborn County, Ind., September 6, 1822; attended the common schools and Franklin College, Franklin, Ind.; taught in the public schools; studied law; was admitted to the bar and practiced; judge of the probate court 1843-1846; prosecuting attorney 1847-1849; member of the State constitutional convention in 1850; member of the state house of representatives in 1851 and 1852; judge of the court of common pleas 1852-1856; elected as a Democrat to the Thirty-sixth, Thirty-seventh, and Thirty-eighth Congresses (March 4, 1859-March 3, 1865); not a candidate for reelection to the Thirty-ninth Congress; elected to the Fortieth and to the four succeeding Congresses (March 4, 1867-March 3, 1877); chairman, Committee on Appropriations (Forty-fourth Congress), Committee on Public Buildings and Grounds (Forty-fourth Congress); was not a candidate for election to the Forty-fifth Congress; elected to the Forty-seventh and to the six succeeding Congresses (March 4, 1881-March 3, 1895); chairman, Committee on Public Lands (Fiftieth Congress), Committee on Appropriations (Fifty-second Congress), Committee on Indiana Affairs (Fifty-third Congress); unsuccessful candidate for reelection to the Fifty-fourth Congress; again elected to the Fifty-fifth Congress and served from March 4, 1897, until his death in Washington, D.C., April 22, 1897; interment in Veraestau Cemetery, Aurora, Ind.

HOVEY, ALVIN P., (1821-1891) - governor of Indiana (1889- 1891), was born on September 6, 1821 in Posey County, Indiana, the son of Abiel and Frances (Peterson) Hovey. As a boy, Hovey received his education at common schools. He later studied law, was admitted to the bar, and began to practice in Mount Vernon, Indiana. During the

Mexican War he was commissioned first lieutenant in a company of the 2nd Indiana Regiment, but his company was never called into service. He stayed in Indiana and from 1850 to 1854 was a circuit court judge. When a seat was left vacant on the State Supreme Court, Hovey was appointed to fill the position from May, 1854 to December, 1855. In 1856, he was named U.S. district attorney and served for two years.

A supporter of the Democratic Party during his early years, about 1858, Hovey joined the Republicans and soon after ran as a Republican candidate for Congress but was not elected. When the Civil War began in 1861, he returned to military service as colonel of the 1st Regiment, 1st Brigade Indiana Legion. Later that summer he took command of the 24th Indiana Regiment. Less than a year after that, he was promoted to brigadier general, and two years later to major general. He served until October, 1865.

In December of 1865, Hovey was sent to Peru as U.S. minister to that country. He remained in Lima until 1870. Returning to Indiana, he practiced law in Mount Vernon. The Republicans offered him the nomination for governor in 1872, but he declined. Instead he continued with his law practice, and in 1886 began a term in the U.S. Congress. In 1888, the Republicans offered him the gubernatorial nomination again and he accepted, and went on to a narrow win in the general election. During his administration, Hovey was at odds with the Democrat-controlled Legislature, especially on the issue of appointive powers. Also, changes were made in public school policy as the State Board of Education was given responsibility for selecting textbooks.

Hovey died while still governor, on November 23, 1891. He was married twice: to Mary Ann James in 1844, who died in 1863, and to Rose Alice Smith Carey in 1865. He had four children from his first marriage.

HOWARD, JONAS GEORGE, (1825-1911) - a U.S. Representative from Indiana; born on a farm near New Albany, Floyd County, Ind., May 22, 1825; attended private school, Indiana Asbury College (now De Pauw University), Greencastle, Ind., and Louisville (Ky.) Law School; was graduated from the law department of Indiana University at Bloomington in 1851; was admitted to the bar in 1852 and commenced the practice of law in Jeffersonville, Clark County, Ind.; city attorney of Jeffersonville in 1854, 1865, 1871-1873, and 1877-1879; member of the city council 1859-1863; member of the State house of representatives tives1863-1866; elected as a Democrat to the Forty-ninth and Fiftieth Congresses (March 4, 1885-March 3, 1889); unsuccessful candidate for renomination in 1888; returned to Jeffersonville, Ind., where he resumed the practice of law; also engaged in agricultural pursuits; died in Jeffersonville, Ind., October 5, 1911; interment in Walnut Ridge Cemetery.

HOWARD, TILGHMAN ASHURST, (1797-1844) - a U.S. Representative from Indiana; born near Pickensville, S.C., November 14, 1797; attended the public schools; moved to Knoxville, Tenn., in 1816; studied law; was admitted to the bar in 1818 and commenced practice in Knoxville; member of the State senate in 1824; moved to Bloomington, Ind., in 1830 and resumed the practice of law; moved to Rockville, Ind., in 1833 and continued the practice of law; appointed by President Jackson district attorney for Indiana and served from 1833 to 1837; unsuccessful candidate for election to the United States Senate in 1838; elected as a Democrat to the Twenty-sixth Congress on August 5, 1839, and served until his resignation on July 1, 1840; unsuccessful candidate for election as Governor of Indiana in 1840, and for United States Senator in 1843; appointed Charge d'Affaires to the Republic of Texas on June 11, 1844; died in Washington, Tex., August 16, 1844; interment in Rockville Cemetery, Rockville, Parke County, Ind.

HUDNUT, WILLIAM HERBERT, III, (1932-   ) - a U.S. Representative from Indiana; born in Cincinnati, Hamilton County, Ohio, October 17, 1932; educated at Darrow School, New Lebanon, N.Y., 1946-1950; A.B., Princeton University, 1954; B.D., Union Theological Seminary, 1957; clergyman, ordained in Rochester, N.Y., 1957; member, Indianapolis Board of Public Safety, 1970- 1972; elected as a Republican to the Ninety-third Congress (January 3, 1973-January 3, 1975); unsuccessful candidate for reelection in 1974 to the Ninety-fourth Congress; elected mayor of Indianapolis in 1975; reelected in 1979, 1983, and 1987 and served from January 1976 to present; is a resident of Indianapolis, Ind.

HUGHES, JAMES, (1823-1873) - a U.S. Representative from Indiana; born in Baltimore County, Md., November 24, 1823; attended the common schools and Indiana University at Bloomington; studied law; was admitted to the bar in 1842 and commenced practice in Indiana; served in the Mexican War; served as judge of the sixth judicial circuit of Indiana from 1852 until 1856, when he resigned; professor of law in Indiana University 1853-1856; elected as a Democrat to the Thirty-fifth Congress (March 4, 1857-March 3, 1859); unsuccessful candidate for reelection in 1858 to the Thirty-sixth Congress; appointed judge of the Court of Claims and served from January 18, 1860, to December 1864, when he resigned; member, State house of representatives 1864-1866; cotton agent of Treasury Department 1866-1868; died in Wattsville, Md., on October 21, 1873; interment in Rose Hill Cemetery, Bloomington, Ind.

HUMPHREYS, ANDREW, (1821-1904) - a U.S. Representative from Indiana; born near Knoxville, Tenn., March 30, 1821; moved with his parents to Owen County, Ind., in 1829; afterwards moved to Putnam County and located near Manhattan; attended the common schools; moved to Greene County in 1842; member of the State house of representatives 1849-1852 and from January 8 to March 9, 1857; appointed Indian agent for Utah by President Buchanan in 1857; delegate to the Democratic National Convention in 1872 and 1888; served in the State senate 1874-1876, 1878-1882, and 1896- 1900; elected as a Democrat to the Forty-fourth Congress to fill the vacancy caused by the resignation of James D. Williams and served from December 5, 1876, to March 3, 1877; resumed agricul tural pursuits in Greene County, Ind.; attended almost every Democratic State convention during his political life; died in Linton, Ind., June 14, 1904; interment in Moss Cemetery.

HUNTER, MORTON CRAIG, (1825-1896) - a U.S. Representative from Indiana; born in Versailles, Ripley County, Ind., on February 5, 1825; completed a preparatory course;

was graduated from the law department of Indiana University at Bloomington in 1849; was admitted to the bar and practiced; member of the State house of representatives in 1858; enlisted in the Union Army August 27, 1862; commanded the First Brigade, Third Division, Fourteenth Army Corps; brevetted brigadier general of Volunteers; honorably discharged June 24, 1865; elected as a Republican to the Fortieth Congress (March 4, 1867-March 3, 1869); elected to the Forty-third, Forty-fourth, and Fortyfifth Congresses (March 4, 1873-March 3, 1879); operated a quarry in the Indiana limestone district; died in Bloomington, Ind., October 25, 1896; interment in Rose Hill Cemetery.

J

JACKSON, EDWARD, (1873-1954) - governor of Indiana (1925- 1929), was born on December 27, 1873 in Howard County, Indiana, the son of Presley and Mary (Howell) Jackson. The young man attended the local public schools and after graduation decided to study law. He passed the bar in the early 1890's, and opened an office in Kennard, Indiana.

Jackson became the prosecuting attorney for Henry County in 1901, and remained at that post for five years. By 1907 he had been appointed judge of the Henry County Circuit Court. The following year he won election to that office, and continued as a judge for the next six years. Seeking higher office in 1916 he won the election for secretary of state. His tenure in office, however, ended in 1917 when he resigned to become a captain in the Army during World War I.

After two years of military service, Jackson resumed his law career in Lafayette. He had been barely settled when, early in 1920, the State Administration reappointed him secretary of state. Destined, it seemed, to hold this office, Jackson was reelected in November, 1920. By 1924 the Republican Party nominated him for governor, and he went on to win the election. Governor Jackson continued his predecessors expansion of the State Park system, and began the

George Rogers Clark Memorial in Vincennes. As the jazz age finished, he retired to his farm near Orleans, Indiana. Edward Jackson died on November 18, 1954. He was married to Rosa Wilkinson in 1897, and had two children.

JACKSON, SAMUEL DILLON, (1895-1951) - a U.S. Senator from Indiana; born near Zanesville, Allen County, Ind., May 28, 1895; attended the public schools of Fort Wayne, Ind.; graduated from the Indiana University Law School at Indianapolis in 1917, and was admitted to the bar the same year; during the First World War, served as a captain of Infantry 1917-1919; engaged in the practice of law at Fort Wayne, Ind., in 1919; prosecuting attorney of Allen County, Ind., 1924-1928; unsuccessful Democratic candidate for election in 1928 to the Seventy-first Congress; attorney general of Indiana 1940-1941; appointed as a Democrat to the United States Senate to fill the vacancy caused by the death of Frederick Van Nuys and served from January 28, 1944, to November 13, 1944, when a duly elected successor qualified; was not a candidate for election to fill the vacancy; unsuccessful Democratic candidate for Governor of Indiana in 1944; resumed the practice of law; died in Fort Wayne, Ind., March 8, 1951; interment in Lindenwood Cemetery.

JACOBS, ANDREW, (1906-   ) - (father of Andrew Jacobs, Jr.), a U.S. Representative from Indiana; born near Gerald, Perry County, Ind., February 22, 1906; attended the public schools in Gerald, Ind., and St. Benedict's College, Atchison, Kans.; was graduated from Ben Harrison Law School, Indianapolis, Ind., in 1928; was admitted to the bar in June 1927 and commenced the practice of law in Indianapolis, Ind.; public defender in Marion County Felony Court, 1930-1933; elected as a Democrat to the Eighty-first Congress (January 3, 1949- January 3, 1951); was an unsuccessful candidate for reelection in 1950 to the Eighty-second Congress; delegate to the Democratic National Conventions in 1952 and 1956; resumed the practice of law; judge, criminal court of Marion County, 1975-1977; elected to the 89th Congress and to each suceeding Congress. Is a resident of Indianapolis, Ind.

JACOBS, ANDREW, JR., (1932-   ) - (son of Andrew Jacobs), a Representative from Indiana; born in Indianapolis, Marion County, Ind., February 24, 1932; graduated from Shortridge High School in 1949; served in the infantry, United States Marine Corps, 1950-1952; resumed studies and graduated from Indiana University in 1955 and from the law school of the same university in 1958; was admitted to the bar in 1958 and commenced the practice of law in Indianapolis, Ind.; member of the State house of representatives in 1959 and 1960; elected as a Democrat to the Eighty-ninth and to the three succeeding Congresses (January 3, 1965-January 3, 1973); unsuccessful candidate for reelection in 1972 to the Ninety-third Congress; returned to Indianapolis and engaged in the private practice of law and teaching, 1973-1975; elected as a Democrat to the Ninety-fourth and to the six succeeding Congresses (January 3, 1975-January 3, 1989); is a resident of Indianapolis, Ind.

JENCKES, VIRGINIA ELLIS, (1877-1975) - a U.S. Representative from Indiana; born in Terre Haute, Vigo County, Ind., November 6, 1877; attended the public and high schools; engaged in agricultural pursuits in 1912; secretary of Wabash Maumee Valley Improvement Association, 1926-1932; elected as a Democrat to the Seventy-third and to the two succeeding Congresses (March 4, 1933-January 3, 1939); unsuccessful candidate for reelection in 1938 to the Seventy-sixth Congress; United States delegate to the Interparliamentary Union in Paris, France, in 1937; after leaving Congress, remained in Washington, D.C., for many years and worked for the American Red Cross; returned to her native Terre Haute, Ind., in the early 1970s; died in Terre Haute, Ind., January 9, 1975; interment in Highland Lawn Cemetery.

JENNER, WILLIAM EZRA, (1908-1985) - a U.S. Senator from Indiana; born in Marengo, Crawford County, Ind., July 21, 1908; attended public and preparatory schools; graduated from Indiana University at Bloomington in 1930 and from that university's law school in 1930; admitted to the bar in 1930 and commenced practice in Paoli, Ind., in 1932; member, State senate 1934-1942, serving as minority leader 1937-1939 and majority leader and president pro tempore 1939-1941; resigned his seat in 1942 to serve in the Second World War; served overseas and retired as a captain in the Army Air Corps in 1944; elected as a Republican to the United States Senate on November 7, 1944, to fill the vacancy caused by the death of Frederick Van Nuys and served from November 14, 1944, to January 3, 1945; was not a candidate for election to the full term; elected to the United States Senate in 1946 for the term commencing January 3, 1947; reelected in 1952, and served from January 3, 1947, until January 3, 1959; was not a candidate for renomination in 1958; co-chairman, Joint Committee on Printing (Eightieth and Eighty-third Congresses), chairman, Committee on Rules and Administration (Eighty-third Congress); resumed the practice of law; died in Redford. Ind.. March 9, 1985; interment at Crest Haven Memorial Gardens, Bedford, Ind.

JENNINGS, JONATHAN, (1787-1834) - first state governor of Indiana (1816-1822), was born in 1787, probably in Hunterdon County, New Jersey, the son of Jacob and Mary (Kennedy) Jennings. As a boy he received a common school education and attended grammar school in Canonsburg, Pennsylvania. At the age of nineteen, he went west to the Indiana Territory and settled in Clark County. He was admitted to the bar in 1807 and served as a land clerk and as a member of the Board of Vincennes University.

In 1809, he ran for territorial delegate to Congress on the anti-slavery platform and was elected, defeating Thomas Randolph, then Attorney- General of the Indiana Territory. Jennings was reelected in 1811, 1812, and 1814, and during his terms as delegate concerned himself with such matters as internal improvements to the Territory, land purchases, and protection of settlers from Indian attacks. On August 8, 1811, Jennings married Ann Gillmore Hay. She died in 1826, and the following year, he was married to Clarissa Barbee. He had no children.

In 1815, Jennings presented a petition to Congress from the Indiana Territorial Legislature requesting statehood. The Enabling Act, passed the following year, made provisions for a constitutional convention to begin the process of statehood. Jennings served as president of that convention. That same year, 1816, he was elected governor of the new state, defeating Thomas Posey, Indiana Territorial Governor.

As governor, Jennings worked to establish a banking system and an educational system. He supported the enactment of laws to protect free blacks, and he assisted in the negotiation of treaties with the Delaware, Wea, Potawatomi, and Miami Indians. He was reelected to the governorship and served until 1822, when he became a member of Congress. He remained in Congress until 1830, then retired to his farm near Charlestown, where he died four years later on July 26, 1834.

JOHNSON, HENRY UNDERWOOD, (1850-1939) - a U.S. Representative from Indiana; born in Cambridge City, Wayne County, Ind., October 28, 1850; attended the Centerville Collegiate Institute and Earlham College, Richmond, Ind.; studied law; was admitted to the bar in 1872 and commenced practice in Centerville, Wayne County, Ind.; moved to Richmond, Ind., in 1876 and continued the practice of his profession; prosecuting attor ney of Wayne County 1876-1880; member of the State senate 1887- 1889; elected as a Republican to the Fifty-second and to the three succeeding Congresses (March 4, 1891-March 3, 1899); chairman, Committee on Elections No. 2 (Fifty-fourth and Fifty- fifth Congresses); was not a candidate for renomination in 1898; affiliated with the Democratic Party upon the expiration of his congressional career; moved to St. Louis, Mo., in 1899 and continued the practice of law until 1900 when he returned to Richmond, Ind., to resume his former law practice; died in Richmond, Ind., June 4, 1939; interment in Earlham Cemetery.

JOHNSON, NOBLE JACOB, (1887-1968) - a U.S. Representative from Indiana; born in Terre Haute, Vigo County, Ind., August 23, 1887; attended public schools; studied law; was admitted to the bar in 1911 and commenced practice in Terre Haute; deputy prosecuting attorney for the forty-third judicial circuit of Indiana in 1917 and 1918; prosecuting attorney for the same judicial circuit 1921-1924; elected as a Republican to the Sixty- ninth, Seventieth, and Seventy-first Congresses (March 4, 1925- March 3, 1931); unsuccessful candidate for reelection in 1930 to the Seventy-second Congress, and for election in 1936 to the

Seventy-fifth Congress; elected to the Seventysixth and to the four succeeding Congresses and served from January 3, 1939, until his resignation on July 1, 1948; appointed a judge of the United States Court of Customs and Patent Appeals and served from July 2, 1948, to July 19, 1956, and as chief judge from July 20, 1956, until his retirement August 7, 1958; resided in Washington, D.C., until his death March 17, 1968; interment in Bethesda Cemetery, West Terre Haute, Ind.

JOHNSTON, JAMES THOMAS, (1839-1904) - a U.S. Representative from Indiana; born near Greencastle, Putnam County, Ind., January 19, 1839; attended the common schools; studied law; during the Civil War enlisted as a private in Company C, Sixth Indiana Cavalry, in July 1862; transferred to Company A, Eighth Tennessee Cavalry, in September 1863 and commissioned as second lieutenant, serving until January 1864, when he resigned; afterwards served as commissary sergeant of the One Hundred and Thirty-third Regiment, Indiana Volunteer Infantry; commissioned lieutenant and assistant quartermaster of the One Hundred and Forty-ninth Regi ment, Indiana Volunteer Infantry, and mustered out in September 1865; was admitted to the bar in March 1866 and commenced practice in Rockville, Parke County, Ind.; prosecuting attorney 1866-1868; member of the State house of representatives in 1868; served in the State senate 1874-1878; elected as a Republican to the Forty-ninth and Fiftieth Congresses (March 4, 1885-March 3, 1889); unsuccessful candidate for reelection; resumed the practice of law; commander of the Grand Army of the Republic, Department of Indiana, in 1893; died in Rockville, Ind., July 19, 1904; interment in the Rockville Cemetery.

JONTZ, JAMES PRATHER, (1951-   ) - a U.S. Representative from Indiana; born in Indianapolis, Ind., December 18, 1951; attended public schools; A.B., Indiana University, Bloomington, 1973; graduate studies at Purdue University, West Lafayette, Ind., and Butler University, Indianapolis; program director, Lake Michigan Federation and Indiana Conservation Council; public relations director, Sycamore Girl Scout Council; instructor, Butler University; member,

Indiana State house of representatives, 1974-1984; member, Indiana State senate, 1984- 1986; elected as a Democrat to the One Hundredth Congress (January 3, 1987-January 3, 1989); is a resident of Brookston, Ind.

JULIAN, GEORGE WASHINGTON, (1817-1899) - a U.S. Representative from Indiana; born near Centerville, Wayne County, Ind., on May 5, 1817; attended the common schools; studied law; was admitted to the bar in 1840 and commenced practice in Green field, Ind.; member of the State house of representatives in 1845; delegate to the Buffalo Free-Soil Convention in 1848; elected as a Free-Soiler to the Thirty-first Congress (March 4, 1849-March 3, 1851); unsuccessful candidate for election in 1850 to the Thirty-second Congress; unsuccessful candidate for Vice President of the United States on the Free-Soil ticket in 1852; delegate to the Republican National Convention in 1856; elected as a Republican to the Thirty-seventh and to the four succeeding Congresses (March 4, 1861-March 3, 1871); chairman, Committee on Public Lands (Thirtyeighth through Forty-first Congresses), Committee on Expenditures in the Department of the Navy (Thirty- ninth Congress); appointed by President Cleveland surveyor gener al of New Mexico and served from July 1885 until September 1889; returned to Indiana and settled in Irvington; engaged in literary pursuits; died in Irvington, a suburb of Indianapolis, Ind., July 7, 1899; interment in Crown Hill Cemetery, Indianapolis, Ind.

K

KAHN, ALBERT A., (1869-1942) - architect, was born in Rhaunen, in the province of Westphalia, Germany. After receiving his early education in the school of Luxembourg, he came to America with his parents in 1881 and settled in Detroit. Kahn began his formal architectural training in Detroit in 1883 when he joined the firm of Mason & Rice. In 1890 and 1891 he studied abroad, with the help of an American Architect scholarship. While working with Mason and Rice, Kahn was best known for commercial and industrial architecture, including the General Motors building, one of the largest office buildings in the world. He left that firm in 1894 when he entered into the partnership of Nettleton, Kahn and Trowbridge.

Some of the buildings Kahn is credited with having designed are: the Fisher building, awarded the New York Architectural League's silver medal; the Chalmers, Ford, Hudson, Lozier and Packard automobile plants; and the *Evening News* and Detroit's *Free Press* buildings. While consulting architect for the University of Michigan, Kahn designed the Hill Auditorium and the University Hospital in addition to the literature, engineering, medical, natural science and physics buildings.

Kahn was married to Ernestine Krolik in 1896, and they had four children. He received both national and international awards in recognition of his outstanding work. Besides being one of the foremost architects in Michigan, Kahn was an active supporter of the arts. During World War II, Kahn's firm was in charge of several of the U.S. government's important constructions, including aeronautical and tank arsenal plants. He died in Detroit.

KENNEDY, ANDREW, (1810-1847) - (cousin of Case Broderick), a U.S. Representative from Indiana; born in Dayton, Ohio, July 24, 1810; moved with his parents to a farm on the Indian reserve near Lafayette, Ind.; soon afterward moved to Connersville, Ind.; became a blacksmith's apprentice; attended the common schools; studied law; was admitted to the bar in 1833 and recommenced practice in Connersville; moved to Muncie (then Muncytown), Ind., in 1834 and continued the practice of law; is member of the State house of representatives in 1835; served; in the State senate in 1838; elected as a Democrat to the Twenty-seventh, Twenty-eighth, and Twenty-ninth Congresses (March 4, 1841-March 3, 1847); Democratic caucus nominee for United States Senator in 1847; was stricken with a smallpox on the eve of the legislative joint convention and died in Indianapolis, Ind., December 31, 1847; interment in Greenlawn Cemetery; reinterment in Beech Grove Cemetery, Muncie, Ind.

KERN, JOHN WORTH, (1849-1921) - a U.S. Senator from Indiana; born in Alto, Howard County, Ind., December 20, 1849; attended the common schools and the normal college at Kokomo, Ind.; taught school; graduated from the law department of the University of Michigan at Ann Arbor in 1869; was admitted to the bar the same year and commenced practice in Kokomo; unsuccessful candidate for election to the State house of representatives in 1870; city attorney of Kokomo 1871-1884; reporter of the Indiana Supreme Court 1885-1889; member, State senate 1893-1897; special assistant United States district attorney 1893-1894; city solicitor of Indianapolis 1897-1901; unsuccessful Democratic candidate for Governor in 1900 and 1904; unsuccessful candidate for Vice President of the United States on the Democratic ticket with William Jennings Bryan in 1908; elected as a Democrat to the United States Senate and served from March 4, 1911, to March 3, 1917; unsuccessful candidate for reelection in 1916; Democratic caucus chairman 1913-1917; chairman, Committee on Privileges and Elections (Sixty-third and Sixty-fourth Congresses); died in Asheville, N.C., August 17, 1917; interment on the Kern estate near Hollins, Va.; reinterment in Crown Hill Cemetery, Indianapolis, Ind., in 1929.

KERR, MICHAEL CRAWFORD, (1827-1876) - a U.S. Representative from Indiana; born in Titusville, Crawford County, Pa., March 15, 1827; attended the common schools and Erie Academy; was graduated from the law department of Louisville (Ky.) University in 1851; was admitted to the bar and commenced practice in New Albany, Ind., in 1852; city attorney in 1854; prosecuting attorney of Floyd County in 1855; member of the State house of representatives in 1856 and 1857; reporter of the supreme court of Indiana 1862-1865; elected as a Democrat to the Thirty-ninth and to the three succeeding Congresses (March 4, 1865-March 3, 1873); unsuccessful candidate for reelection in 1872 to the Forty-third Congress; elected to the Fortyfourth Congress and served from March 4, 1875, until his death; Speaker of the House of Representatives (Forty-fourth Congress); died at Rockbridge Alum Springs, Rockbridge County, Va., on August 19, 1876; interment in Fairview Cemetery, New Albany, Ind.

KETCHAM, JOHN CLARK, (1873-1941) - U. S. Representative from Michigan; born in Toledo, Ohio, January 1, 1873; moved with his parents to Maple Grove, near Nashville, Michigan, the same year; attended the common schools of Barry County and high school at Nashville; was graduated from Hastings High School in 1892; taught in rural and high schools from 1890 to 1899; county commissioner of schools for Barry County 1899-1907; chairman of the Republican county committee 1902-1908; postmaster of Hastings 1907-1914; master of the Michigan State Grange 1912-1920; lecturer of the National Grange 1917-1921; elected as a Republican to the Sixty-seventh and to the five succeeding Congresses (March 4, 1921-March 3, 1933); unsuccessful candidate for reelection in 1932 to the Seventy-third Congress; president of the National Bank of Hastings 1933-1937; State commissioner of insurance 1935-1941; died in Hastings, Michigan, December 4, 1941; interment in Riverside Cemetery.

KINNARD, GEORGE L., (1803-1836) - a U.S. Representative from Indiana; born in Pennsylvania in 1803; moved with his widowed mother to Tennessee and completed preparatory studies; moved to Indianapolis, Ind., in 1823; studied law; was admitted to the bar and practiced in Marion County, Ind.; assessor for Marion County in 1826 and 1827; member of the State house of representatives 1827-1830; county surveyor 1831-1835; State auditor for several years; colonel of the State militia; elected as a Jacksonian to the Twenty-third and Twenty-fourth Congresses and served from March 4, 1833, until his death from injuries received in an explosion on the steamer *Flora* on the Ohio River November 26, 1836; interment probably in Presbyterian Burying Ground (now Washington Park), Cincinnati, Ohio.

KLEINER, JOHN JAY, (1845-1911) - a U.S. Representative from Indiana; born in West Hanover, Dauphin County, Pa., February 8, 1845; moved to Medina County, Ohio, in 1850 with his parents, who settled near Wadsworth; attended the public schools and assisted his father in agricultural pursuits; during the Civil War enlisted on June 20, 1863, in Company G, Eighty-sixth Regiment, Ohio Volunteer Infantry, and served until February 10, 1864; returned to Wadsworth, Ohio, where he resided until 1867; moved to Evansville, Ind., in 1867; taught in the Evansville Business College and edited the Saturday Argus of that city; member of the city council of Evansville in 1873; engaged in the manufacture and sale of lumber; mayor of Evansville 1874-1880; elected as a Democrat to the Forty-eighth and Forty-ninth Congresses (March 4, 1883-March 3, 1887); unsuccessful candidate for reelection; en gaged in the real estate business and stock raising at Pierre, s.Dak., in 1887; moved to Washington, D.C., in 1890 and engaged in the real estate business until his death in Takoma Park, Md., April 8, 1911; interment in Rock Creek Cemetery, Washington, D.C.

KORBLY, CHARLES ALEXANDER, (1871-1937) - a U.S. Representative from Indiana; born in Madison, Jefferson County, Ind., March 24, 1871; attended the parochial schools of Madison and St. Joseph's College, near Effingham, Ill.; reporter and editor of the Madison Herald; studied law; was admitted to the bar in 1892 and commenced practice in Madison, Ind.; moved to Indianapolis, Ind., in 1895 and continued the practice of law; elected as a Democrat to the Sixty-first, Sixty-second, and Sixty-third Congresses (March 4, 1909-March 3, 1915); chairman, Committee on Railways and Canals (Sixty-second Congress); unsuccessful candidate for reelection in 1914 to the Sixty-fourth Congress; served as receiver general of insolvent national banks in Washington, D.C., 1915-1917; member of the legal staff of the Alien Property Custodian in 1918; served with the War Labor Board until it dissolved in 1919 and with the Shipping Board until 1922; resumed the practice of law in Washington, D.C., in 1922; also engaged in literary pursuits; died in Washington, D.C., July 26, 1937; interment in Mount Olivet Cemetery.

KRUSE, EDWARD H., (1918-) - a U.S. Representative from Indiana; born in Fort Wayne, Allen County, Ind., October 22, 1918; attended the public schools; graduated from the Indiana University Law School in Indianapolis in January 1942; also attended Butler University at Indianapolis; admitted to the bar in 1942; enlisted in the United

States Naval Reserve in January 1942; commissioned an ensign in October 1942 and served in the Pacific; commenced the private practice of law in Fort Wayne, Ind.; elected as a Democrat to the Eightyfirst Congress (January 3, 1949-January 3, 1951); unsuccessful candidate for reelection in 1950 to the Eighty-second Congress; judge of Allen County Superior Court No. 2, Fort Wayne, Ind., in 1952; trust officer of two national banks, 1953-1957; member of an actuarial and pension consulting firm, 1959-1965; president, consulting actuarial firm since January 1966; is a resident of Fort Lauderdale, Fla.

L

LA FOLLETTE, CHARLES MARION, (1898-1974) - (great-grandson of William Heilman), a U.S. Representative from Indiana; born in New Albany, Floyd County, Ind., February 27, 1898; moved with his parents to Evansville, Ind., in 1901; attended the public schools and entered Wabash College at Crawfordsville, Ind., in September 1916; during the First World War enlisted in the United States Army and served with the One Hundred and Fifty-first Infantry, Thirty-eighth Division, 1917-1919, with four months overseas; attended Wabash College until June 1921; studied law at Vanderbilt University, Nashville, Tenn., in 1921 and also in law offices in Dayton, Ohio, and Evansville, Ind.; was admitted to the bar in 1925 and commenced practice in Evansville, Ind.; member of the State house of representatives 1927-1929; elected as a Republican to the Seventy-eighth and to the Seventy-ninth Congresses (January 3, 1943-January 3, 1947); was not a candidate for reelection in 1946 but was an unsuccessful candidate for the Republican nomination for United States Senator; deputy chief of counsel for war crimes, Nuremberg, Germany, from January 4, 1947, to December 15, 1947; director of the Office of Military Government for Wurttemberg-Baden, Germany, from December 15, 1947, to January 16, 1949; appointed a director of Americans for Democratic Action on July 1, 1949, serving until May 1,

1950; member of first Subversive Activities Contol Board, 1950-1951; died in Trenton, N.J., June 27, 1974; cremated; ashes interred at Locust Hill Cemetery, Evansville, Ind.

LAMB, JOHN EDWARD, (1852-1914) - a U.S. Representative from Indiana; born in Terre Haute, Ind., December 26, 1852; attended the common schools and was graduated from the Terre Haute High School; studied law; was admitted to the bar in 1873 and commenced practice in Terre Haute; prosecuting attorney of the fourteenth judicial circuit 1875-1880; elected as a Democrat to the Forty-eighth Congress (March 4, 1883-March 3, 1885); resumed the practice of law in Terre Haute; appointed United States district attorney for Indiana July 10, 1885, and served until August 16, 1886; delegate to the Democratic National Conventions in 1892, 1896, 1904, 1908, and 1912; died in Terre Haute, Ind., August 23, 1914; interment in Calvary Cemetery.

LANDERS, FRANKLIN, (1825-1901) - a U.S. Representative from Indiana; born near the village of Landersdale, Morgan County, Ind., March 22, 1825; attended local schools; at the age of twentyone engaged in teaching school; was associated with his brother in mercantile pursuits at Waverly, Ind.; laid out the town of Brooklyn, Ind., where he engaged in mercantile pursuits and stock raising; member of the State senate 1860-1864; moved to Indianapolis in 1865 and engaged in the drygoods business; in 1873 became the head of a pork-packing house; elected as a Democrat to the Forty-fourth Congress (March 4, 1875-March 3, 1877); unsuccessful candidate for reelection in 1876 and for election as Governor of Indiana in 1880; engaged in the management of his farming lands; died in Indianapolis, Ind., September 10, 1901; interment in Crown Hill Cemetery.

LANDGREBE, EARL FREDRICK, (1916-1986) - a U.S. Representative from Indiana; born in Valparaiso, Porter County, Ind., January 21, 1916; attended Union Township Elementary and Wheeler High School; elected to the Indiana State senate, 1959- 1968; owner and operator, Landgrebe Motor Transport, Inc.; elect ed as a Republican to the Ninety-first and to the two succeeding Congresses (January

3, 1969-January 3, 1975); unsuccessful candidate for reelection in 1974 to the Ninetyfourth Congress; was a resident of Valparaiso, Ind., until his death there June 29, 1986; interment in Blachly Cemetery, Crown Point, Ind.

LANDIS, CHARLES BEARY, (1858-1922) - (brother of Frederick Landis), a U.S. Representative from Indiana; born in Millville, Butler County, Ohio, July 9, 1858; attended the public schools of Logansport, Ind., and was graduated from Wabash College, Crawfordsville, Ind., in 1883; editor of the Logansport Journal 1883-1887 and at the time of his nomination for Congress was editor of the Delphi (Ind.) Journal; president of the Indiana Republican Editorial Association in 1894 and 1895; elected as a Republican to the Fifty-fifth and to the five succeeding Congresses (March 4, 1897-March 3, 1909); unsuccessful candidate for reelection; resumed newspaper work in Delphi, Ind.; died in Asheville, N.C., where he had gone because of impaired health, April 24, 1922; interment in Mount Hope Cemetery, Logansport, Ind.

LANDIS, FREDERICK, (1872-1934) - (brother of Charles Beary Landis), a U.S. Representative from Indiana; born at Sevenmile, Butler County, Ohio, August 18, 1872; moved with his parents to Logansport, Ind., in 1875; attended the public schools; was graduated from the law department of the University of Michigan at Ann Arbor in 1895; was admitted to the bar the same year and commenced practice at Logansport, Ind.; elected as a Republican to the Fifty-eighth and Fifty-ninth Congresses (March 4, 1903- March 3, 1907); unsuccessful candidate for reelection in 1906 to the Sixtieth Congress; returned to Logansport and engaged in writing and lecturing; one of the organizers of the Progressive Party in 1912 and temporary chairman of its first State convention in Indiana; delegate to the National Progressive Convention at Chicago in 1912; unsuccessful candidate for Governor on the Progressive ticket in 1912; unsuccessful candidate for the nomination for Governor on the Republican ticket in 1928; author and lecturer; elected to the Seventy- fourth Congress on November 6, 1934, but died in a hospital in Logansport, Ind., November 15, 1934, before

Congress had convened; interment in Mount Hope Cemetery.

LANDIS, GERALD WAYNE, (1895-1971) - a U.S. Representative from Indiana; born in Bloomfield, Greene County, Ind., February 23, 1895; attended the public schools of Linton, Ind.; served as a lieutenant in the Infantry of the United States Army in 1918 and 1919; was graduated from Indiana University at Bloomington in 1923 and received master's degree in 1938; taught in the high schools at Linton, Ind., 1923-1938; elected as a Republican to the Seventy-sixth and to the four succeeding Congresses (January 3, 1939-January 3, 1949); unsuccessful candidate for reelection in 1948 to the Eighty-first Congress; delegate to the Republican National Convention in 1944 and Indiana State convention in 1964; assistant to the Administrator, Commodity Stabilization Service, Department of Agriculture, from April 1954 to January 1961; died in Linton, Ind., September 6, 1971; interment in Fairview Cemetery.

LANE, HENRY S., (1811-1881) - governor of Indiana (1861), was born on February 11, 1811 in Kentucky, the son of James and Mary (Higgins) Lane. He was educated at home by tutors and later studied law and was admitted to the bar. He moved to Crawfordsville, Indiana in 1835 and practiced law. Soon after, he won a seat in the Indiana House of Representatives and served from 1837 to 1838. He ran for U.S. Congress in a special election in 1840 and won. The following year he was reelected. However, in the 1849 congressional election, Lane lost to his opponent, Joseph McDonald.

When the Mexican War began in 1846, Lane mustered volunteers and became major of the First Indiana Regiment. He rose to the rank of lieutenant colonel before he completed his service in 1848. Back in Indiana, Lane was a major promoter of the new Republican Party, and in 1860 was nominated governor by the Republicans. In the election that followed, he defeated Democrat Thomas A. Hendricks by 10,000 votes. He took office on January 14, 1861, but resigned after only two days, when the Legislature elected him to the U.S. Senate.

In the Senate, Lane supported the Union as the Civil War raged throughout the country. He served until 1867, then returned to his home state. From 1869 to 1871, he was special Indian commissioner in Indiana, and in 1872 he served as commissioner for improvement of the Mississippi River. He died on June 19, 1881 in Crawfordsville, Indiana. Lane was married twice: in 1833 to Pamela Bledsoe Jameson who died in 1842, and to Joanna Elston in 1845.

LANE, JAMES HENRY, (1814-1866) - (son of Amos Lane), a U.S. Representative from Indiana and a Senator from Kansas; born in Lawrenceburg, Ind., June 22, 1814; attended the public schools; studied law; was admitted to the bar in 1840 and commenced practice in Lawrenceburg; member of the city council; served in the Mexican War; lieutenant governor of Indiana 1849-1853; elected as a Democrat to the Thirty-third Congress (March 4, 1853-March 3, 1855); moved to the Territory of Kansas in 1855; member of the Topeka constitutional convention 1855; elected to the United States Senate by the legislature that convened under the Topeka constitution in 1856, but the election was not recognized by the United States Senate; president of the Leavenworth constitutional convention in 1857; elected as a Republican to the United States Senate in 1861; reelected in 1865 and served from April 4, 1861, until his death; chairman, Committee on Agriculture (Thirty-eighth Congress); appointed by President Abraham Lincoln brigadier general of volunteers and saw battle during the Civil War; deranged and charged with financial irregularities, Lane shot himself on July 1, 1866, but lingered ten days, dying on July 11, near Fort Levenworth, Kans.; interment in the City Cemetery, Lawrence, Kans.

LARRABEE, WILLIAM HENRY, (1870-1960) - a U.S. Representative from Indiana; born on a farm near Crawfordsville, Montgomery County, Ind., February 21, 1870; attended the public schools, Indiana Central Normal School at Danville, and Indiana State Normal School at Terre Haute; taught in public schools at New Palestine, Ind., 1889-1895; was graduated from the Indiana School of Medicine at Indianapolis in 1898; commenced practice of medicine and surgery in New Palestine, Ind., in 1898; secretary of Hancock County Board of Health in 1917 and 1918; served on the city council of New Palestine, Ind., 1916-1920; member of the State house of representatives 1923-1925; elected as a Democrat to the Seventy-second and to the five succeeding Congresses (March 4, 1931-January 3, 1943); chairman, Committee on the Census (Seventy-fourth and Seventy-fifth Congresses), Committee on Education (Seventy-fifth through Seventy-seventh Congresses); unsuccessful candidate for reelection in 1942 to the Seventy- eighth Congress; resumed the practice of medicine and surgery; died in New Palestine, Ind., November 16, 1960; interment in New Palestine Cemetery.

LEIGHTY, JACOB D., (1839-1912) - a U.S. Representative from Indiana; born near Greensburg, Westmoreland County, Pa., November 15, 1839; in 1844 moved with his parents to De Kalb County, Ind., where they settled on a farm at Spencerville; attended the public schools; taught in district schools; spent two years at a commercial school at Fort Wayne and then entered Wittenberg College, Springfield, Ohio; on July 1, 1861, after two years in college, he left to enlist in the Union Army and became a member of Company E, Eleventh Indiana Volunteer Zouave Infantry; engaged in farming and general merchandising with his father until 1875, when he established the town of St. Joe, Ind.; member of the State house of representatives 1886-1888; elected as a Republican to the Fifty-fourth Congress (March 4, 1895-March 3, 1897); unsuccessful candidate for reelection in 1896 to the Fifty-fifth Congress; United States pension agent at Indianapolis 1897-1901; died at St. Joe, De Kalb County, Ind., on October 18, 1912; interment in Riverview Cemetery.

LESLIE, HARRY G., (1878-1937) - governor of Indiana (1929- 1933), was born in West Lafayette, Indiana on August 6, 1878, the son of Daniel and Mary Ann (Burkhardt) Leslie. He attended the local schools and was a successful student. He worked several years before entering Purdue University in 1901. After graduation in 1905 he attended Indiana University Law School and received a law degree in 1907. Leslie settled in Lafayette, and began a profitable law practice.

At the age of thirty-four he was elected treasurer of Tippecanoe County, an office he faithfully executed for the next five years. By 1923 Leslie ran for and was elected to the Indiana House of Representatives. He rose quickly and became the speaker of the House in 1925. At fifty, Leslie ran for governor on the Republican ticket and defeated his Democratic opponent. Although his administration started out in the Great Bull stock market, the Depression arrived in 1930. He struggled with issues of public relief and in 1932 called a special session of the Legislature to reduce property taxes. After his term ended in 1932, he organized the Standard Life Insurance Company of Indiana. Harry Leslie died in Miami, Florida on December 10, 1937. He was married to Martha Morgan in 1910, and they had three sons.

LIEB, CHARLES, (1852-1928) - a U.S. Representative from Indiana; born in Flehingen, Germany, May 20, 1852; immigrated to the United States in 1868 and settled in Rockport, Ind.; attended the public schools, the Rockport Collegiate Institute, and Bryant and Stratton's Business College, Louisville, Ky.; employed as a bookkeeper and accountant; mernber of the Rockport City Council 1879-1884; engaged in the lumber business and as a contractor in 1882; postmaster of Rockport 1893-1897; member of the State house of representatives 1907-1913; elected as a Democrat to the Sixty- third and Sixty-fourth Congresses (March 4, 1913-March 3, 1917); was not a candidate for renomination in 1916; delegate to the Democratic National Convention in 1916; served as president and director of the Farmers' Bank, Rockport, Ind.; also engaged in agricultural pursuits; died in Rockport, Ind., September 1, 1928; interment in Sun Set Hill Cemetery.

LIEBER, RICHARD, (1869 - 1944) was a conservationist and architect of the Indiana state park system.

Lieber was born in St. Johann Saarbrucken, Germany on September 5, 1869 and was educated at the Municipal Lyceum and Royal Lyceum in Dusseldorf. He emigrated to the U.S. in 1891 and became a naturalized citizen in 1901. From 1892 to 1900, Lieber worked for two newspapers, the *Indianapolis Journal* and the *Indianapolis Tribune*. He was later employed by an Indianapolis-based importer (1905-18).

Lieber accepted his first conservation-related position in 1912, when he became chairman of the board of governors for the Fourth National Conservation Congress. He became chairman of the Indiana State Park Commission (1915-19) and chairman of the Indiana Board of Forestry (1917-19). In 1919, the Indiana Department of Conservation was formed by the consolidation of all state conservation agencies. Lieber became the new department's first director and remained so until his resignation in 1933.

In addition to his efforts to develop state parks in Indiana, Lieber worked with the National Conference on State Parks, the American Planning and Civic Association, and the National Park Service. His literary contribution to the field of conservation includes numerous official reports and one book, *America's Natural Wealth: A Story of the Use and Abuse of our Natural Resources* (1942). His work in building and administering the Indiana park system was officially recognized in 1932, when a monument was erected in his honor at Turkey Run State Park.

Lieber died on April 5, 1944.

LITTLE TURTLE, (1752 - 1812) - was a chief of the Miami Indians of Indiana who, in 1786, organized the Indian confederacy that defeated General Joseph Harmar in 1790 and General Arthur St. Clair in 1791. His victory in a 1790 battle with French soldiers who had attacked his village served to destroy the prestige of the French in the Northwest Territory.

Little Turtle's tribe settled in Indiana about 1763 after having inhabited several different regions. The Miami under the leadership of Little Turtle long resisted the movement of white settlers to their area. Through various treaties from 1795 to 1854, however, the ceded their Ohio and Indiana land claims and moved west to the Mississippi. Little Turtle served as the spokesman of the Miami at the signing of many of these treaties, including the 1795 Treaty of Greenville. Little Turtle spent his last years counseling peace with the white man, travelling to Philadelphia to meet President Washington in 1797. He died at Fort Wayne on July 14, 1812.

LOCKHART

LOCKHART, JAMES, (1806-1857) - a U.S. Representative from Indiana; born in Auburn, Cayuga County, N.Y., February 13, 1806; attended the public schools; moved to Ithaca, N.Y., about 1826 and operated a woolen mill; moved to Indiana in 1832; studied law; was admitted to the bar in 1832 and commenced practice in Evansville, Ind., in 1834; city clerk in 1836 and 1837; prosecuting attorney of Vanderburg County 1841-1845; judge of the fourth judicial district from 1846 until 1851, when he resigned; delegate to the State constitutional convention in 1850; elected as a Democrat to the Thirty-second Congress (March 4, 1851-March 3, 1853); was not a candidate for reelection in 1852 to the Thirty-third Congress; resumed the practice of his profession in Evansville; appointed by President Pierce superintendent of construction of the marine hospital at Evansville in 1853; elected to the Thirty-fifth Congress and served from March 4, 1857, until his death in Evansville, Ind., on September 7, 1857; interment in Oak Hill Cemetery.

LONG, JILL, (1952-   ) - Democrat, of Larwill, IN, born in Warsaw, IN on July 15, 1952; attended Etna-Troy Elementary School in Whitley County, IN; graduated from Columbia City Joint High School; B.S., Valparaiso University, IN, 1974; M.B.A. (1978), Ph.D. (1984), Indiana University; farmer and college professor; assistant professor, Valparaiso University; adjunct assistant professor, Indiana Purdue University, Fort Wayne; elected to the Valparaiso City Council, 1984-86; unsuccessful candidate for election to the U.S. Senate, 1986, and to the U.S. House of Representatives, 1988; elected by special election on March 28, 1989 to fill the vacancy caused by the resignation of Dan Coats; reelected to the 102nd Congress on November 6, 1990.

LOWRY, ROBERT, (1824-1904) - a U.S. Representative from Indiana; born in Killeleigh, County Down, Ireland, April 2, 1824; immigrated to the United States and settled in Rochester, N.Y.; educated in private schools and had partial academic course; librarian of Rochester Athenaeum and Young Men's Association; studied law; moved to Fort Wayne, Ind., in 1843; city recorder in 1844 and 1845; was admitted to the bar in 1846 and commenced practice in Go-

120

shen, Ind.; auditor of Elkhart County in 1852; circuit judge in 1852; president of the Democratic State convention; delegate to the Democratic National Conventions at Baltimore in 1860 and 1872; served as circuit judge from 1864 until January 1875, when he resigned; judge of the superior court in 1877 and 1878; elected the first president of the Indiana State Bar Association in July 1879; elected as a Democrat to the Forty-eighth and Forty-ninth Congresses (March 4, 1883-March 3, 1887); chairman, Committee on Expenditures in the Department of the Treasury (Forty-ninth Congress); unsuccessful candidate for reelection in 1886 to the Fiftieth Congress; resumed the practice of law; died in Fort Wayne, Allen County, Ind., January 27, 1904; interment in Linderwood Cemetery.

LUDLOW, LOUIS LEON, (1873-1950) - a U.S. Representative from Indiana; born on a farm near Connersville, Fayette County, Ind., June 24, 1873; attended the grade and high schools; moved to Indianapolis, Ind., in 1892 and became a reporter and later a political writer; Washington correspondent for Indiana and Ohio newspapers and member of the Congressional Press Galleries 1901- 1929; elected as a Democrat to the Seventy-first and to the nine succeeding Congresses (March 4, 1929-January 3, 1949); election to the Seventy-first Congress was unsuccessfully contested by Ralph E. Updike; was not a candidate for renomination in 1948 to the Eighty-first Congress; resumed work as a newspaper correspondent until his death in Washington, D.C., November 28, 1950; interment in Rock Creek Cemetery.

LUGAR, RICHARD GREEN, (1932-   ) - a U.S. Senator from Indiana; born in Indianapolis, Marion County, Ind., April 4, 1932; attended the public schools of Indianapolis; graduated, Denison University, Granville, Ohio, 1954; attended Pembroke College, Oxford, England, as a Rhodes scholar and received a graduate degree in 1956; businessman, involved in the manufac turing of food production equipment, livestock and grain operations; United States Navy 1957-1960; member, Indianapolis Board of School Commissioners 1964-1967; mayor, Indianapolis 1968-1975; unsuccessful Republican candidate for the United States Senate in 1974; elected as a Republican to the United

States Senate in 1976 for the term commencing January 3, 1977; reelected in 1982 for the term ending January 3, 1989; chairman, Republican Senatorial Campaign Committee (Ninety-eighth Congress), Committee on Foreign Relations (Ninety-ninth Congress).

LUHRING, OSCAR RAYMOND, (1879-1944) - a U.S. Representative from Indiana; born in Haubstadt, Gibson County, Ind., February 11, 1879; attended the public schools; was graduated in law from the University of Virginia at Charlottesville in 1900; was admitted to the bar the same year and commenced practice in Evansville, Vanderburg County, Ind.; member of the State house of representatives in 1903 and 1904; deputy prosecuting attorney of the same circuit 1908-1912; elected as a Republican to the Sixty- sixth and Sixty-seventh Congresses (March 4, 1919-March 3, 1923); unsuccessful candidate for reelection in 1922 to the Sixty-eighth Congress; special assistant to the Secretary of Labor 1923-1925; appointed by President Coolidge to be Assistant Attorney General of the United States on September 9, 1925; appointed by President Hoover as an associate justice of the supreme court for the District of Columbia (now United States District Court) on July 3, 1930, and served until his death in Washington, D.C., August 20, 1944; interment in the Abbey Mausoleum, adjoining Arlington National Cemetery.

M

MACE, DANIEL, (1811-1867) - a U.S. Representative from Indiana; born in Pickaway County, Ohio, September 5, 1811; attended the public schools; studied law; was admitted to the bar in 1835 and practiced in LaFayette, Ind.; member of the State house of representatives in 1836; clerk of the State house of representatives in 1837; United States attorney for Indiana 1849- 1853; elected as a Democrat to the Thirty-second and Thirty-third Congresses (March 4, 1851-March 3, 1855); reelected as a Republican to the Thirty-fourth Congress (March 4, 1855,-March 3, 1857);

chairman, Committee on the Post Office and Post Roads (Thirty-fourth Congress); resumed the practice of law; postmaster of LaFayette from September 22, 1866, until his death in LaFayette, July 26, 1867; interment in Greenbush Cemetery.

MADDEN, RAY JOHN, (1892-1987) - a U.S. Representative from Indiana; born in Waseca, Waseca County, Minn., February 25, 1892; attended the public schools and Sacred Heart Academy in his native city; the law department of Creighton University, Omaha, Nebr., LL.B., 1913; was admitted to the bar the same year and commenced practice in Omaha, Nebr.; elected municipal judge of Omaha, Nebr., in 1916, resigning during the First World War to serve in the United States Navy; engaged in the practice of law in Gary, Ind.; city comptroller of Gary 1935-1938; treasurer of Lake County, Ind., 1938-1942; delegate to every State convention since 1936; delegate to every Democratic National Convention from 1940 through 1968; elected as a Democrat to the Seventy-eighth and to the sixteen succeeding Congresses (January 3, 1943-January 3, 1977); co-chairman, Joint Committee on Organization of Con gress (Eighty-ninth and Ninetieth Congresses), chairman, Committee on Rules (Ninety-third and Ninety-fourth Congresses); unsuccessful candidate for renomination in 1976 to the Ninety- fifth Congress; was a resident of Washington, D.C., until his death there on September 28, 1987; interment in Arlington National Cemetery.

MANSON, MAHLON DICKERSON, (1820-1895) - a U.S. Representative from Indiana; born in Piqua, Ohio, February 20, 1820; attended the common schools; moved to Montgomery County, Ind., and taught school for a year; studied medicine at the Ohio Medical College at Cincinnati; served as captain of Volunteers in the Mexican War October 8, 1847-July 28, 1848; member of the State house of representatives 1851 and 1852; engaged in the retail drug business at Crawfordsville; commissioned captain of the Tenth Regiment, Indiana Volunteer Infantry, April 17, 1861, and promoted through the ranks to brigadier general of Volunteers March 24, 1862; resigned December 21, 1864; unsuccessful Democratic candidate for Lieutenant Governor of

Indiana in 1864; elected as a Democrat to the Forty-second Congress (March 4, 1871-March 3, 1873); unsuccessful candidate for reelection in 1872 to the Forty-third Congress; elected auditor of Indiana in 1878; elected Lieutenant Governor in 1884; appointed collector of internal revenue of the seventh district of Indiana August 11, 1886, and resigned November 5, 1889; died in Crawfordsville, Montgomery County, Ind., on February 4, 1895; interment in Oak Hill Cemetery.

MARSHALL, THOMAS R., (1854-1925) - governor of Indiana (1909-1913), was born in North Manchester, Indiana on March 14, 1854, the son of Daniel and Martha (Patterson) Marshall. As a boy he lived in Illinois, Missouri, Kansas, and Indiana. He received his education at public schools and at Wabash College, from which he graduated in 1873. Following college, he studied law in Fort Wayne and Columbia City, and passed the bar. An attorney, Marshall soon became known for his abilities as a public speaker. He was an ardent Democrat, and in 1908 ran for governor of Indiana on the Democratic ticket. He won over Republican, James Watson by nearly 15,000 votes.

Marshall worked for a new state constitution during his administration, terming the old one obsolete due to changes in the way business was conducted in the State. His efforts, however, were not successful. Marshall also had no success with his attempts to pass legislation to protect bank and trust company depositors, and to require that building and loan companies be examined by the state. His accomplishments included the passage of the Child Labor Law and strides in the enforcement of state anti-gambling laws.

Marshall ran on the ticket with Woodrow Wilson in 1912 and 1916 and was elected vice president of the United States. At the end of his two terms, he returned to Indianapolis to write his memoirs, which were published in 1925 under the title, *Recollections*. He also toured the country, giving lectures, and served on the Board of Trustees of Wabash College. He died on June 1, 1925 in Washington, D.C. Marshall was married in 1895 to Lois Kimsey and had an adopted son who died in early childhood.

MARTIN, AUGUSTUS NEWTON, (1847-1901) - a U.S. Representative from Indiana; born near Whitestown, Butler County, Pa., March 23, 1847; attended the common schools and Witherspoon Institute, Butler, Pa., and was graduated from Eastman College, Poughkeepsie, N.Y., in February 1867; enlisted July 3, 1863, in Company I, Fifty-eighth Regiment, Pennsylvania Volunteer Militia; enlisted again February 22, 1865, in Company E, Seventy-eighth Regiment, Pennsylvania Volunteer Infantry, and served until discharged for disability August 30, 1865; taught school; studied law in Bluffton, Wells County, Ind., in 1869; was admitted to the bar in 1870 and practiced; member of the State house of representatives in 1875; elected reporter of the Supreme Court of Indiana in 1876 and served four years; unsuccessful candidate for reelection in 1880; resided in Austin, Tex., 1881-1883; returned to Bluffton, Ind., in 1883; elected as a Democrat to the Fifty- first, Fifty-second, and Fifty-third Congresses (March 4, 1889- March 3, 1895); chairman, Committee on Invalid Pensions (Fifty-second and Fifty-third Congresses); unsuccessful candidate for reelection to the Fifty-fourth Congress; engaged in the practice of law in Bluffton, Ind., until his death at the Soldiers' Home Hospital, Marion, Ind., July 11, 1901; interment in Fairview Cemetery, Bluffton, Ind.

MATSON, COURTLAND CUSHING, (1841-1915) - a U.S. Representative from Indiana; born in Brookville, Franklin County, Ind., April 25, 1841; was graduated from Indiana Asbury (later De Pauw) University in 1862; during the Civil War enlisted as a pri vate in the Sixteenth Regiment, Indiana Volunteers; after one year's service entered the Sixth Regiment, Indiana Volunteer Cavalry (Seventy-first Volunteers), and served until October 1865, and was subsequently promoted to the rank of colonel; studied law; was admitted to the bar and commenced practice in Greencastle, Putnam County, Ind.; was three times elected prosecuting attorney of the county; chairman of the Democratic State central committee in 1878; elected as a Democrat to the Forty-seventh and to the three succeeding Congresses (March 4, 1881-March 3, 1889); chairman, Committee on Invalid Pensions (Forty-eighth through Fiftieth Congresses); was not a candidate for renomination; unsuccessful Democratic candidate for Governor of Indiana in 1888; resumed the practice of law in Greencastle, Ind.; member of the board of tax commissioners 1909-1913; died in Chicago, Ill., September 4, 1915; interment in Forest Hill Cemetery, Greencastle, Ind.

MATTHEWS, CLAUDE, (1845-1898) - governor of Indiana (1893- 1897), was born on December 14, 1845 in Bethel, Kentucky, the son of Thomas and Eliza (Fletcher) Matthews. He attended Centre College in Danville, Kentucky and graduated in 1867. Soon after, he moved to Indiana, bought a farm, and began to breed fine livestock. He won his first public office in 1876 when he was elected as a Democrat to the Indiana House of Representatives. He made a bid for the State Senate in 1882, but lost the election. In between his political service, Matthews continued on his farm with the breeding of livestock. From 1891 to 1893, he was the Indiana Secretary of State. He received the Democratic nomination for governor in 1892, and later that year was elected, defeating the Republican candidate, Ira Chase.

While governor, Matthews was called upon to deal with various labor disputes. During a bitter coal miners' strike, the Governor ordered out the National Guard to restore the peace. Matthew's administration was also taken up by his campaign against the formal organization and promotion of prize fighting and racing, which he only managed to suppress against heavy opposition. Matthews left office in 1897. He died the following year, on April 28. Claude Matthews was married in 1868 to Martha Whitcomb and had three children.

MC NUTT, PAUL V(ORIES), (1891 -1955) was the 34th governor of Indiana and a politician of great sagacity and national stature.

McNutt was born in Franklin, Indiana on July 19, 1891, the son of a prominent lawyer. A Phi Beta Kappa, he was graduated from Indiana University in 1913 and Harvard Law School in 1916. He began his law practice in his father's office in Martinsville, and became an assistant professor of law at Indiana University in 1917. Within one year he joined the U.S. Army, and at the end of World War

I returned to Indiana Unversity as a professor of law. In 1925, again at Indiana University, he became one of the nation's youngest deans of a law school.

McNutt's rise in politics was based on his position with the American Legion. He became state commander in 1927 and national commander in 1928-29. He was director of the American Legion Publication Corporation from 1928 to 1931. From these posts he gained the political power to be elected governopr of Indiana in 1933.

A man with the gift of accepting the sound ideas of others and making them work, McNutt guided Indiana through the Great Depression. He imposed strict economic measures throughout the administration, but did not reduce the budget of the school system.

Because he was the first Democratic governor in 16 years, McNutt had little party organization to support him. He reorganized the state's 169 departments and agencies into eight, giving him complete control as well as a more reasonable budget. The party was not only without power, but without financial resources. One solution was the issuance of liquor franchises, following repeal of Prohibition, to those willing to contribute to the party's funds.

McNutt's most publicized innovation - and one the Republicans quickly adopted when they returned to power - was the establishment of the "Two Per Cent Club." Not an actual club, it wa a system of collection of two percent of the salaries of all state employees for the coffers of the party in power. The practice was not changed until 1974.

It is generally believed that McNutt was given a series of federal posts after his governorship because his political power made him a possible presidential rival of Franklin D. Roosevelt. His posts included those of U.S. high commissioner (1937-39, 1945-46) and ambassador (1946-47) to the Philippines, head of the Federal Security Agency (1939-45), director of Defense, Health and Welfare Services (1941-43), and chairman of the War Manpower Commission (1942-45). McNutt served as chairman of the board of the Philippine-American Life Insurance Company after 1948 and practiced law in New York City and Washington, D.C. He died March 24, 1955.

MCCARTY, JOHNATHAN, (1795-1852) - a U.S. Representative from Indiana; born in Culpeper County, Va., August 3, 1795; attended the public schools; moved to Indiana in 1803 with his father, who settled in Franklin County; engaged in mercantile pursuits; member of the State house of representatives in 1818; moved to Connersville, Fayette County, Ind.; clerk of the county court 1819-1827; elected as a Jacksonian to the Twenty-second Congress; reelected to the Twenty-third Congress and reelected as an Anti-Jacksonian to the Twentyfourth Congress (March 4, 1831-March 3, 1837); unsuccessful candidate for reelection in 1836 to the Twenty-fifth Congress; presidential elector on the Whig ticket in 1840; moved to Keokuk, Iowa, where he died March 30, 1852; interment in Oakland Cemetery.

MCCLELLAN, CHARLES A.O., (1835-1898) - a U.S. Representative from Indiana; born in Ashland, Ashe County, Ohio, May 25, 1835; moved to Auburn, Ind., in 1856; attended the public schools; studied law in Auburn and Waterloo, Ind.; was admitted to the bar in 1863 and commenced practice in Waterloo; became engaged in banking in 1868; appointed judge of the fortieth judicial circuit of Indiana by Governor Williams in 1879, and served for two years; elected as a Democrat to the Fifty-first and Fifty-second Congresses (March 4, 1889-March 3, 1893); chairman, Committee on Expenditures in the Department of the Navy (Fifty-second Congress); was not a candidate for renomination in 1892; again engaged in banking and the practice of law; died in Auburn, Ind., January 31, 1898; interment in Waterloo Cemetery, Waterloo, Ind.

MCCLOSKEY, FRANCIS XAVIER, (1939-   ) - a U.S. Representative from Indiana; born in Philadelphia, Pa., June 12, 1939; graduated, Bishop Kendrick High School, Norristown, Pa., 1957; A.B., Indiana University, Bloomington, 1968; J.D., Indiana University School of Law, 1971; served, United States Air Force, 1957-1961; newspaper reporter, 1961-1968; admitted to the Indiana bar, 1971, and commenced practice in Bloomington; mayor of Bloomington, 1972-1982; elected as a Democrat to the Ninety- eighth Congress (January 3, 1983-January 3, 1985); reelected to the Ninety-ninth Congress pursuant to H. Res. 146, taking his seat on May 1, 1985, and reelected to the One Hundredth Congress (May 1, 1985-January 3, 1989); is a resident of Bloomington, Ind.

MCCRAY, WARREN, (1865-1938) - governor of Indiana, was born on February 4, 1865 near Kentland, Indiana, the son of Greenberry and Martha (Galey) McCray. He grew up in Kentland where his father had gone into the banking business. By the age of fifteen he joined his father's firm as a bank teller and gradually rose in its administration. In addition to his banking business, McCray ran a grain elevator business in northern Indiana, and became a highly successful breeder of Hereford cattle.

As a prominent businessman, he served on the Indiana Board of Agriculture from 1912 until 1916. During the first World War he was chairman of Indiana's Food Conservation Committee, and shortly thereafter a trustee of Purdue University. Setting his sights on politics, McCray ran for and was elected governor of Indiana in 1920 after defeating his Democratic opponent, Carleton McCulloch.

Unfortunately his administration paralleled Warren Harding's scandal-ridden national administration, and Warren McCray resigned from office on April 29, 1924 following his conviction in a mail fraud case. He served the next three years in a federal prison, finally gaining release in 1927. Considered to have paid his debt, McCray received a pardon from President Herbert Hoover in 1930. Warren McCray died on December 19, 1938 near his hometown of Kentland. He was married to Ella M. Ade, and fathered three children.

MCDOWELL, JAMES FOSTER, (1825-1887) - a U.S. Representative from Indiana; born in Mifflin County, Pa., December 3, 1825; moved with his parents to Ohio in 1835; attended the public schools; worked in a printing office; studied law; was admitted to the bar in 1846 and practiced; prosecuting attorney of Darke County, Ohio, in 1848; moved to Marion, Ind., in 1851 and engaged in the practice of law; established the Marion Journal in 1851; elected as a Democrat to the Thirty-eighth Congress (March 4, 1863-March 3, 1865); unsuccessful candidate for reelection in 1864 to the Thirty-ninth Congress; delegate to the

Democratic National Convention in 1876; engaged in the practice of law in Marion, Ind., until his death in that city April 18, 1887; interment in Odd Fellows Cemetery.

MCGAUGHEY, EDWARD WILSON, (1817-1852) - a U.S. Representative from Indiana; born near Greencastle, Putnam County, Ind., January 16, 1817; attended the public schools; deputy clerk of Putnam County; studied law; was admitted to the bar in 1835 and commenced practice in Greencastle, Ind.; member of the State house of representatives in 1839 and 1840; served in the State senate for the session December 5, 1842, to February 13, 1843; resigned before the beginning of the next session; unsuccessful candidate for election to the Twenty-eighth Congress; elected as a Whig to the Twenty ninth Congress (March 4, 1845-March 3, 1847); unsuccessful candidate for reelection in 1846 to the Thirtieth Congress; moved to Rockville, Parke County, Ind., in 1846 and resumed the practice of law; elected to the Thirty-first Congress (March 4, 1849-March 3, 1851); unsuccessful candidate for reelection in 1850 to the Thirty-second Congress; nominated by President Taylor as Governor of Minnesota Territory in 1849, but the Senate failed to confirm the nomination; moved to California in 1852; died in San Francisco, Calif., August 6, 1852; interment in Yerba Buena Cemetery.

MCNAGNY, WILLIAM FORGY, (1850-1923) - a U.S. Representative from Indiana; born in Talmadge, Summit County, Ohio, April 19, 1850; moved in early life to Whitley County, Ind.; attended the public schools and the Springfield Academy, South Whitley, Ind.; taught school; worked on his father's farm for six years; station agent for the Pennsylvania Railroad Co. at Larwill, Ind., 1868- 1875; studied law; was admitted to the bar in 1875 and commenced practice in Columbia City, Whitley County, Ind.; elected as a Democrat to the Fifty-third Congress (March 4, 1893-March 3, 1895); unsuccessful candidate for reelection in 1894 to the Fifty-fourth Congress; resumed the practice of law in Columbia City, Ind., and died there August 24, 1923; interment in Masonic Cemetery.

MERRILL, D. BAILEY, (1912-   ) - a U.S. Representative from Indiana; born in Hymera, Sullivan County, Ind., November 22, 1912; attended the public schools; was graduated from Indiana State Teachers College, Terre Haute, Ind., in 1933; taught high school in Hymera, Ind., 1933-1935; graduated from Indiana University Law School, Bloomington, Ind., 1937; was admitted to the bar in 1937 and began practice in Terre Haute, Ind.; moved to Evansville, Ind., in 1939 and continued law practice; in 1942 volunteered as a private in the field artillery and served overseas with the Two Hundred and Ninety-first Field Artillery Observation Battalion; was released from active duty as a captain in March 1946; resumed the practice of law; elected as a Republican to the Eighty-third Congress (January 3, 1953-January 3, 1955); was an unsuccessful candidate for reelection in 1954 to the Eighty-fourth Congress and for election in 1956 to the Eighty-fifth Congress; resumed law practice until his retirement in 1977; is a resident of Evansville, Ind.

MIERS, ROBERT WALTER, (1848-1930) - a U.S. Representative from Indiana; born near Greensburg, Decatur County, Ind., January 27, 1848; attended the common schools; was graduated from the academic department of Indiana University at Bloomington in 1870 and from its law department in 1871; was admitted to the bar in April 1872 and commenced practice in Bloomington, Ind.; prosecuting attorney for the tenth judicial circuit of Indiana 1875-1879; member of the State house of representatives in 1879; member of the board of trustees of Indiana University 1879-1897; appointed judge of the tenth judicial circuit of Indiana in 1883, elected in 1884 and again in 1890, and served until September 1896, when he resigned to become a candidate for Congress; unsuccessful Democratic nominee for secretary of state in 1886 and in 1888; elected as a Democrat to the Fifty-fifth and to the three succeeding Congresses (March 4, 1897-March 3, 1905); unsuccessful candidate for reelection in 1904 to the Fifty-ninth Congress; resumed the practice of law; again elected judge of the tenth circuit of Indiana on November 3, 1914, and served until November 22, 1920; continued the practice of law in Bloomington, Ind., until 1928; died while on a visit in Martinsville, Ind., February 20, 1930; interment in Rosehill Cemetery, Bloomington, Ind.

MILLER, SMITH, (1804-1872) - a U.S. Representative from Indiana; born near Charlotte, N.C., May 30, 1804; moved to Gibson County, Ind., with his parents who settled in Patoka in 1813; re ceived a limited schooling; engaged in agricultural pursuits; member of the State house of representatives 1835-1839 and in 1846; served in the State senate 1841-1844 and 1847-1850; delegate to the State constitutional convention in 1850; elected as a Democrat to the Thirty-third and Thirty-fourth Congresses (March 4, 1853-March 3, 1857); resumed agricultural pursuits; delegate to the Democratic National Convention at Charleston, S.C., in 1860; died near Patoka, Ind., March 21, 1872; interment in Robb Cemetery.

MITCHELL, EDWARD AREHIBALD, (1910-1979) - a U.S. Representative from Indiana; born in Binghamton, Broome County, N.Y., December 2, 1910; attended the grade and high schools and had three years of college training at the American Institute and Columbia University, New York City; moved to Evansville, Ind., in September 1937; engaged as a warehouseman and later as district manager for a large food distributor 1934-1937; in 1937 purchased a half interest in a food marketing and brokerage company and served as president; served in the United States Navy from November 1942 until his discharge as a lieutenant commander in January 1946, having been commanding officer of underwater demolition teams in the Pacific Theater for two years; awarded the Silver Star Medal at Okinawa; elected as a Republican to the Eightieth Congress (January 3, 1947-January 3, 1949); unsuccessful candidate for reelection in 1948 to the Eighty-first Congress; delegate in 1952 and 1956 to Republican National Conventions; resided in Evansville, Ind., where he died December 11, 1979; interment in Sunset Memorial Park.

MITCHELL, WILLIAM, (1807-1865) - a U.S. Representative from Indiana; born in Root, Montgomery County, N.Y., January 19, 1807; attended the public schools; studied law; was admitted to the bar in 1836; moved to Kendallville,

Noble County, Ind., and commenced the practice of law; appointed first postmaster of Kendallville December 7, 1836, and served until a successor was appointed March 7, 1846; member of the State house of representatives in 1841; justice of the peace; elected as a Republican to the Thirty-seventh Congress (March 4, 1861-March 3, 1863); unsuccessful candidate for reelection in 1862 to the Thirty-eighth Congress; engaged in the cotton business; died in Macon, Ga., September 11, 1865; interment in Lake View Cemetery, Kendallville, Ind.

MOORES, MERRILL, (1856-1929) - a U.S. Representative from Indiana; born in Indianapolis, Ind., April 21, 1856; attended the public schools, Butler University, Indianapolis, Ind., and Willamette University, Salem, Oreg.; was graduated from Yale Uni versity in 1878 and from the Central Law School of Indiana (now Indiana Law School) at Indianapolis in 1880; was admitted to the bar in 1880 and commenced practice in Indianapolis, Ind.; chairman of the Marion County Republican committee 1892-1896; assistant attorney general of Indiana 1894-1903; president of the Indiana State Bar Association and of the Indianapolis Bar Association in 1908; Indiana commissioner of the National Conference on Uniform State Laws 1909-1925; member of the executive council of the Interparliamentary Union in 1919; elected as a Republican to the Sixty-fourth and to the four succeeding Congresses (March 4, 1915-March 3, 1925); unsuccessful candidate for renomination in 1924 and for nomination in 1926; resumed the practice of law in Indianapolis, Ind.; served as vice president of the American Systems and Audit Co.; died October 21, 1929, in Indianapolis, Ind.; interment in Crown Hill Cemetery.

MORRISON, MARTIN ANDREW, (1862-1944) - a U.S. Representative from Indiana; born in Frankfort, Clinton County, Ind., April 15, 1862; attended the public schools; was graduated from Butler College, Irvington, Ind., in June 1883 and from the law department of the University of Virginia at Charlottesville in 1886; was admitted to the bar the same year and commenced practice in Frankfort, Ind.; county attorney of Clinton County in 1905 and 1906; member of the board of education 1907-1909; elected as a

Democrat to the Sixty-first and to the three succeeding Congresses (March 4, 1909-March 3, 1917); chairman, Committee on Patents (Sixty-fourth Congress); was not a candidate for renomination in 1916; resumed the practice of law; president of the United States Civil Service Commission from March 1919 to July 1921; became a member of the legal staff of the chief counsel of the Federal Trade Commission at Washington, D.C., on December 10, 1925, and served until his retirement on April 30, 1942, maintaining his residence in Washington, D.C.; died in Abingdon, Va., July 9, 1944, while on a vacation; interment in Bunnell Cemetery, Frankfort, Ind.

MORTON, OLIVER P., (1823-1877) - governor of Indiana (1861- 1867), was born on August 4, 1823 in Salisbury, Indiana, the son of James and Sarah (Miller) Morton. He attended Miami University in Oxford, Ohio from 1843 to 1845, then studied law and was admitted to the bar. In 1852, he became circuit court judge in Centreville. He was an early supporter of the Republican Party, and in 1856 was chosen as the Republican nominee for governor. Democrat, Ashbel P. Willard defeated him in the general election. Four years later, Morton returned as the Republican contender for lieutenant governor. Just two days after inauguration, the new Republican governor, Henry S. Lane resigned to take a seat in the U.S. Senate and Morton was sworn in as governor. Morton was elected governor in his own right in 1864.

Governing during the Civil War, Morton managed to answer the Union call for troops despite a lack of funds and only mixed support for the war among Indiana residents. The Legislature voted against war appropriations so Morton obtained the capital to outfit troops by taking out loans of nearly a million dollars. Governor Morton suffered a stroke in 1865 and was unable to perform his duties as governor for a time. During his recovery, Lieutenant Governor Conrad Baker assumed executive responsibilities.

Recuperated from his stroke, in 1867, Governor Morton won a seat in the U.S. Senate. He resigned the governorship on January 24, 1867. In 1872, he was reelected to the Senate. After his terms ended, he returned to live in Indianapolis. He died there on November 1, 1877. Morton was married in 1843 to Lucinda Burbank. They had five children.

MOSS, RALPH WILBUR, (1862-1919) - a U.S. Representative from Indiana; born in Center Point, Clay County, Ind., April 21, 1862; educated in the common schools of the township and attended Purdue University, West Lafayette, Ind., for two years; taught school in Sugar Ridge Township; principal of the graded schools in Harmony, Ind.; subsequently became engaged in agricultural pursuits; member of the State senate 1905-1909; elected as a Democrat to the Sixty-first and to the three succeeding Congresses (March 4, 1909-March 3, 1917); chairman, Committee on Expenditures in the Department of Agriculture (Sixty-second Congress); unsuccessful candidate for reelection in 1916 to the Sixty-fifth Congress and for election in 1918 to the Sixty-sixth Congress; retired to his farm near Ashboro, Clay County, Ind., where he died on April 26, 1919; interment in Moss Cemetery, near his home.

MOUNT, JAMES A., (1843-1901) - governor of Indiana (1897- 1901), was born in Montgomery County, Indiana on March 24, 1843, the son of Atwell and Lucinda (Fullenwider) Mount. When he was young he lived on a farm and was educated at common schools. He served in Company D of the 72nd Indiana Regiment for three years during the Civil War and attained the rank of sergeant. After the war, he returned to Lebanon, Indiana and attended the Presbyterian Academy. He bought a farm soon after, and became a well-respected lecturer on agricultural matters.

Mount's appearances on the lecture circuit led him to seek public office, and in 1888 he ran as a Republican for the Indiana Senate and was elected. He lost a bid for U.S. Congress in 1890, but in 1896 made a political comeback, winning the Indiana governorship by a margin of 6,000 votes. Mount served as governor during the Spanish-American War. While in office, he worked to overhaul the prison system. He also saw the establishment of the Medical Examining Board and the Office of Labor Commissioner.

Mount completed his term in January, 1901. He died only a few days after leaving office, on January 16. He was married in 1867 to Catharine Boyd and had three children.

MYERS, JOHN THOMAS, (1927-   ) - a U.S. Representative from Indiana; born in Covington, Fountain County, Ind., February 8, 1927; attended the public schools of Covington, Ind.; graduated from Indiana State University in 1951; served in the United States Army in the European Theater, 1945-1946; cashier and trust officer with The Fountain Trust Co. in Covington, Ind., 1952-1966; owns and operates a grain and livestock farm in Fountain County, Ind.; elected as a Republican to 1, the Ninetieth and to the ten succeeding Congresses (January 13, 1967- January 3, 1989); is a resident of Covington, Ind.

MYERS, WILLIAM RALPH, (1836-1907) - a U.S. Representative from Indiana; born near Wilmington, Clinton County, Ohio, June 12, 1836; moved with his parents to Anderson, Madison County, Ind., in October 1836; attended the common schools and later taught; surveyor of Madison County 1858-1860; during the Civil War enlisted as a private in Company G, Forty-seventh Regiment, Indiana Volunteer Infantry; was promoted to orderly sergeant, second lieutenant, first lieuten'ant, and captain, and served four years and three months; after returning from the Army taught school; superintendent of the public schools of Anderson, Ind., in 1868 and 1869; member of the school board of Anderson 1871- 1879; studied law; was admitted to the bar in 1871 and commenced practice in Anderson; elected as a Democrat to the Forty-sixth Congress (March 4, 1879-March 3, 1881); unsuccessful candidate for reelection in 1880 to the Forty-seventh Congress; secretary of State of Indiana 1882-1886; purchased the Anderson Democrat in 1886 and was its editor; unsuccessful Democratic candidate for Governor; again secretary of state 1892-1894; resumed the practice of law; died in Anderson, Ind., April 18, 1907; interment in East Maplewood Cemetery.

N

NEW, JEPTHA DUDLEY, (1830-1892) - a U.S. Representative from Indiana; born in Vernon, Jennings County, Ind., November 28, 1830; was graduated from Vernon (Ind.) Academy and Bethany (W.Va.) College; studied law; was admitted to the bar in 1851 and practiced in Vernon, Ind., until 1864; mayor of Vernon 1852-1854; prosecuting attorney of Jennings County, Ind., 1860-1864; judge of the district court of common pleas 1864-1868; resumed the practice of law in Vernon; elected as a Democrat to the Forty- fourth Congress (March 4, 1875-March 3, 1877); declined to be a candidate for reelection in 1876 to the Forty-fifth Congress; elected to the Forty-sixth Congress (March 4, 1879-March 3, 1881); was not a candidate for reelection in 1880; judge of the sixth judicial circuit of Indiana 1882-1888; appellate judge in 1891; was nominated by the Democratic Party as a candidate for judge of the supreme court of Indiana in 1892, but died before the election in Vernon, Ind., July 9, 1892; interment in Vernon Cemetery.

NIBLACK, WILLIAM ELLIS, (1822-1893) - (cousin of Silas Leslie Niblack), a U.S. Representative from Indiana; born in Dubois County, Ind., May 19, 1822; attended the country schools and the Indiana University at Bloomington; studied law; was admitted to the bar in 1843 and commenced practice in Vincennes, Ind.; surveyor of Dubois County; member of the State house of representatives in 1849 and 1850; served in the State senate 1850-1853; judge of the circuit court of the third judicial district from January 1854 until October 1859, when he resigned; moved to Vincennes, Ind., in 1855; elected as a Democrat to the Thirty-fifth Congress to fill the vacancy caused by the death of James Lockhart; reelected to the Thirty-sixth Congress and served from December 7, 1857, to March 3, 1861; was not a candidate for renomination in 1860; again a member of the State house of representatives in 1862 and 1863; delegate to the Democratic National Conventions in 1864,

1868, and 1876; elected to the Thirty-ninth and to the four succeeding Congresses (March 4, 1865-March 3, 1875); was not a candidate for renomination in 1874; resumed the practice of law; judge of the supreme court of Indiana 1877-1889; moved to Indianapolis in 1889 and retired from public life; died in Indianapolis, Ind., May 7, 1893; interment in Crown Hill Cemetery.

NICHOLSON, MEREDITH, (1866 - 1947) - was a writer of best- selling novels and an essayist of distinction whose fondness for Indiana shone through his works.

Born at Crawfordsville on Dec, 1866, Nicholson spent most of his life in Indianapolis. After nine years in the public schools, he spurned further formal education to the regret of his mother, a nurse for the South during the Civil War. His father had fought with Indiana troops for the North.

Nicholson held a variety of jobs before he became involved in newspaper journalism. His writing career was established in 1900 with the publication of *The Hoosiers*, a book of essays about many aspects of Indiana life and lore, including the mysterious origin of the Hoosier sobriquet. His novels, fashioned into the literary mold of the day, were smoothly written in a highly readable style. Publication of *The Main Chance* (1903) and *Zelda Dameron* (1904) brought him national reknown. His *The House of a Thousand Candles* (1905) drew warm notices in France.

Nicholson, a Jeffersonian Democrat held deep beliefs in democracy, in self-government, and in tolerance. For years he worked and wrote for the Democratic Party. He was named U.S. minister to Paraguay (1933-34), Venezuela (1935-38), and Nicaragua (1938-41).

After his foray into diplomacy, Nicholson returned to Indianapolis, where he had been a great friend of the poet James Whitcomb Riley. Nicholson's *The Poet* (1914) is a fictionalized biography of Riley. Heeding his mother's advice about education, he taught himself Latin, Greek, French, and Italian. Nicholson was awarded several honorary degrees, honorary membership in Phi Beta Kappa, and membership in the American Academy of Arts and Letters. He died Dec. 20, 1947.

NOBLE, JAMES, (1785-1831) - a U.S. Senator from Indiana; born near Berryville, Clarke County, Va., December 16, 1785; moved with his parents to Campbell County, Ky., in 1795; studied law; was admitted to the bar and practiced; moved to Indiana and settled in Brookville; ferryboat operator; judge; member of the convention to draft the constitution of the State in 1816; member, first State house of representatives 1816; elected as a Republican to the United States Senate in 1816; reelected in 1821 and again in 1827 and served from December 11, 1816, until his death in Washington, D.C., on February 26, 1831; chairman, Committee on Pensions (Fifteenth through Eighteenth and Twentieth Congresses), Committee on the Militia (Sixteenth and Seventeenth Congresses); interment in the Congressional Cemetery.

NOBLE, NOAH, (1794-1844) - governor of Indiana (1831-1837), was born on January 14, 1794 in Berryville, Virginia, the son of Dr. Thomas and Elizabeth (Sedgewick) Noble. His family moved to Kentucky around 1800 and Noble attended common schools there. He settled in Brookville, Indiana in 1816 and the next year was commissioned a lieutenant colonel in the Indiana Militia. In 1820, he was promoted to the rank of colonel.

While in Brookville, Noble was involved in various business endeavors, including wool carding, a fulling mill, and real estate speculation. He was elected sheriff of Franklin County in 1820 and 1822. In 1824, he won a seat in the Indiana House of Representatives, and in 1825 he was named receiver general of public monies for the Indianapolis Land Office, a post he held for four years. Nobel was a commissioner and assisted in the locating of the Michigan Road in 1830.

In 1831, Noble was elected governor of Indiana. Accomplishments during his administration included the construction of new roads and canals, and the revision of the tax law. Noble left office in 1837. He was a candidate for U.S. Senate in 1836 and 1838 but lost both times. He did however continue to serve in public posts: from 1839 to 1840 on the Internal Improvements Board, and in 1841 as fund commissioner.

Noble died on February 8, 1844 in Indianapolis. He was married to Catherine Stull Van Swearington, and had a son and a daughter.

NOLAND, JAMES ELLSWORTH, (1920-   ) - a U.S. Representative from Indiana; born in La Grange, Lewis County, Mo., April 22, 1920; with his parents moved to Indiana; attended the public schools of Spencer and Bloomington, Ind.; graduated from Indiana University in 1942 and from Harvard Graduate School of Business Administration in 1943; commissioned a second lieutenant in June 1943 in the Army Transportation Corps and assigned to the New Orleans Port of Embarkation and served until discharged as a captain on May 26, 1946; unsuccessful Democratic candidate for election in 1946 to the Eightieth Congress; graduated from Indiana University Law School in 1948; was admitted to the bar and commenced the practice of law; elected as a Democrat to the Eighty-first Congress (January 3, 1949-January 3, 1951); unsuccessful r candidate for reelection in 1950 to the Eighty-second Congress; resumed the practice of law; delegate, Democratic Naitional Convention, 1964; assistant state attorney general, Indiana, 1952; assistant city attorney, Indianapolis, 1956-1957; Democratic member of Indiana State Election Board, Democratic State committee, 1959, 1958-1966; secretary, 1966 to 1966; Federal judge, southern district of Indiana, Present; chief judge, 1984 to present; is a resident of Indianapolis, Ind.

O

O'NEALL, JOHN HENRY, (1838-1907) - a U.S. Representative from Indiana; born in Newberry, Newberry County, S.C., October 30, 1838; was left an orphan when eight years of age and was reared by his grandfather, who resided in Daviess County, Ind.; attended country schools and was graduated from Indiana University at Bloomington in 1862; was graduated from the law department of the University of

Michigan at Ann Arbor in 1864; was admitted to the bar the same year and practiced in Terre Haute and later in Washington, Ind.; served in the State legislature in 1866; appointed prosecuting attorney for the eleventh judicial circuit in 1873; elected to the office in 1874, but resigned before his term was completed; elected as a Democrat to the Fiftieth and Fifty-first Congresses (March 4, 1887-March 3, 1891); was not a candidate for renomination in 1890; resumed the practice of law in Washington, Ind.; school trustee of Washington for fifteen years; delegate to the Democratic National Convention in 1896; city attorney of Washington 1899-1907; organized the Federal Trust Co. in 1899 and was its president until 1902, when it was made a national bank; died in Washington, Daviess County, Ind., July 15, 1907; interment in St. John's Cemetery.

ORR, ROBERT D., (1917-   ) - governor of Indiana (1981- 1989), was born on November 17, 1917 in Ann Arbor, Michigan, the son of Samuel Lowry and Louis (Dunkerson) Orr. His family lived in Evansville, Indiana and he received his early education there and at Hotchkiss School in Connecticut. He went on to Yale University, where he graduated with a B.A. in history in 1940, and then entered the Harvard Graduate School of Business Administration. During World War II, he enlisted in the Army and served in the Pacific.

In 1946, after the war, Orr returned to Evansville and worked as a manager for the Orr Iron Company, his family's business. He also became involved in other business ventures in Evansville, and served on the boards of various companies there, including Sign Crafters, Hahn, Erie Investments, Sterling Brewers, Product Analysis and Research Industries, and Evansville Metal Products.

Starting in 1965, Orr served as chairman of the Vanderburgh County Republican Central Committee for six years. Meanwhile, in 1968, he won a seat in the Indiana State Senate. He was nominated for lieutenant governor by the Republicans in 1972, and running on a ticket with Otis R. Bowen, won in the general election later that year. In 1976, he was reelected and served for a second time under Governor Otis.

At the end of two terms, in 1980, the outgoing Governor Otis endorsed Orr as the Republican gubernatorial candidate, and Orr won a smashing victory over his Democratic rival, John Hillenbrand II in the fall election. Orr was reelected in 1984. Entering office in the midst of a recession, Orr saw the State's surplus quickly become a deficit. As unemployment rose to 20 percent in parts of the State, public dissatisfaction grew. Orr attempted to ameliorate these problems by pushing for job creation and opposing tax increases. By 1983, however, Indiana's deficit exceeded $450 million and Orr called a special session of the Legislature which resulted in an increase in the state income tax from 1.9 percent to 3 percent, and state sales tax from 4 percent to 5 percent.

Orr's second administration struggled to help the State recover economically by improving educational programs and luring foreign investors. In 1988, Indiana was successful in bringing the Isuzu/Subaru light truck and auto plant to the State. Orr left office in January, 1989 and was succeeded by Birch Evans Bayh III.

Robert Orr was married in 1944 to Joanne "Josie" Wallace, and had three children.

ORTH, GODLOVE STEIN, (1817-1882) - a U.S. Representative from Indiana; born in Lebanon, Pa., on April 22, 1817; attended the Gettysburg College, Pennsylvania; studied law; was admitted to the bar in 1839 and commenced practice in LaFayette, Ind.; member of the State senate 1843-1848 and served one year as president; presidential elector on the Whig ticket in 1848; delegate to the peace convention held in Washington, D.C., in 1861 in an effort to devise means to prevent the impending war; served as captain of a company of Volunteers during the Civil War; elected as a Republican to the Thirtyeighth and to the three succeeding Congresses (March 4, 1863-March 3, 1871); chairman, Committee on Private Land Claims (Fortieth and Forty-first Congresses), Committee on Foreign Affairs (Forty-third Congress); was not a candidate for reelection in 1870 to the Forty-second Congress; elected to the Forty-third Congress (March 4, 1873- March 3, 1875); was not a candidate for renomination in 1874; appointed Envoy Extraordinary and Minister Plenipotentiary to Austria-Hungary

March 9, 1875, and served until May 23, 1876, when he resigned; elected as a Republican to the Forty-sixth and Forty-seventh Congresses and served from March 4, 1879, until his death in LaFayette, Tippecanoe County, Ind., December 16, 1882; interment in Springvale Cemetery.

OVERSTREET, JESSE, (1859-1910) - a U.S. Representative from Indiana; born in Franklin, Johnson County, Ind., December 14, 1859; attended the schools of his native city; was graduated from the Franklin High School in 1877 and from Franklin College in 1882; studied law; was admitted to the bar in 1886 and commenced practice in Franklin; member of the Republican State central committee of Indiana in 1892; elected as a Republican to the Fifty-fourth and to the six succeeding Congresses (March 4, 1895- March 3, 1909); chairman, Committee on Expenditures in the Department of Justice (Fifty-sixth and Fifty-seventh Congresses), Committee on the Post Office and Post Roads (Fifty-eighth through Sixtieth Congresses); unsuccessful candidate for reelection in 1908 to the Sixty-first Congress; resumed the practice of his profession; died in Indianapolis, Ind., May 27, 1910; interment in the Columbus City Cemetery, Columbus, Ind.

OWEN, ROBERT DALE, (1801-1877) - a U.S. Representative from Indiana; born in Glasgow, Scotland, November 7, 1801; studied under private teachers and attended the Emanuel von Fellenberg School at Hofwyl, near Berne, Switzerland, 1820-1823; immigrated to the United States in 1825 with his parents, who settled in Posey County, Ind.; aided his father in the establishment of the social community of New Harmony, Ind., and on the failure of that project he returned to Europe for further study; returned to the United States in 1827 and became a citizen; was the founder and editor of the Free Enquirer, published in New York, 1828-1832; returned to New Harmony in 1832; member of the State house of representatives 1835-1838; unsuccessful candidate for election in 1838 to the Twenty-sixth Congress and in 1840 to the Twenty- seventh Congress; elected as a Democrat to the Twenty-eighth and Twenty-ninth Congresses (March 4, 1843-March 3, 1847); chairman, Committee on Roads and Canals (Twenty-eighth

Congress); unsuccessful candidate for reelection in 1846 to the Thirtieth Congress; member of the State constitutional convention in 1850; member of the State house of representatives in 1851; appointed by President Franklin Pierce as Charge d'Affaires to the Two Sicilies May 24, 1853, and Minister Resident June 29, 1854, serving until September 20, 1858; devoted the remainder of his life to writing on social problems; died at his summer home""""Cosy Cove," at Crosbyside, on Lake George, N.Y., June 24, 1877; interment in the Village Cemetery at Lake George, Warren County, N.Y.

OWEN, WILLIAM DALE, (1846-1906) - a U.S. Representative from Indiana; born in Bloomington, Ind., on September 6, 1846; attended Indiana University at Bloomington in 1865 and entered upon the study of law; relinquished law for the ministry; pastor of the Logansport (Ind.) Christian Church until 1878; elected as a Republican to the Forty-ninth, Fiftieth, and Fifty-first Congresses (March 4, 1885-March 3, 1891); unsuccessful candidate for reelection in 1890 to the Fifty-second Congress; elected secretary of state of Indiana and served from January 16, 1895, to January 15, 1899; engaged in real estate speculation and interested in rubber plantations in Mexico; in 1906 went to Europe, where he died.

OWINGS, NATHANIEL ALEXANDER, (1903-) - architect, was born in Indianapolis, Indiana on February 5, 1903.

After graduation from high school, he went on a trip to Europe and when he saw the beautiful cathedrals there he immediately knew that architecture would be his life's work.

In 1921, he enrolled in the University of Illinois to study architectural engineering. After one year, he became ill and had to leave. When he was able to return to school, he switched to Cornell University, where he received his B.S. degree in architecture and engineering in 1927.

He then did a year of apprenticeship as a draftsman at the New York architecture firm of York and Sawyer and so impressed his superiors that he got promoted to a designing assignment. In 1933, he was made development supervisor at the Century Progress Exposition in Chicago and worked closely with the Exposition's chief designer, Louis Skidmore. In 1936, the two men formed a partnership in Chicago. In 1939, they added one more partner, making the firm name, Skidmore, Owings & Merrill. Eventually, along with the Chicago and New York offices, they opened branches in San Francisco, Washington D.C. and Portland, Oregon.

The commissions given to the firm were both numerous and impressive. They included: several buildings for the 1939-40 New York World's Fair; the secret town of Oak Ridge, Tennessee, where the atomic bomb was to be developed during World War II; the H.J. Heinz Company in Tracy, California; New York University-Bellevue Medical Center; the Lever House in New York; the Air Force Academy near Colorado Springs; the Chase Manhattan Bank in downtown Manhattan; the Alcoa Building in San Francisco and both the John Hancock Center and the Sears Tower in Chicago.

Owings felt that one of his most prestigious assignments was being named chairman of the Temporary Commission on Pennsylvania Avenue in 1964. He had been appointed to their advisory council in 1962, by President John F. Kennedy. As chairman, through the administrations of Presidents Johnson and Nixon, Owings supervised the creation of a master plan for an extensive remodeling of Pennsylvania Avenue in Washington D.C., from the Capitol to the White House. He became a member of the Permanent Commission on Pennsylvania Avenue in 1973.

During this period, he and his company took on the task of designing an eighteen mile strip of Highway Interstate 95, running through the center of Baltimore. He brought in a team of experts to examine the feasibility of the construction versus the preservation of landmarks and residential districts. One of Owings most admired qualities was his ability to negotiate with all parties involved, in order to achieve the correct balance of the situation.

In 1968, he wrote a book entitled, *The American Aesthetic.* He also wrote his autobiography in 1973, called *The Spaces In Between: An Architect's Journey,* in which he gave his vision for environmental planning which would include a high-density city and "the clear, clean air of the open country around it." He felt that "the hope for the future lies in going back to the roots of man--where we do not depend on systems or forumulas but on a corpus of myth, fable and miracle. We can do this through living in harmony with the laws of Nature- -not the contrived, plastic ones of man." Owing was married twice and had four children from his first wife.

P

PACKARD, JASPER, (1832-1899) - a U.S. Representative from Indiana; born in Austintown, Mahoning County, Ohio, February 1, 1832; moved with his parents to Indiana in 1835; attended the public schools and was graduated from the University of Michigan at Ann Arbor in 1855; taught school; settled in La Porte, Ind.; studied law and was admitted to the bar in 1861; during the Civil War enlisted in the Union Army as a private in the Forty-eighth Regiment, Indiana Volunteer Infantry, October 24, 1861; promoted to first lieutenant January 1, 1862; captain September 12, 1862; lieutenant colonel of the One Hundred and Twenty-eighth Regiment, Indiana Volunteer Infantry, March 17, 1864; colonel June 26, 1865; brevetted brigadier general March 13, 1865," ""for meritorious services"; mustered out April 10, 1866; auditor of La Porte County from November 15, 1866, to March 1, 1869, when he resigned; elected as a Republican to the Forty-first, Forty second, and Forty-third Congresses (March 4, 1869-March 3, 1875); chairman, Committee on Expenditures in the Department of State (Forty-third Congress), Committee on Private Land Claims (Forty- third Congress); was not a candidate for renomination in 1874; engaged in newspaper pursuits; appointed July 1, 1899, commandant of the State soldiers' home at Lafayette, Ind., and died there December 13, 1899; interment in the Soldiers' Home Cemetery.

PAIGE, ROBERT, (1910-1987) - actor, newscaster, was born in Indianapolis, Indiana.

Paige began his career as a radio announcer and then started working in films in the 1940's. Some of his movies were *Cain and Mabel, Hellzapoppin, Raging Waters* and *Bye Bye Birdie*. He was in the television series, *Run Buddy Run* in 1966.

He also was a co-host, with Bess Myerson, of the game show *The Big Payoff*, produced in New York. He returned to Los Angeles and was a long-time newscaster for local station KABC-TV. After that, he began his own television sales promotion company, Paige-Ludden Enterprises, in tandem with his wife, Jo Anne Ludden, whom he married in 1961.

PAPAKEECHA, (fl. 19th century) - Miami Indian, also known as Flat Belly, was chief of a village of Miami Indians--commonly known as Flat Belly's Village--near Turkey Lake in Noble County, Indiana.

PARKE, BENJAMIN, (1777-1835) -a Delegate from the Territory of Indiana; born in New Jersey on September 22, 1777; received a limited schooling; moved to Lexington, Ky., in 1797; studied law and was admitted to the bar; moved to Vincennes, Territory of Indiana, in 1799 and practiced; attorney general of the Territory 1804-1808; member of the Territorial house of representatives in 1805; when the Territory was formed, was elected the first Delegate to the Ninth and Tenth Congresses and served from December 12, 1805, until March 1, 1808, when he resigned; served on the staff of Gov. William Harrison; Territorial judge 1808-1817; judge of the United States District Court for Indiana 1817- 1835; was the first president of the Indiana Historical Society; died in Salem, Washington County, Ind., July 12, 1835; interment in Crown Hill Cemetery.

PARKER, SAMUEL WILSON, (1805-1859) - a U.S. Representative from Indiana; born near Watertown, Jefferson County, N.Y., September 9, 1805; pursued academic studies; was graduated from Miami University, Oxford, Ohio, in 1828; studied law; was admitted to the bar in 1831 and commenced practice in Connersville, Fayette County, Ind.; served as prosecuting attorney of Fayette County from December 10, 1836, to December 10, 1838; member of the

State house of representatives in 1839 and 1843; served in the State senate 1841-1843; unsuccessful can didate for election in 1849 to the Thirty-first Congress; elected as a Whig to the Thirty-second and Thirty-third Congresses (March 4, 1851-March 3, 1855); did not seek renomination in 1855; died near Sackets Harbor, N.Y., February 1, 1859; interment in the private cemetery on the Old Elm farm, near Sackets Harbor.

PATTON, DAVID HENRY, (1837-1914) - a U.S. Representative from Indiana; born in Flemingsburg, Fleming County, Ky., November 26, 1837; attended the Collegiate Institute, Waveland, Ind.; en listed in the Thirty-eighth Indiana Regiment in 1861 and was mustered out in July 1865, after having attained the rank of colonel; was graduated from the Chicago Medical College in 1867 and practiced medicine in Remington, Jasper County, Ind.; pension examiner at Remington 1886-1890; delegate to the Democratic National Convention in 1892 and 1900; elected as a Democrat to the Fifty-second Congress (March 4, 1891-March 3, 1893); was not a candidate for renomination in 1892; moved to Woodward, Woodward County, Indian Territory (now Oklahoma), in 1893; appointed receiver of public lands for Oklahoma in 1893, and later resumed the practice of medicine; member of the district board of health of Woodward, Okla.; appointed pension examiner at Woodward; died in Otterbein, Benton County on July 17, 1914.

PAULEY, EDWIN WENDELL, (1903-   ) - oil corporation executive, was born in Indianapolis, Indiana on January 7, 1903.

He attended the University of California's College of Commerce and Business Administration, where he received his B.S. in 1922 and his M.S. in 1923. He worked himself through school by selling encyclopedias and also by working as a "mucker" in the California oil fields, where he continued to move up through the ranks from roughneck, to derrick man, driller, buyer and refinery evaluator.

After graduation, he began to teach economics at the university until he was severely injured in a plane crash. Realizing he was not going to be able to pay a years worth of hospital bills on an instructor's salary, he decided to put his oil company experience to work and with some other investors, he leased an oil refinery. He became the president of his new company, called the Petrol Corporation of Los Angeles. The company expanded to include not only refining, but oil production, transportation and marketing. Within fifteen years, Pauley was a millionaire and became the president of two more oil companies.

Pauley was a great admirer of Franklin Delano Roosevelt. He campaigned for him in 1932 and 1936, and in the 1940 race, he was asked to help raise campaign funds in eleven states.

After he made a suggestion to President Roosevelt concerning the shipping of oil to Great Britain, he was appointed to act as a liaison and troubleshooter with both Britain and Russia regarding petroleum lend-lease supplies.

Pauley became the secretary of the Democratic National committee in 1941, and the next year, President Roosevelt gave him the post of the Democratic Party Treasurer and asked him to eliminate its $750,000 debt, which Pauley accomplished within two years time.

In 1945, he was appointed as ambassador to the Allied Commission on Reparations and two years later he was named Special Adviser on Reparations to the Secretary of State. He made inspection tours of both Germany and Japan and returned home to make his recommendations to President Truman and Secretary of State George C. Marshall. He was also named Special Assistant to the Secretary of the Army, in 1947.

Besides being an independent oil man, Pauley was a founder of the People's Bank of California, serving on its board of directors.

Pauley was married to Barbara McHenry in 1937, and they had four children.

PAULEY, JANE, (ne Margaret Jane Pauley) - (1950-) - broadcast journalist, was born in Indianapolis, Indiana on October 31, 1950.

She attended Indiana University where she received a B.A. degree in 1971. After graduation, she went to work as an aide to New York Mayor John V. Lindsay during his 1971 Presidential campaign. When his political efforts failed, Pauley returned home and found a position with the Indiana Democratic Central Committee.

In 1972, she became a cub reporter at WISH-TV, the CBS affiliate in Indianapolis, even though she had no experience. However, in a little more than a year's time, she was coanchoring the midday news broadcasts and anchoring the weekend evening newscasts.

During that time, she was noticed by executives at WMAQ-TV in Chicago, who suggested she try out for the position of coanchor on their nightly newscast. She had decided before her audition that they weren't about to hire a twenty-four year old woman, so feeling like she had nothing to lose, she was confident and relaxed. The situation worked in her favor and she was hired in September of 1975 to coanchor the 5:00 PM and 10:00 PM newscasts with veteran Floyd Kalber, making her the first female coanchor in Chicago broadcasting.

The reaction to her hiring was swift and derogatory. The critics had a field day with her youth, her looks and her limited experience. The news ratings continuted to decline and Pauley was relegated to doing only the 5:00 PM newscast. However, she still provided special reports to the later newscast, and continued to quietly learn and pay her dues.

Meanwhile, Barbara Walters, co-host of the *Today* show, had made her infamous defection from NBC to ABC, and NBC executives were looking at videotapes for her replacement. Out of over 250 applicants, six people were chosen for on-the-air tryouts on the *Today* show, including Jane Pauley. Approximately 2,000 viewers were asked who they liked the best, and Jane Pauley was, without question, the number one choice. Based on those results, she was
hired in October of 1976 to coanchor the *Today* show with Tom Brokaw.

The decision once again drew barbs from the critics, but Pauley immediately proved her mettle in interviews and as a co- host. She was meticulous in researching her assignments and learned to be persistent in her questioning, and within two weeks of her hiring, the ratings began to climb. For the next thirteen years, Pauley became a comfortable presence to early morning viewers. In 1982, Tom Brokaw left the show and Bryant Gumbel became a part of the team, while different people, such as Chris Wallace and John Palmer sat at the news desk.

In September of 1989, Palmer was replaced by Deborah Norville. The thirty-one year old Norville was brought in to lure back the 18 to 49 year old demographic group that the network felt they were losing. However, it was a move that backfired. Norville was also invited to share hosting duties, as well as deliver the news, but it was a surprise to Pauley and eventually created a highly awkward atmosphere. Unfortunately, it became a media free-for-all, with Norville being cast as an ambitious predator, which both Norville and Pauley emphatically denied. However, it did make Pauley re-examine her role on the show, as well as the question of where her career was headed. She resigned from the *Today* show at the end of 1989, but continues to work with NBC on other projects such as a prime-time news program, and to occasionally fill in for Tom Brokaw on the NBC Nightly News.

In June of 1980, she married *Doonesbury* cartoonist, Garry Trudeau and they have three children.

PEELLE, STANTON JUDKINS, (1843-1928) - a U.S. Representative from Indiana; born near Richmond, Wayne County, Ind., February 11, 1843; attended the common schools and Winchester Seminary; enlisted in Company G, Eighth Regiment, Indiana Volunteers, August 5, 1861 and served until near the close of the war; studied law; was admitted to the bar in 1866 and commenced practice in Winchester, Ind.; moved to Indianapolis in 1869; deputy district attorney of Marion County in 1872 and 1873; member of the State house of representatives 1877-1879; elected as a Republican to the Forty-seventh Congress (March 4, 1881-March 3, 1883); presented credentials as a Member-elect to the Forty-eighth Congress and served from March 4, 1883, to May 22, 1884, when he was succeeded by William E. English, who contested his election; delegate to the Republican National Convention in 1892; appointed judge of the United States Court of Claims in 1892 and served until January 1, 1906, when he was advanced to chief justice and served until February 11, 1913, when he resigned; Professor of law at George Washington University (D.C.) 1901-1911; member of the board of trustees of Howard University, Washington, D.C., 1906-1925; president of the board of the Washington College of Law 1910-1925; resided in Washington, D.C., until his death there September 4, 1928; interment in Rock Creek Cemetery.

PESHEWAH, (1761-I841) - Miami Indian, also known as Johm Richardville or Jean Baptiste Richardville, born on St. Mary's River, Indiana, was principal Miami chief, and, at his death perhaps the wealthiest Indian in North America. Although he managed to prevent the Miami nation from selfdestruction caused by internal disagreements, he was unexcelled in meeting U.S. demands for Indian land and removal, and in increasing his family's wealth through tribal lands. Peshewah was a politician and businessman whose authority rested on his ability to manipulate treaties and his support from the Bureau of Indian Affairs.

PETTIT, JOHN UPFOLD, (1820-1881) - a U.S. Representative from Indiana; born in Fabius, Onondaga County, N.Y., September 11, 1820; received an academic education; attended Hamilton College, Clinton, N.Y., and was graduated from Union College, Schenectady, N.Y., in 1839; studied law; was admitted to the bar in 1841 and commenced practice in Wabash, Wabash County, Ind.; American consul to Maranham, Brazil, 1850-1853; elected as a Republican to the Thirty-fourth, Thirtyfifth, and Thirty-sixth Congresses (March 4, 1855-March 3, 1861); chairman, Committee on Expenditures in the Post Offlce Department (Thirty-fourth Congress); member of the State house of representatives in 1865 and served as speaker; judge of the twenty-seventh judicial district of Indiana 1872-1880; died in Wabash, Ind., March 21, 1881; interment in Falls Cemetery.

PHILLIPS, DAVID GRAHAM, (1867-1911); novelist, was born in Madison, Indiana on October 31, 1867.

Phillips, whose pen name was John Graham, was educated in his home state of Indiana, as well as at Princeton.

He wrote for various newspapers, such as the Cincinnati *Times-Star*, the New York *Tribune*, the New York *Sun* and the New York *World*. Between the years 1901 to 1911, he published many articles including a series in *Cosmopolitan*, in 1906, entitled *The Treason of the Senate*.

His style of writing was always described as being of the "muckraking" variety, because he wrote mostly about society's ills and political corruption. Some of his books included, *The Great God Success, Light-Fingered Gentry* and *The Price She Paid*. He wrote one play, entitled *The Worth of a Woman*, in 1908, which dealt with the changing attitudes of women in that era. His most important novel was, *Susan Lenox: Her Fall and Rise*, written in 1917.

David Phillips was murdered on January 24, 1911, by a deranged gunman who believed that Phillips had disparaged his sister in his book, *The Fashionable Adventures of Joshua Craig*, written in 1909.

PORTER, ALBERT G., (1824-1897) - governor of Indiana (1881- 1885), was born on April 20, 1824 in Lawrenceburg, Indiana, the son of Thomas and Miranda (Tousey) Porter. He received his education at Hanover College and Indiana Asbury College. After graduation in 1843, he moved to Indianapolis where he worked as an attorney. From 1853 to 1857, he was a reporter for the State Supreme Court.

Originally a Democrat, Porter's affiliation changed with the rise of the new Republican Party. He ran for U.S. Congress as a Republican and was elected in 1858 and 1860. Once again in Washington, he served as controller of the U.S. Treasury from 1878 to 1880. In 1880, Porter received the Republican nomination for governor of Indiana. He went on to win in the general election later that year against Democrat, Franklin Landers. As governor, Porter gave attention to the issue of medical care in Indiana. Hospitals were erected in Richmond, Evansville, and Logansport, and the State Board of Health was established. A drive to clear up swamplands was put into action and the Kankakee Swamp and other marshlands were drained.

After leaving office, Porter was named U.S. minister to Italy and served there from 1889 to 1892. He returned to Indiana and lived his final years in Indianapolis. He died on May 3, 1897. Porter was married in 1846 to Minerva Brown, and had four children. Minerva died in 1875. In 1881, he remarried to Cornelia Stone.

PORTER, COLE, (1892 - 1964) was a composer who wrote songs for more than 30 musical comedies including *Kiss Me Kate* and *Can Can*.

Porter was born in Peru, Indiana on June 9, 1892. He received considerable musical training during his childhood in a wealthy farm environment. While he studied for a bachelor of arts degree at Yale University (1909-13), he wrote music and lyrics for programs sponsored by his fraternity and the Yale Dramatic Association. He attended Harvard Law School for one semester during 1914, and then entered the unversity's graduate music school (1915-16). During this time he wrote *See America First* (1916) his first Broadway musical comedy and his most dismal failure.

Porter then went to North Africa to entertain the French Foreign Legion. He served in the French army during World War I and had a brief period of study with the French composer, Vincent d'Indy. After returning to New York City, he wrote the scores and lyrics for two mildly successful Broadway musicals, *Hitchy- koo* (1919) and *Greenwich Village Follies* (1924). An unproductive period ended in 1927 when Porter wrote the score for the musical *Paris* (1928), for which he composed one of his most popular tunes, "Let's Do It Again." Porter's reputation as one of the most talented lyricist of his time was further enhanced by his composition of scores for a string of successful musicals such as *Fifty Million Frenchman* (1929), *The Gay Divorcee* (1932), *Anything Goes* (1934), and *Jubilee* (1935). From these and some of his other musicals came the songs most associated with the Porter name - "Night and Day," "Just One of Those Things," "You're the Top," "I Get a Kick Out of You," "Begin Things," "Anything Goes," and "In the Still of the Night."

In 1937, Porter was severely crippled in an accident while horseback riding. He continued his highly prolific career, however, with productions such as *DuBarry Was a Lady* (1939; and *Kiss Me Kate* (1948), which some critics consider to be his best work. His last two musicals - *Can Can* (1953) and *Silk Stockings* (1955) - also enjoyed high levels of success. Ill health and the amputation of his right leg in 1958 led him to a self-imposed confinement which lasted until his death in Santa Monica, California on October 15, 1964.

PORTER, GENE (VA) STRATTON, (1863 - 1924) - novelist and naturalist.

Geneva Stratton was born on a farm in Wabash County, Indiana on August 17, 1863, the twelfth child of a Methodist minister. In October, 1874, Geneva and her family moved to Wabash, Indiana where marriage to Charles D. Porter in 1866, the couple moved to Geneva, Indiana where Gene spent a great deal of her time in Limberlost Swamp where she took nature photographs for *Recreation* magazine.

Her first literary work, "Laddie, the Princess and the Pie" wsa published in *Metropolitan* magazine in 1901. She later returned to writing novels which, in some cases were geared strictly toward her interest in nature. In other cases, her novels combined the elements of romance, adventure and sentimentality. Such works include: *Laddie* (1913), *Freckles* (1904), *A Girl of the Limberlost (1909), The Song of the Cardinal* (1902), *The Harvester* (1911), *Birds of the Limberlost* (1914) and *Moths of the Limberlost.*

After World War I Porter and her family moved to California where she wrote editorials for *McCalls* Magazine and organized a company to make movies based on her novels.

By the time of her death in an automobile accident on Dec. 6, 1924, Porter's books had sold more than ten million copies. Her biography, *The Lade of the Limberlost* (1928) was written posthumously by her daughter, Jeanette Porter Meehan.

POSEY, FRANCIS BLACKBURN, (1848-1915) - a U.S. Representative from Indiana; born in Petersburg, Pike County, Ind., April 28, 1848; attended the public schools, Blythewood Academy, and Indiana Asbury (now De Pauw) University, Greencastle, Ind.; was graduated from the law department of the Indiana University at Bloomington in 1869; was admitted to the bar the same year and commenced practice in Petersburg, Ind.; delegate to the Republican National Convention in 1884; unsuc cessful Republican candidate for election in 1888 to the Fifty- first Congress; was subsequently elected to the Fiftieth Congress to fill the vacancy caused by the resignation of Alvin P. Hovey and served from January 29, 1889, to March 3, 1889;

resumed the practice of law in Evansville, Ind.; surveyor of the port of Evansville 1903-1913; died in Rockport, Spencer County, Ind., on October 31, 1915; interment in Walnut Hills Cemetery, Petersburg, Ind.

PRATT, DANIE) DARWIN, (1813-1877) - a U.S. Senator from Indiana; born in Palermo, Maine, October 26, 1813; moved to New York with his parents, who settled in Fenner, Madison County; attended the public schools and Cazenovia Seminary; graduated from Hamilton College, Clinton, N.Y., in 1831; moved to Indiana in 1832 and taught school; settled in Indianapolis in 1834 and was employed in the office of the secretary of State; studied law; was admitted to the bar and commenced practice in Logansport, Ind., in 1836; member, State house of representatives in 1851, 1853; elected in 1868 as a Republican to the Forty-first Congress but resigned January 27, 1869, before the beginning of the congressional term, having been elected to the United States Senate; served as a Republican in the Senate from March 4, 1869, to March 3, 1875; chairman, Committee on Pensions (Forty-second and Fortythird Congresses); appointed by President Ulysses Grant as Commissioner of Internal Revenue 1875-1876; died in Lo gansport, Cass County, Ind., June 17, 1877; interment in Mount Hope Cemetery.

PRICE, BYRON, (1891-1981) - journalist, United States Director of Censorship, was born in Topeka, Indiana on March 25, 1891.

He attended Wabash College, where he received his B.A. degree in 1912. After graduation, he went to work for United Press for a few months and then switched to the Associated Press and was eventually sent to their Washington D.C. office.

In 1917, Price enlisted in the Army and upon his discharge in 1919, he resumed work at his former job in Washington. For five years, he was the news editor, and in 1927, he was promoted to the position of chief. Ten years later, he was named executive editor of the whole organization, which gave him complete responsibility for the Associated Press' 250,000-word daily news stories.

On December 16, 1941, Price was appointed to the office of Director of Censorship. Since World War II had just begun, Price had his work cut out for him, especially since the office was still governed by the rules of the Espionage Act of 1917. The rules were so general and ill-defined that the press was "virtually" at the mercy of the censor." News writers had to tread carefully in order not to inadvertantly give information to the enemy. Any article concerning the military or a diplomatic situation was to be shown to the censor in advance.

As per this Act, Price had the authority to levy fines and have the Department of Justice prosecute anyone who did not comply. By July of 1942, Price had come up with a new list of rules. These rules not only covered newspapers, but radio broadcasts, cables and letters. A staff of over 13,000 people was hired, with a major portion of them handling the postal and cable censorship departments. This list was eventually questioned by members of the press as being too stringent, especially regarding news stories sent overseas. But Price stuck to his guns, saying that his office felt there was a necessity to censor editorial comments which "emphasize disunity in this country instead of stating the facts as they are." Price pointed out that Axis agents who were trying to pass military information had been caught because of the censorship enforcement.

He served in this position until 1945, when he was chosen by President Harry S. Truman to be a personal representative on a special mission to Germany. The next year, he became the Vice President of the Motion Picture Association of America and from 1947 to 1954, he was the Assistant Secretary General for the United Nations.

Price was given numerous awards during his career, including the Medal of Merit from President Truman. He also won a Pulitzer Prize in 1944 for his creation of media censorship codes.

He was married to Priscilla Alden in 1920. They had no children. Byron Price died of a heart attack on August 6, 1981.

PRINCE, WILLIAM, (1772-1824) - a U.S. Representative from Indiana; born in Ireland in 1772; immigrated to the United States and settled in Indiana; studied law; served in the State senate in 1816; delegate to the State constitutional convention in 1816; served as captain in the Battle of Tippecanoe; member of the State house of representatives in 1821 and 1822; was elected to the Eighteenth Congress and served from March 4, 1823, until his death near Princeton, Gibson County, Ind., September 8, 1824; interment in the Old Cemetery, near Princeton, Ind.

PROFFIT, GEORGE H., (1807-1847) - a U.S. Representative from Indiana; born in New Orleans, La., September 4, 1807; completed preparatory studies; moved to Petersburg, Pike County, Ind., in 1828; engaged in mercantile pursuits in Petersburg and Portersville, Ind.; studied law; was admitted to the bar and commenced practice in Petersburg, Ind.; member of the State house of representatives in 1831, 1832, and 1836-1838; elected as a Whig to the Twenty-sixth and Twenty-seventh Congresses (March 4, 1839-March 3, 1843); was not a candidate for renomination in 1842; appointed by President Tyler as Envoy Extraordinary and Minister Plenipotentiary to Brazil and served from June 7, 1843, to August 10, 1844, when he returned home, the Senate having refused to confirm his appointment; died in Louisville, Ky., September 7, 1847; interment in Walnut Hills Cemetery, Petersburg, Ind.

PURNELL, FRED SAMPSON, (1882-1939) - a U.S. Representative from Indiana; born on a farm near Veedersburg, Fountain County, Ind., October 25, 1882; attended the common schools and the high school at Veedersburg; was graduated from the law department of Indiana University at Bloomington in 1904; was admitted to the bar the same year and commenced practice in Attica, Fountain County, Ind.; city attorney of Attica 1910-1914; resumed the practice of his profession; unsuccessful candidate for election in 1914 to the Sixtyfourth Congress; elected as a Republican to the Sixty-fifth and to the seven succeeding Congresses (March 4, 1917- March 3, 1933); unsuccessful candidate for reelection in 1932 to the Seventy-third Congress and for election in 1934 to the Seventy-fourth Congress; resumed the practice of law in Attica, Ind.; moved to Washington, D.C., in April 1939 and served as an attorney in the General Accounting Office until his resignation on October

1, 1939; died in Washington, D.C., October 21, 1939; interment in Rockfield Cemetery, near Veedersburg, Ind.

Q

QUAYLE, J. DANFORTH (DAN), (1947-   ) - a U.S. Representative, Senator, and Vice-President from Indiana; born in Indianapolis, Marion County, Ind., February 4, 1947; attended the public schools of Huntington, Ind.; graduated, DePauw University, Greencastle, Ind., 1969; graduated, Indiana University, Indianapolis, 1974; admitted to the Indiana bar in 1974 and commenced practice in Huntington; served in the Indiana National Guard 1969-1975; associate publisher of the Huntington Herald Press; elected as a Republican to the Ninety-fifth Congress in 1976; reelected to the Ninety-sixth Congress (January 3, 1977- January 3, 1981); was not a candidate in 1980 for reelection to the House of Representatives, but was elected to the United States Senate for the term commencing January 3, 1981; reelected in 1986 for the term ending January 3, 1993; chairman, Select Committee to Study the Committee System (Ninety-eighth Congress); was elected as Vice President in 1988; was defeated in the 1992 election.

R

RALSTON, SAMUEL, (1857-1925) - governor of Indiana (1913- 1917), was born on December 1, 1857 in New Cumberland, Ohio, the son of John and Sarah (Scott) Ralston. His family stayed in Ohio during the Civil War, but immediately thereafter moved to Owen County in Indiana. The young boy attended the public schools and achieved a good record. Still not twenty, he began teaching school, but within a few years had matriculated into the Central Normal College at Danville, Indiana. While at school he met and married Mary Josephine Backous who tragically died the following year. Graduating in 1884, Ralston began to study law, and was admitted to the Indiana bar in 1886.

For the next fourteen years he successfully practiced the legal profession in Lebanon, Indiana. Shortly after his fortieth birthday in 1898, Ralston decided to go into politics. He became the Democratic Party's candidate for secretary of state, but lost to his Republican rival. This defeat ended his political career until 1908 when he ran for the Democratic nomination for governor, but lost to fellow Democrat, Thomas R. Marshall. A third try for high office succeeded four years later in 1912 when he was nominated by the Democrats for governor and went on to win in the general election.

Coming to office at the peak of the Progressive era in politics, Ralston initiated a number of reform measures. Following disastrous floods in 1913 he backed legislation for state flood control efforts. Governor Ralston appointed a non- partisan commission to plan the building of public roads, and began the State Park System. With his prodding the Legislature passed a Workmen's Compensation Law, and provided aid to the blind. His administration was considered successful by the people of Indiana who elected him their Senator in 1922. Senator Ralston died in 1925, halfway through his first term in the U.S. Senate. He was married to Jennie Craven in 1889, and had three children.

RANDALL, JAMES GARFIELD, (1881-1953) - teacher, American historian, was born in Indianapolis, Indiana on June 24, 1881.

Randall attended Butler College and then went to the University of Chicago where he received a doctor's degree in history, in 1911.

He taught at numerous colleges including, Illinois College, the University of Michican, Roanoke College, Harvard and the University of California at Los Angeles. In 1920, he began teaching at the University of Illinois where he stayed for thirty-two years, until his retirement in 1949.

Most of his books concerned President Abraham Lincoln and the Civil War, and he was regarded as an authority on the subject. Some of his books included *Constitutional*

Problems Under Lincoln, Civil War and Reconstruction, Lincoln and the South and *Lincoln the Liberal Statesman.*

He attempted what was to be a definitive four-volume biography of Abraham Lincoln. His first was *Lincoln From Springfield to Bull Run*, in 1945. Next came *Lincoln the President: From Bull Run to Gettysburg*, also in 1945. In 1952, he published *Midstream: Lincoln the President*. He wrote the first eight chapters for the fourth volume, but died before he could complete it. Richard N. Current finished the book, entitled, *Last Full Measure*, using Randall's notes. It was published in 1955.

J.G. Randall died of leukemia on February 20, 1953. He was seventy-one.

RARIDEN, JAMES, (1795-1856) - a U.S. Representative from Indiana; born near Cynthiana, Harrison County, Ky., February 14, 1795; received a limited schooling; moved to Brookville, Ind., and thence to Salisbury; deputy clerk of court; studied law; was admitted to the bar in 1818 and began practice in Centerville, Ind., in 1820; prosecuting attorney 1822-1825; served in the State senate in 1823; member of the State house of representatives in 1829, 1830, 1832, and 1833; elected as a Whig to the Twenty-fifth and Twenty-sixth Congresses (March 4, 1837- March 3, 1841); moved to Cambridge City, Ind., in 1846; delegate to the State constitutional convention in 1850; died in Cambridge City, Wayne County, Ind., October 20, 1856; interment in Riverside Cemetery.

RAUCH, GEORGE WASHINGTON, (1876-1940) - a U.S. Representative from Indiana; born on a farm near Warren in Salamonie Township, Huntington County, Ind., February 22, 1876; attended the common schools and Valparaiso (Ind.) Normal School (now Valparaiso University); was graduated from the Northern Indiana Law School at Valparaiso in 1902; was admitted to the bar the same year and commenced the practice of law in Marion, Grant County, Ind.; elected as a Democrat to the Sixtieth and to the four succeeding Congresses (March 4, 1907-March 3, 1917); unsuccessful candidate for reelection in 1916 to the Sixty-fifth Congress; resumed the practice of his profession in Marion, Ind., served on the board of directors of the Motor

Securities Corporation and as president and treasurer of the Davis Records Co.; appointed a Federal bank receiver for banks in Swayzee, Sheridan, and Marion, Ind., serving from 1930 to 1939; member of the city school board 1927-1933; died in Marion, Ind., November 4, 1940; interment in Masonic Cemetery, Warren, Ind.

RAY, JAMES BROWN, (1794-1848) - governor of Indiana (1825- 1831), was born on February 19. 1794 in Jefferson County, Kentucky, the son of William and Phebe Ann (Brown) Ray. As a young man, he read law in Cincinnati, and in 1818 moved to Indiana where he was admitted to the bar. He ran for state representative and in 1821 was elected to the Indiana House. The following year he served in the State Senate.

In 1824, Lt. Governor Boon Ratliff resigned his office and Ray became president pro tempore of the Senate. He was reelected the following year. Then in 1825 Governor Hendricks resigned to take a seat in the U.S. Senate and Ray was named governor of Indiana. Later that year, he was elected governor in his own right. He served two terms. During his administration the construction of the Michigan Road from the Michigan border to the Ohio River and the Wabash and Erie Canal were major objectives. In 1826, Ray served as a commissioner in negotiating land concessions from the Miami and Potawatomi Indians. Ray had strong opposition from the Legislature during his second term; his attempts to revise the penal code were overridden, and his appointments to the State Supreme Court were challenged. He left office in 1831 and practiced law in Indianapolis. In 1833, with business partner, W. M. Tannehill, he started the Greencastle, Indiana newspaper *The Hoosier*.

Ray died of cholera on August 4, 1848 in Cincinnati. He was married twice: 1) to Mary Riddle in 1818, who died in 1823, and 2) to Esther Brooker in 1825. Ray had six children.

REXROTH, KENNETH, (1905-1982) - poet, critic, translator, was born in South Bend, Indiana on December 22, 1905.

Rexroth was orphaned at a young age and at twelve years old, he dropped out of school and found his way to Chicago, deciding on self-education. Eventually, he took some art courses at the Art Institute of Chicago and later at the New York Art Students League. He made a living at many different jobs, including harvest hand, fruit picker, forest patrolman and as an attendant in an insane asylum.

His talents were numerous. He became one of the first abstract painters, and held one-man art shows in New York, Chicago, Los Angeles, Paris and San Francisco. He also wrote poetry and was considered one of the most admired avant-garde literary minds of Chicago's underground society in the 1920's and '30s.

He moved to San Francisco and became a co-founder of the San Francisco Poetry Center. He was enmeshed in the various literary movements of that time, most notably the Beat Movement. Some of his peotry books included, *The Phoenix and the Tortoise*, *The Signature of All Things*, *The Hearts Garden, the Garden's Heart* and *The Morning Star*.

In 1953, he became the San Francisco correspondent for New York's *The Nation* and for ten years, beginning in 1958, he was a columnist for the San Francisco *Examiner*. Later on, he became a columnist for *San Francisco Magazine* and the *San Francisco Bay Guardian*.

He wrote one ballet, *Original Sin*, which was performed by the San Francisco Ballet in 1961. He had a mastery of several languages and translated numerous books of Oriental poetry, such as *One Hundred Poems From the Japanese*, in 1955, *One Hundred Poems From the Chinese*, in 1956, and *The Orchid Boat: The Women Poets of China*, in 1973.

He continued his writing, with books of essays, including *Bird in the Bush* and *The Alternative Society*. He also wrote about his Chicago childhood in *An Autobiographical Novel*, published in 1966. He won the Guggenheim fellowship in poetry in
1948 and 1949.

Rexroth was married three times and had two daughters by his third marriage.

RICKEY, GEORGE WARREN, (1907-   ) - sculptor, educator, was born in South Bend, Indiana on June 6, 1907.

From the age of five, Rickey was brought up in Scotland, after his father was transferred there by his employer. He attended Trinity College, a boys' boarding school in 1921, and then went to Balliol College in 1926, with plans to be a teacher. He received his B.A. degree in 1929, and then went on to get an M.A. degree with honors from Oxford in 1941.

While at Oxford, he took classes in painting and drawing at the Ruskin School of Drawing and Fine Art. One of his teachers suggested that he go to Paris to study modern art, which he did for almost a year.

In 1930, he returned to the United States and began teaching history at Groton School in Massachusetts. However, the pull of his art was too strong and after three years, he returned to Paris to pursue his painting.

He had his first one-man show at the Caz-Delbo Gallery in New York, in 1933, and eventually made New York his home. In 1936, he did a short stint as a copy editor for *Newsweek* magazine, but he knew art was to be his life's work. In 1938, he was commissioned by the U.S. Treasury Department to do a mural for the Selingrove, Pennsylvania Post Office, which he called *Susquehanna Countryside*.

He received grants from the Carnegie Corporation periodically, and was able to begin teaching at various colleges such as Olivet College in Michigan, where he was an artist-in- residence from 1937 to 1939, Kalamazoo College from 1938 to 1940, Knox College in Illinois in 1940 and Muhlenberg College in Pennsylvania in 1941.

In 1942, he joined the Army Air Corps and was assigned to troubleshoot ballistics problems involving computers. After his
military discharge in 1945, he enrolled at the New York University Institute of Fine Arts on the G.I. Bill, where he went for his graduate study in art history.

He continued to combine his academic and artistic worlds by serving as chairman of the art department at Muhlenberg College from 1946 to 1948 and teaching art history at the University of Washington in 1948.

During this time, Rickey had been studying kinetic sculpture and in 1949, began creating sculptures by joining parts of different kinds of materials such as glass, plastic, copper, steel and brass. He would then take those finished pieces and make mobiles of them by hanging them with wires. Some of his titles included, *Square and Catenary*, *Machine For a Low Ceiling*, *Flag-Waving Machine With Quarterings* and *Little Machine of Unconceived Use*.

He progressed from his "movement" pieces to his "line" series of sculptures, and had his *Two Lines Temporal I* displayed at Documenta III in Kassel, West Germany in 1964, and then it was shown at the Museum of Modern Art in New York.

In 1966, his commissioned work, *Three Red Lines* became part of the Hirshhorn Museum and Sculpture Garden's permanent collection in Washington, D.C. His next progression was the geometric plane, with which he created *Four Squares in a Square* and *Two Rectangles Vertical Gyratory*.

In 1971, the University of California gave a retrospective of his work and the Guggenheim Museum in New York did the same in 1979. In 1967, he published a book on the constructivist movement, entitled, *Constructivism: Origins and Evolution*.

He married Edith Leighton in 1947 and they had two sons.

RILEY, JAMES WHITCOMB, (1849 -1916) - Riley was born on October 7, 1849. He was a writer whose dialect poems about the lives of the country people of Indiana earned him the reputation of "The Hoosier Poet." Riley left school at the age of 16 to travel around Indiana painting signs and advertisements on houses, barns, and fences. Further travels as a musician in a medicine show ended when he returned to Greenville, Indiana where he joined the staff of the Greenville *Times*. Riley later became the local editor of the Anderson *Democrat*. He was forced to resign from this position as a result of the so called "Leonainei hoax" in which Riley, wishing to prove the instant popularity awarded a poem assumed to be written by an established writer, wrote a poem in the style of Edgar Allen Poe. The poem was published in a rival paper under the pretense of a newly discovered work of "a genius known to fame". The poem caused quite a stir among prominent literary critics until the true identity of the author was revealed.

From 1877 to 1885, Riley was affiliated with the Indianapolis *Journal* from whom he wrote the folksy poems in Hoosier dialect which were to make him famous. Riley published his poems under the pen name of Benjamin F. Johnson of Boone whom the readers were led to believe was an area farmer. During this time, Riley wrote one of his most famous works - "When Frost is on the Punkin".

Riley's collection of poems *The Old Swimmin' Hole and 'Leven More Poems* (1883) sold more than half a million copies and was followed by 40 more books in which he created such literary characters as "Little Orphan Annie," "The Raggedy Man," and "Nine Little Goblins." He died July 22, 1916.

ROBINSON, ARTHUR RAYMOND, (1881-1961) - a U.S. Senator from Indiana, born in Pickerington, Fairfield County, Ohio, on March 12, 1881; attended the common schools; graduated from the Ohio Northern University at Ada in 1901, the Indiana Law School at Indianapolis in 1910, and the University of Chicago, Chicago, Ill., in 1913; was admitted to the bar in 1910 and commenced practice in Indianapolis, Ind.; member, State senate 1914-1918, and was the Republican floor leader during the entire period; during the First World War served in the army as a first lieutenant, captain, and major; served in France in the Army of Occupation; resumed the practice of law; judge of Marion County Superior Court 1921-1922; resumed the practice of law in Indianapolis, Ind., in 1922; appointed as a Republican to the United States Senate and subsequently elected on November 2, 1926, to fill the vacancy caused by the death of Samuel M. Ralston; reelected in 1928, and served from October 20, 1925, to January 3, 1935; was an unsuccessful candidate for reelection in 1934; chairman, Committee on Pensions (Seventieth through Seventysecond Congresses); practiced law in Indianapolis, Ind., until his death there March 17, 1961; interment in Washington Park Cemetery East.

ROBINSON, JAMES MCCLELLAN, (1861-1942) - a U.S. Representative from Indiana; born on a farm near Fort Wayne, Allen County, Ind., May 31, 1861; attended the public schools; studied law; was admitted to the bar in 1882 and commenced practice in Fort Wayne, Ind.; prosecuting attorney for the thirty-eighth judicial circuit of Indiana 1886-1890; resumed the practice of law; elected as a Democrat to the Fifty-fifth and to the three succeeding Congresses (March 4, 1897-March 3, 1905); unsuccessful candidate for reelection in 1904 to the Fifty-ninth Congress; continued the practice of law in Fort Wayne, Ind., until 1908; moved to Los Angeles, Calif., in 1911; died in Los Angeles, January 16, 1942; interment in Lindenwood Cemetery, Fort Wayne, Ind.

ROBINSON, JOHN LARNE, (1813-1860) - a U.S. Representative from Indiana; born near Maysville, Mason County, Ky., May 3, 1813; attended the public schools; moved to Rush County, Ind.; engaged in the mercantile business in Milroy, Ind.; county clerk of Rush County, Ind., 1841-1845; elected as a Democrat to the Thirtieth, Thirty-first, and Thirty-second Congresses (March 4, 1847-March 3, 1853); chairman, Committee on Roads and Canals (Thirty-first and Thirty-second Congresses); appointed by President Pierce as United States marshal for the southern district of Indiana in 1853; reappointed by President Buchanan in 1858 and served until his death;, appointed brigade inspector of the fourth military district of Indiana in 1854; trustee of Indiana University at Bloomington 1856-1859; died at Rushville, Ind., March 21, 1860; interment in East Hill Cemetery.

ROBINSON, MILTON STAPP, (1832-1892) - a U.S. Representative from Indiana; born in Versailles, Ripley County, Ind., April 20, 1832; received a limited schooling; studied law; was admitted to the bar in 1851 and began practice in Anderson, Ind.; presi dential elector on the Republican ticket in 1856; appointed a director of the Indiana State Penitentiary at Michigan City in 1861, but resigned after a few months; entered the Union Army in September 1861 as lieutenant colonel of the Fortyseventh Regiment, Indiana Volunteer Infantry and served until March 29, 1864; brevetted brigadier general March 13, 1865; served in the State senate 1866-1870; delegate to the Republican National Convention in 1872; elected as a Republican to the Forty-fourth and Forty-fifth Congresses (March 4, 1875-March 3,

1879); was not a candidate for renomination in 1878; resumed the practice of law; appointed associate justice of the appellate court of Indiana in March 1891; subsequently appointed chief justice and served until his death in Anderson, Ind., July 28, 1892; interment in Maplewood Cemetery.

ROCKHILL, WILLIAM, (1793-1865) - a U.S. Representative from Indiana; born in Burlington, N.J., February 10, 1793; attended the public schools; moved to Fort Wayne, Ind., in 1822; engaged in agricultural pursuits; commissioner of Allen County, Ind., in 1825 justice of the peace; member of the first city council of Fort Wayne and also city assessor; member of the State house of representatives 1834-1837; served in the State senate 1844-1847; elected as a Democrat to the Thirtieth Congress (March 4, 1847-March 3, 1849); resumed agricultural pursuits; died at Fort Wayne, Allen County, Ind., January 15, 1865; interment in Lindenwood Cemetery.

ROCKNE, KNUTE KENNETH, (1888 - 1931) was a football coach born on March 4, 1888, who, with an alchemy all his own, molded the nation into a vast fan club for the University of Notre Dame football teams.

Rockne was born in Voss, Norway, and emigrated with his family to Chicago, Illinois, when he was five years of age. After high school he worked for four years in the post office to earn enough money to attend the University of Notre Dame in South Bend, Indiana, where he became a football and track star. Rockne was graduated in 1914 and returned to the university as a teacher of chemistry and an assistant football coach. He was head football coach from 1918 until his death in an airplane crash in Kansas.

Rockne taught summer football schools across the country at the height of his career. He accepted numerous after-dinner speaking invitations and was the author of many articles on sports. A stickler for details, which he often carried out himself, he nonetheless had time to talk kindly with parents whose sons had not won a coveted position on Rockne's team. For the boys who played for him, he pricked with wit any ballooning football ego. He understood the players, and they responded enthusiastically.

As a strategist, Coach Rockne had no peer. He brought new concepts to the game including the forward pass, the Notre Dame shift, and the substitution of entire teams during a game. Even while he lived, legends grew about him. He coached such famous players as George Gipp and the Four Horsemen. His 13-year record was 105 victories, 12 defeats, and 5 ties, with 5 undefeated seasons.

Newspapers across the country carried column after column about Rockne when he died on March 31, 1931. Damon Runyon said: "The entire world of sport will mourn his passing. And the nation generally must deplore the death of a man who was one of its greatest men makers and one of its finest influences for good."

ROEMER, TIM, (1956-) - Democrat, of South Bend, Indiana; born in South Bend, In, October 30, 1965; attended Schmucker Middle School, Mishawaka, IN; graduated, Penn High School, Mishawaka, IN, 1975; B.A., political science, University of California, San Diego, CA, 1979; M.A. and Ph.D., international relations, University of Notre Dame, South Bend, IN, 1985; staff assistant, Congressman John Brademas, U.S. Congress; defense, trade, and foreign policy advisor to Senator Dennis DeConcini; adjunct professor, the American University; married to the former Sarah Lee Johnston, 1989; elected to the 102nd Congress, November 6, 1990.

ROREM, NED, (1923-) - composer, was born in Richmond, Indiana on October 23, 1923.

When he was young, his father moved the family to Chicago. At the age of ten, he was introduced to the music of Ravel and Debussy by a piano teacher, and his life's passion for music was set.

He attended the Music School of Northwestern University in 1940 and two years later he won a scholarship to study for a year with Gian Carlo Menotti at the Curtis Institute of Music in Philadelphia. He then finished his education at the Juilliard School of Music in New York City, where he received his B.A. degree in 1947 and his M.A. degree in 1949. He also won the $1,000 George Gershwin Memorial Prize for music composition.

He worked for Virgil Thomson as a music copyist for which he received $20.00 and orchestration lessons. He continued his music study on a scholarship at the Berkshire Music Center in 1946 and the following year, studied under famed composer Aaron Copland.

He had already begun to write songs, including a musical version of Paul Goodman's poem, *The Lordly Hudson*, which the Music Library Association voted the best published song of 1948.

In 1949, after a stop in Paris, Rorem went to Morocco, where he admitted he was at his most prolific. Beginning that year, he composed: a ballet entitled *Melos*; *Symphony No. 1; an opera; A Childhood Miracle* (with libretto by Elliott Stein) and a number of poems set to music, such as, *Penny Arcade, Flight For Heaven* and *Another Sleep*.

In 1951, Rorem went back to Paris to live and on a Fulbright fellowship, studied with Arthur Honegger. He had the right combination of youth, looks and talent to immediately become the darling of Paris' upper echelon. He found a benefactor and companion in the Vicomtesse Marie Laure de Moailles, who fed and clothed him and gave him a place to live, as well as providing him with three pianos and sponsoring his concerts. She also introduced him to the high society of Paris. He wrote a book about his Paris experience in 1966, entitled, *The Paris Diary of Ned Rorem*, which covered the years from 1951 to 1955.

During that period, his music was being heard in both France and America. His Piano Sonata No. 2 was played at the Theatre des Champs Elysees, and it was recorded on London Records, and in the United States, his music was presented at Carnegie Hall in New York in 1954.

In 1957, Rorem returned to the United States and he soon received the American Woodwind Ensemble grant and a Guggenheim fellowship. He continued to write and present orchestral pieces, as well as music for voice. His work received hosannas from the critics, who called it "dazzling" and "genuinely beguiling."

He also wrote incidental music for the theater, for plays such as *Suddenly Last Summer*, *Motel*, and *The Milk Train Doesn't Stop Here Any More*.

From 1959 to 1961, Rorem was professor of composition and composer-in-residence at New York State University at Buffalo, where he continued to write music, including the music for a Martha Graham ballet. He then became the composer-in-residence at the University of Utah from 1965 to 1967.

He published other books, such as *Music From Inside Out, The New York Diaries of Ned Rorem, Music and People, Critical Affairs* and *Pure Contraption*.

ROUDEBUSH, RICHARD LOWELL, (1918-   ) - a U.S. Representative from Indiana; born on a farm in Hamilton County, near Noblesville, Ind., January 18, 1918; attended Hamilton County schools; graduated from Butler University, Indianapolis, Ind., in 1941; served in the United States Army from November 18, 1941, to August 12, 1944, as a demolition specialist for the Ordnance Department in Middle Eastern, North African, and Italian Campaigns; farmer; partner in livestock commission company; National Commander of Veterans of Foreign Wars in 1957-1958; chairman of Indiana Veterans Commission, 1954-1960; elected as a Republican to the Eighty-seventh and to the four succeeding Congresses (January 3, 1961-January 3, 1971); was not a candidate in 1970 for reelection but was an unsuccessful candidate for election to the United States Senate; administrator of Veterans Affairs, Veterans Administration, 1971-1977; is a resident of Noblesville, Ind.

ROUSH, JOHN EDWARD, (1920-   ) - a U.S. Representative from Indiana; born in Barnsdall, Osage County, Okla., September 12, 1920; moved with parents to Huntington, Ind., in 1924; attended the public schools in Huntington; was graduated from Huntington College in 1942; served as an Infantry officer with the United States Army 1942-1946; graduated from Indiana University School of Law in 1949; was admitted to the bar in 1949 and commenced the practice of law in Huntington, Ind.; served one term in the Indiana State legislature in 1949; in 1950 was recalled to active duty in the United States Army and served as a Counterintelligence Corps agent until separated from the service in June 1952; elected prosecuting attorney of Huntington County in 1954 for a four-year term and served until elected to Congress; vice president of the board of trustees of Huntington College 1958-1960; elected as a

Democrat to the Eighty-sixth and to the four succeeding Congresses (January 3, 1959-January 3, 1969); unsuccessful candidate for reelection in 1968 to the Ninety-first Congress; resumed the practice of law; elected to the Ninety-second and to the two succeeding Congresses (January 3, 1971-January 3, 1977); unsuccessful candidate for reelection in 1976 to the Ninety-fifth Congress; Director, regional and intergovernmental operations for the Environmental Protection Agency, 1977-1979; resumed the practice of law in 1979; chairman of the board of Huntington College, 1981-1987; is a resident of Huntington, Ind.

ROYSE, LEMUEL WILLARD, (1847-1946) - a U.S. Representative from Indiana; born near Pierceton, Kosciusko County, Ind., January 19, 1847; attended the common schools; studied law; was admitted to the bar in 1874 and commenced practice in Warsaw, Kosciusko County, Ind.; prosecuting attorney for the thirtythird judicial circuit of Indiana in 1876; mayor of Warsaw 1885-1891; member of the Republican State central committee from 1886 to 1890; delegate to the Republican National Convention in 1892; elected as a Republican to the Fiftyfourth and Fifty-fifth Congresses (March 4, 1895-March 3, 1899); chairman, Committee on Elections No. 2 (Fifty-fifth Congress); unsuccessful candidate for renomination in 1898; resumed the practice of law in Warsaw, Ind.; judge of the Kosciusko County Circuit Court 1904-1908; resumed the practice of his profession; reelected circuit judge and served from 1920 to 1932; again resumed the practice of law until his retirement in 1940; died in Warsaw, Ind., December 18, 1946; interment in Oakwood Cemetery.

S

SAMPLE, SAMUEL CALDWELL, (1796-1855) - a U.S. Representative from Indiana; born in Elkton, Cecil County, Md., on August 15, 1796; attended the rural school; learned the trade of carpenter and assisted his father, who was a contractor; moved with his father's family to Connersville,

Ind., about 1823; studied law; was admitted to the bar in 1833 and commenced practice in South Bend, St. Joseph County, Ind.; elected prosecuting attorney in 1834; elected judge of the ninth judicial circuit in 1836 and served until 1843, when he resigned; was the first president of the First National Bank of South Bend; elected as a Whig to the Twenty-eighth Congress (March 4, 1843-March 3, 1845); unsuccessful candidate for reelection in 1844 to the Twenty-ninth Congress; resumed the practice of his profession in South Bend, Ind., and died there December 2, 1855; interment in the City Cemetery.

SANDERS, EVERETT, (1882-1950) - a U.S. Representative from Indiana; born near Coalmont, Clay County, Ind., March 8, 1882; attended the public schools and the Indiana State Normal School at Terre Haute; was graduated from the law department of Indiana University at Bloomington in 1907; was admitted to the bar the same year and practiced his profession in Terre Haute, Ind.; elected as a Republican to the Sixty-fifth and to the three succeeding Congresses (March 4, 1917-March 3, 1925); declined to be a candidate for renomination in 1924; was director of the speakers' bureau of the Republican National Committee in 1924; appointed secretary to President Calvin Coolidge on March 4, 1925, and served until March 4, 1929; served as Republican National Chairman from 1932 to 1934; resumed the practice of law in Washington, D.C., where he died May 12, 1950; interment in Highland Lawn Cemetery, Terre Haute, Ind.

SAYLER, HENRY BENTON, (1836-1900) - (cousin of Milton Sayler), a Representative from Indiana; born in Montgomery County, Ohio, March 31, 1836; moved to Clinton County, Ind.; attended the common schools of the county; studied law; was ad mitted to the bar in 1856 and commenced practice in Eaton, Preble County, Ohio; during the Civil War served in the Union Army as lieutenant, captain, and major; elected as a Republican to the Forty-third Congress (March 4, 1873- March 3, 1875); was not a candidate for renomiantion in 1874; judge of the Twenty-eighth judicial circuit court of Indiana 1875-1900; died in Huntington, Huntington County, Ind., June 18, 1900; interment in Mount Hope Cemetery.

SCHRICKER, HENRY F., (1883-1966) - governor of Indiana (1941-1945, 1949-1953), was born in North Judson, Indiana on August 20, 1883, the son of Christopher and Magdalena (Meyer) Schricker. He received his early education at common schools in Starke County. At the age of twenty-five he took over publication of the *Starke County Democrat,* a Knox, Indiana weekly newspaper. He continued with the paper for nine years, selling it in 1919 to take a position with the Farmers' Bank and Trust Company. In 1932, he ran for State Senate and was elected. Four years later, the Democrats chose him as their candidate for lieutenant governor, and he won in the election, and served under Governor Townsend. Schricker ran for governor in 1940 and was elected by a margin of 4,000 votes over his Republican opponent, Glenn Hills.

During his administration, he was at odds with the Republican-controlled Legislature. In 1941, the Legislature attempted to centralize state government and revoke the Governor's appointive powers as laid out in laws passed in 1933. Governor Schricker rejected this and the Indiana Supreme Court agreed with him, striking down the new legislation as unconstitutional. Schricker was elected to another gubernatorial term in 1948. In his second administration, he faced a Republican-controlled Legislature once again. He worked to make welfare available to the needy and sought in a special session of the Legislature to preserve federal funding for the State.

Schricker left office in 1953 and became associated with the Wabash Fire and Casualty Company in Indianapolis. He died at the age of eighty-three in Knox, Indiana on December 28, 1966. Schricker was married in 1914 to Maude L. Brown and had three children.

SCHULTE, WILLIAM THEODORE, (1890-1966) - a U.S. Representative from Indiana; born in St. Bernard, Platte County, Nebr., August 19, 1890; attended the public schools of St. Bernard, Nebr.; moved with his parents to Hammond, Ind., where he attended high school and received a business training; engaged in the theatrical business until 1918; also interested in agricul tural pursuits; member of the city council of Hammond, Ind., 1918-1922; resumed the theatrical business until 1932; elected as a Democrat to the

Seventy-third and to the four succeeding Congresses (March 4, 1933-January 3, 1943); unguccessful candidate for renomination in 1942 to the Seventy-eighth Congress, coordinator of field operations in the labor division of the War Production Board, Washington, D.C., 1942-1944; returned to Lake County, Ind., and engaged in agricultural pursuits, engaged in the automobile business at Michigan City, Ind., from October 1947 to March 1949; sales representative of a construction machinery firm; died in Hammond, Ind., on December 7, 1966; interment in St. Andrew's Cemetery.

SCOTT, HARVEY DAVID, (1818-1891) - a U.S. Representative from Indiana; born near Ashtabula, Union County, Ohio, October 18, 1818; attended the public schools and the Asbury (now De Pauw) University at Greencastle, Ind.; studied law; was admitted to the bar and commenced practice in Terre Haute, Ind.; held several local offices; elected as a Republican to the Thirty fourth Congress (March 4, 1855-March 3, 1857); resumed the practice of law; judge of the circuit court of Vigo County, 1881- 1884; moved to California in 1887; died in Pasadena, Calif., July 11, 1891; interment in Mountain View Cemetery.

SEXTON, LEONIDAS, (1827-1880) - a U.S. Representative from Indiana; born in Rushville, Rush County, Ind., May 19, 1827; attended the public schools of his native county and was graduated from Jefferson College, Canonsburg, Pa., in 1847; studied law in Rushville and in 1848 and 1849 attended the Cincinnati Law School; was admitted to the Indiana bar in 1850 and commenced the practice of his profession in Rushville, Ind.; member of the State house of representatives in 1856; elected Lieutenant Governor of Indiana and served from January 1873 to January 1877; elected as a Republican to the Fortyfifth Congress (March 4, 1877-March 3, 1879); unsuccessful candidate for reelection in 1878 to the Forty-sixth Congress; died in Parsons, Labette County, Kans., July 4, 1880; interment in East Hill Cemetery, Rushville, Ind.

SHAFER, PAUL WERNTZ, (1893-1954) - a U. S. Representative from Michigan; born in Elkhart, Indiana, April 27, 1893; moved with his parents to Three Rivers, Michigan, and attended the public schools; student at Ferris Institute, Big Rapids, Michigan, and studied law by correspondence with the Blackstone Institute of Chicago, Illinois; reporter, editor, and pubisher of newspaper in Elkhart, Indiana, Battle Creek, Michigan, and Bronson, Michigan; member of Indiana State Militia in 1916 and 1917; municipal judge in Battle Creek, Michigan, 1929-1936; elected as a Republican to the Seventy-fifth and to the eight succeeding Congresses and served from January 3, 1937, until his death; had been renominated in the Republican primary election August 3, 1954, to the Eighty-fourth Congress; died in Walter Reed Hospital, Washington, D.C., August 17, 1954; interment in Memorial Park Cemetery, Battle Creek, Michigan.

SHANKS, JOHN PETER CLEAVER, (1826-1901) - a U.S. Representative from Indiana; born in Martinsburg, Va. (now West Virginia), June 17, 1826; pursued an academic course; studied law; was admitted to the bar in 1848 and commenced practice in Portland, Ind., in 1849; prosecuting attorney of Jay County in 1850 and 1851; member of the State house of representatives in 1855; during the Civil War served in the Union Army as a colonel and aide-de-camp; elected as a Republican to the Thirtyseventh Congress (March 4, 1861-March 3, 1863); unsuccessful candidate for reelection in 1862 to the Thirty-eighth Congress; elected to the Fortieth and to the three succeeding Congresses (March 4, 1867-March 3, 1875); chairman, Committee on Militia (Forty-first Congress); Committee on Indian Affairs (Forty-second Congress); unsuccessful candidate for renomination in 1874; resumed the practice of his profession; was again a member of the State house of representatives in 1879; died in Portland, Jay County, Ind., January 23, 1901; interment in Green Park Cemetery.

SHARP, PHILIP RILEY, (1942-   ) - a U.S. Representative from Indiana; born in Baltimore, Md., July 15, 1942; attended Washington Elementary School, Elwood, Ind.; graduated from Wendell Willkie High School, Elwood, 1960; attended DePauw University, Greencastle, Ind., 1961; B.S., Georgetown University School of Foreign Service, Washington, D.C., 1964; graduate work, Exeter College, Oxford University, 1966; Ph.D., Georgetown University,

1974; aide to United States Senator Vance Hartke, 1964-1969; assistant and later associate professor, Ball State University, Muncie, Ind., 1969-1974; elected as a Democrat to the Ninety-fourth and to the six succeeding Congresses (January 3, 1975-January 3, 1989); is a resident of Muncie, Ind.

SHIVELY, BENJAMIN FRANKLIN, (1857-1916) - a U.S. Representative and a Senator from Indiana; born near Osceola, St. Joseph County, Ind., March 20, 1857; attended the common schools and the Northern Indiana Normal School at Valparaiso, Ind.; taught school 1874-1880; engaged in journalism 1880-1884; secre tary of the National Anti-Monopoly Association in 1883; president of the board of Indiana University in 1884; elected as a National Anti-Monopolist to the Forty-eighth Congress to fill the vacancy caused by the resignation of William H. Calkins and served from December 1, 1884, to March 3, 1885; graduated from the law department of the University of Michigan at Ann Arbor in 1886; was admitted to the bar and commenced practice in South Bend, Ind.; elected as a Democrat to the Fiftieth, Fifty-first, and Fifty-second Congresses (March 4, 1887-March 3, 1893); was not a candidate for renomination in 1892; resumed the practice of law in South Bend, Ind.; unsuccessful Democratic candidate for governor of Indiana in 1896; unsuccessful candidate for election in 1906 to the Sixtieth Congress; elected as a Democrat to the United States Senate in 1909; reelected in 1914 and served from March 4, 1909, until his death in Washington, D.C., March 14, 1916; chairman, Committee on Pacific Railroads (Sixty-second Congress), Committee on Pensions (Sixty-third and Sixty-fourth Congresses); interment in the Brookville Cemetery, Brookville, Pa.

SISSLE, NOBLE, (1889-1975) - lyricist, actor, was born in Indianapolis, Indiana on July 10, 1889.

In 1914, Sissle formed an in-house band for the Severin Hotel in Indiana. The next year, he traveled to Baltimore to work in Bob Young's Band, and then moved on to the Cocoanut Grove in Palm Beach, Florida, where he led his own group of musicians.

In December of 1916, Sissle joined the United States Army, serving as a lieutenant in the 369th Division Band. After his discharge, he toured with Jim Europe's Society Orchestra until Europe's death in 1919.

He met up with Eubie Blake soon after and they formed a team that for years, produced and composed highly successful shows, including, *Shuffle Along*, which was Broadway's first long- running all-Black musical. Two popular songs from that show were, *I'm Just Wild About Harry* and *Love Will Find The Way*. Some of their other shows included *London Calling* (which had the song "You Were Meant For Me"), *Elsie*, *Chocolate Dandies* and *Shuffle Along of 1933*.

Sissle did solo work and then formed a band to do gigs in Paris, Monte Carlo and London, as well as dates in the United States. In the summer of 1936, he sustained injuries in a car crash, but soon recovered. In 1938, he began a twelve year span of working as a bandleader at Billy Rose's Diamond Horseshoe in New York, meanwhile fitting in tours in the United States and overseas for the USO during World War II.

In the 1960's, Sissle managed his own publishing company and eventually had his own nightclub, Noble's. In 1973, he was the subject of a book entitled, *Reminiscing With Sissle and Blake*.

Noble Sissle died on December 17, 1975.

SKELTON, RICHARD BERNARD "RED", (1913 -   ) - a famous U.S. comedian.

Skelton was born in Vincennes, Indiana on July 18, 1913, two months after the death of his father, a circus clown. The indigence of his family caused him to seek employment at an early age and to later leave school while a seventh grade student. His debut an an entertainer came at the age of ten, when he toured with the "Doc" R.E. Lewis Medicine Show. This was followed by tours with a tent show, a minstrel group, a showboat act, and the Hagenbeck and Wallace Circus that had also employed Skelton's father. When 17 years of age, he married Edna Stilwell, who became his partner, scriptwriter, and agent. The couple toured the U.S. and Canada as a vaudeville team during the 1930s, achieving varying degrees of success.

Skelton made his first radio and Broadway guest appearances in 1937. The following year, while entertaining at the White House during President Franklin D. Roosevelt's campaign against infantile paralysis, he met the screen actor Mickey Rooney, who arranged Skelton's first appearance in motion pictures. His career blossomed during the 1940s, when he received numerous motion picture and radio assignments and became a popular entertainer among World War II servicemen. Skelton made more than 30 movies before turning his attention to television during the early 1950s. His biggest success, the *Red Skelton Show*, was broadcast for 18 years. The changing taste of television viewers made an attempt to establish a second program a failure. Skelton retired from show business in 1972, greatly disillusioned by what he considered unfair treatment from television network executives.

SKIDMORE, LOUIS, (1897-1962) - architect, was born in Lawrenceburg, Indiana on April 8, 1897.

After graduating from Bradley Polytechnic Institute in 1917, he went into the United States Army a year later, where he was a sergeant with the Sixteenth Aero Construction Company and helped build airports in England for the American Expeditionary Force.

After the service, Skidmore did his graduate work at the Massachusetts Institute of Technology from 1921 to 1924.

He then worked as a designer for the architectural firm of Maginnis and Walsh for two years. In 1926, he won a fellowship and studied in Europe for three years at the Ecole des Beaux Arts in Paris and the American Academy in Rome. During his trip, he collaborated on the book, *Tudor Homes of England*, with Samuel Chamberlain.

Skidmore was asked to join the team that was designing the Century of Progress Exposition in Chicago. Beginning in 1929, he worked as chief of design and assistant general manager in charge of design, construction and demolition for the Exposition. He was eventually promoted to the position of assistant director of the exhibits department and was responsible for the designing and installation of over 500 exhibits. By the time he'd finished his exposition duties in 1935, he was a partner in the architectural firm of Buckley and Skidmore.

In January of 1936, Skidmore began a new partnership with one of his exposition co-workers, Nathaniel A. Owings. In 1939, a third partner, John O. Merrill, was added, making the firm name, Skidmore, Owings and Merrill.

During the war years, his firm worked almost exclusively for national defense projects, such as housing. They acted as consultants to help develop low-cost prefabricated housing, which was used by employees of a nearby aircraft plant. In 1942, they designed the Reception Center and Welfare Building at the Great Lakes Naval Training Station, and then built the entire community of Oak Ridge, Tennessee within two years, which eventually housed approximately 70,000 employees of the atomic plants.

After the war, the firm was involved in numerous projects that included: a Chicago public housing project; Ohio State University's Medical Center; Terrace Plaza Hotel in Cincinnati; the widely admired Lever House in New York City, plus airline and bus terminals and shopping centers.

The firm continued to expand and believed in hiring top-notch personnel, including young up-and-coming architects. By the year 1950, their office in New York, San Francisco and Chicago, employed 322 people that included architects, designers, engineers, researchers, city planners, etc.

Skidmore was the author of a section in the Encyclopedia Britannica on exposition architecture. He also contributed articles to *American Architect*, *Architectural Forum* and *Architectural Record*. In 1949, he received that Gold Medal of Honor from the New York Chapter of the American Institute of Architects.

He married Eloise Owings in 1930 and they had two sons. Louis Skidmore died on September 27, 1962.

SMITH, CALEB BLOOD, (1808-1864) - a U.S. Representative from Indiana; born in Boston, Mass., April 16, 1808; moved with his parents to Ohio in 1814; attended Miami University, Oxford, Ohio, 1825-1826; studied law; was admitted to the bar in 1828 and commenced practice in Connersville, Fayette County, Ind.; founded and edited the Indiana Sentinel in 1832; member of the State house of representatives 1833-1837, 1840, and 1841, and served as speaker in 1836; unsuccessful candidate for the Twenty-seventh Congress in 1841; elected as a Whig to the Twenty-eighth, Twenty- ninth, and Thirtieth Congresses (March 4, 1843-March 3, 1849); chairman, Committee on Territories (Thirtieth Congress); appointed by President Zachary Taylor a member of the board to investigate claims of American citizens against Mexico; moved to Cincinnati, Ohio, and practiced his profession; member of the peace convention of 1861 held in Washington, D.C., in an effort to devise means to prevent the impending war; appointed Sec retary of the Interior in the Cabinet of President Lincoln and served from March 5, 1861, to January 1, 1863, when he resigned to become judge of the United States District Court for the District of Indiana, in which capacity he served until his death in Indianapolis, Marion County, Ind., January 7, 1864; interment in the City Cemetery, Connersville, Ind.

SMITH, THOMAS, (1799-1876) - a U.S. Representative from Indiana; born in Fayette County, Pa., May 1, 1799; moved to Rising Sun, Ind., in 1818; learned the trade of tanner; moved to Versailles, Ind., in 1821 and established a tanyard; became a colonel in the militia; member of the State house of representatives in 1829, 1830, and 1833-1836; served in the State senate 1836-1839; elected as a Democrat to the Twenty-sixth Congress (March 4, 1839-March 3, 1841); unsuccessful candidate for election in 1840 to the Twenty-seventh Congress; elected to the Twenty-eighth and Twenty-ninth Congresses (March 4, 1843- March 3, 1847); was not a candidate for renomination in 1846; delegate to the State constitutional convention in 1850; died in Versailles, Ripley County, Ind., April 12, 1876; interment in Cliff Hill Cemetery.

SMITH, WALTER BEDELL, (1895-1961) - United States government official, was born in Indianapolis, Indiana on October 5, 1895.

In 1911, while still in school, Smith became a private in the Indiana National Guard. For a short time, he attended Butler University, but soon left in order to support his family while his father was ill. He continued his National Guard training and became an infantry first sergeant at eighteen. In 1917, he became a second lieutenant in the

United States Army and a year later he was fighting with the Fourth Division in France. On his return home, he worked at the Bureau of Military Intelligence in Washington D.C. He was continually transferred to different Army bases and then had a four year stay at the Bureau of the Budget in Washington, beginning in 1925.

Smith served two years in the Phillipines and when he came back to the U.S., he pursued his military education feeling insecure about his "lack of West Point or college training." In 1937, he graduated from the Army War College in Washington, D.C. and was assigned to the faculty of the Fort Benning Infantry School. Two years later, he was promoted from captain to major.

In September of 1941, he became secretary of the War Department General Staff, and after World War II began, he became secretary of the Combined Chiefs of Staff.

In September of 1941, Smith went to England as General Dwight D. Eisenhower's Chief of Staff of the European, North African and Mediterranean theater of operations, a position in which he was responsible for the planning of the invasions of North Africa and Normandy. In 1944, he was named Chief of Staff of the Supreme Headquarters, Allied Expeditionary Forces. Smith was chosen by Eisenhower to sign the Italian surrender document in 1943, and two years later, he was at the helm of the Allied group that was present when Germany gave their unconditional surrender.

When World War II was over, President Harry S. Truman appointed Smith to follow W. Averell Harriman in the position of U.S. Ambassador to the USSR, meanwhile asking Congress to allow Smith to retain his military status as major general.

In September of 1950, President Truman nominated Smith to be Director of the Central Intelligence Agency, and three years later, he was appointed to be Under Secretary of State in the Republican Administration.

Smith wrote of his Russian experiences in the 1950 book, *My Three Years in Moscow*. He also published a series of articles for the Saturday Evening Post, entitled *Eisenhower's Six Great Decisions*.

During his illustrious military career, he has been given numerous medals from foreign countries, and the United

States has bestowed the Distinguished Service Medal with two Oak Leaf Clusters, the National Security Medal, the Legion of Merit and the Bronze Star.

Walter Smith died on August 9, 1961.

SPRINGER, RAYMOND SMILEY, (1882-1947) - a U.S. Representative from Indiana; born on a farm in Rush County, near Dunreith, Ind., April 26, 1882; attended the public schools, Earlham College, Richmond, Ind., and Butler University, Indianapolis, Ind.; was graduated from the Indiana Law School at Indianapolis in 1904; was admitted to the bar in 1904 and commenced practice in Connersville, Fayette County, Ind.; county attorney of Fayette County, Ind., 1908-1914; judge of the thirty seventh judicial circuit of Indiana 1916-1922; during the First World War served as a captain of Infantry, Eightyfourth Division, in 1918; lieutenant colonel of the Officers' Reserve Corps 1918- 1946; unsuccessful candidate for Governor of Indiana in 1932 and 1936; elected as a Republican to the Seventy-sixth and to the four succeeding Congresses and served from January 3, 1939, until his death in Connersville, Ind., August 28, 1947; interment in Dale Cemetery.

STEELE, GEORGE WASHINGTON, (1839-1922) - a U.S. Representative from Indiana; born near Connersville, Fayette County, Ind., December 13, 1839; attended the common schools and Ohio Wesleyan University at Delaware; studied law; was admitted to the bar and commenced practice in Hartford City, Ind.; during the Civil War served with the Twelfth Indiana Regiment and the One Hundred and First Indiana Regiment from May 1861, until the close of the war; commissioned and served in the Fourteenth Regiment, United States Infantry, from February 23, 1866, to February 1, 1876; resigned and engaged in agricultural pursuits and pork packing until 1882; first Governor of Oklahoma Territory in 1890 and 1891; elected as a Republican to the Forty-seventh and to the three succeeding Congresses (March 4, 1881-March 3, 1889); member of the Board of Managers of the National Military Home from April 21, 1890, to December 10, 1904; elected to the Fifty-fourth and to the three succeeding Congresses (March 4, 1895-March 3, 1903); chairman, Committee on Manufactures (Fifty-seventh Congress); governor of the National Military Home in Marion, Ind., from December 11, 1904, to May 31, 1915, when he resigned; died in Marion, Grant County, Ind., July 12, 1922; interment in Odd Fellows Cemetery.

STEELE, THEODORE CLEMENT, (1847 - 1926) - was an accomplished portraitist and still-life artist and founder of the Indiana School of Art.

Steele was born in Owen County, Indiana on September 22, 1847, and educated at Waveland Collegiate Institute, Waveland, Indiana (1859-68). While a student at the Institute, he taught drawing to his fellow classmates and eventually became popular for his exceptional portrait painting abilities.

In 1872 Steele moved to Indianapolis, where he earned a living painting portraits. His reputation in the city as an outstanding artist precipitated the formation of a citizens' group intent upon raising the necessary funds to permit Steele to study abroad. As a result of the efforts of this group, he was able to enter the Royal Academy of Munich in 1880 to study under Gyula Benczur and Ludwig von Lofftz. Steele returned to Indianapolis in 1885 and established the Indiana School of Art four years later. In 1890 he published *The Steele Portfolio*, a volume of photogravure prints of portraits, still lifes, and landscapes. His awards and honors include an honorable mention at the Paris Exposition of 1900 and a 1910 Fine Arts Corporation prize. "Gordon Hill," "Oaks at Vernon," "Portrait of Rev. N.A. Hyde," "Whitewater Valley," and "Landscape" are some of his better known paintings. Steele died July 24, 1926.

STILWELL, THOMAS NEEL, (1830-1874) - a U.S. Representative from Indiana; born in Stilwell, Ohio, August 29, 1830; received a thorough English education; attended Oxford and College Hill Col leges; studied law; was admitted to the bar in 1852 and began practice in Anderson, Ind.; member of the State house of representatives in 1856; served in the Union Army during the Civil War; elected as a Republican to the Thirty-ninth Congress (March 4, 1865-

March 3, 1867); was not a candidate for renomination in 1866; Minister Resident to Venezuela in 1867 and 1868; served as president of the First National Bank of Anderson, Ind., until his death; died in Anderson as the result of a gunshot wound January 14, 1874; interment in Maplewood Cemetery.

STOCKSLAGER, STROTHER MADISON, (1842-1930) - a U.S. Representative from Indiana; born in Mauckport, Harrison County, Ind., May 7, 1842; attended the common schools, Corydon High School, and Indiana University at Bloomington; taught school; served in the Union Army during the Civil War as second lieutenant and captain in the Thirteenth Indiana Volunteer Cavalry, which he had assisted to organize; was mustered out as captain and returned to Mauckport; deputy county auditor of Harrison County 1866-1868; deputy county clerk of Harrison County 1868-1870; appointed by President Andrew Johnson as assessor of internal revenue in 1867, but was not confirmed by the United States Senate; studied law; was admitted to the bar in Corydon, Ind., in 1871 and practiced in Indiana and Kentucky; member of the State senate 1874-1878; editor of the Corydon Democrat 1879- 1882; elected as a Democrat to the Forty-seventh and Forty-eighth Congresses (March 4, 1881-March 3, 1885); chairman, Committee on Public Buildings and Grounds (Forty-eighth Congress); was an unsuccessful candidate for renomination in 1884 to the Forty- ninth Congress; resumed the practice of law in Corydon; appointed assistant commissioner of the General Land Office on October 1, 1885, and commissioner on March 27, 1888; resigned March 4, 1889, but remained in charge until June 20, 1889; continued the practice of law in Washington, D.C.; was an unsuccessful Democratic candidate for election in 1894 to the Fifty-fourth Congress; delegate to the Democratic National Convention in 1896; served as legal expert in the Department of Labor in 1918; resumed the practice of law in Washington, D.C., until his death there on June 1, 1930; interment in Arlington National Cemetery.

T

TAGGART, THOMAS, (1856-1929) - a U.S. Senator from Indiana; born in County Monaghan, Ireland, November 17, 1856; immigrated to the United States in 1861 with his parents, who settled in Xenia, Greene County, Ohio; attended the common schools while working on the railroad; moved to Garrett, Ind., in 1874 and to Indianapolis, Ind., in 1877 and was employed in a restaurant and later engaged in the restaurant and hotel business; auditor of Marion County 1886-1894; mayor of Indianapolis 1895-1901; member of the Democratic National Committee 1900-1916, and served as chairman 1900-1908; president of the French Lick Hotel Co.; appointed as a Democrat to the United States Senate to fill the vacancy caused by the death of Benjamin F. Shively and served from March in 1916 to fill the vacancy; chairman, Committee on Forest Reservations and Game Protection (Sixty-fourth Congress); resumed his former business pursuits in Indianapolis and French Lick, Ind.; banker; died in Indianapolis, Ind., on March 6, 1929; interment in Crown Hill Cemetery.

TAYLOR, ARTHUR HERBERT, (1859-1922) - a U.S. Representative from Indiana; born at Caledonia Springs, Canada, February 29, 1852; moved with his parents to Yates County, N.Y., in 1856; attended the local school; taught school for several years; moved to Indianapolis, Ind., in 1869; studied law; was admitted to the bar in 1873 and commenced practice in Indianapolis, Ind.; moved to Petersburg, Ind., in 1874 and continued the practice of law; prosecuting attorney for the eleventh judicial circuit of Indiana 1880-1884; elected as a Democrat to the Fifty-third Congress (March 4, 1893-March 3, 1895); unsuccessful candidate for reelection in 1894 to the Fiftyfourth Congress; resumed the practice of law in Petersburg, Ind., until his death February 20, 1922; interment in Walnut Hills Cemetery.

TAYLOR, WALLER, (1786-1826) - a U.S. Senator from Indiana; born in Lunenburg County, Va., before 1786; attended the common schools; studied law; was admitted to the bar and practiced in Virginia; member, State house of delegates 1800-1802; moved to Vincennes, Ind., in 1804 and continued the practice of law; appointed chancellor of Indiana Territory in 1807; appointed major in the Territorial militia in 1807; served in the Army during the War of 1812 and was promoted to adjutant general in 1814; upon the admission of Indiana as a State into the Union in 1816 was elected as a Republican to the United States Senate; reelected, and served from December 11, 1816, to March 3, 1825; died in Lunenburg County, Va., August 26, 1826; interment in the family burial ground near Lunenburg, Va.

TECUMSEH, (1768 - 1813) - was a Shawnee chief who organized an Indian confederation in the early 1800s in an unsuccessful attempt to prevent white expansion into the Ohio Valley.

Tecumseh was born in the village of Piqua near present-day Springfield, Ohio. He was the fifth child of the Shawnee chief, Puckeshinwa, who died as a result of Indian-white hostilities when Tecumseh was six years old. He was later adopted by Chief Blackfish who, with Tecumseh's older brothers was responsible for most of his early training as a warrior and a hunter.

About 1787, Tecumseh and a band of Shawnee led by his brother, Cheeseekan, went south to join the Cherokee in their fight against the white settlers. Upon the death of his brother, Tecumseh assumed the leadership of the band, and remained in the South for three years. Soon after his return to the Northwest Territory, he became a scout for the Shawnee chief, Blue Jacket, assisting him in his defeat of General Arthur St. Clair in 1791 and in the Battle of Fallen Timbers of 1794, in which Blue Jacket and Little Turtle were defeated by General Anthony Wayne.

The idea of a league of Indians was first presented at an Indian council held at Greenville in 1807, when Tecumseh strongly denounced the treaties that gave the settlers claim to land north of the Ohio River. Tecumseh believed in the community principle of land ownership, asserting that no one tribe had the right to sign treaties that gave away the land. Tecumseh and his brother, Tenkswatawa, the Shawnee Prophet, began organizing the Indians with the objectives of regaining the land that had been taken and preventing the further signing of treaties such as those that had recently turned nearly half of the present state of Indiana over to the U.S. government.

The confederacy was still in the organizing stages when it suffered irreparable damage with the defeat of Tenkswatawa in the Battle of Tippecanoe in 1811. The battle was ill-planned and unsanctioned by Tecumseh, who was away trying to gain the support of southern Indian tribes. The subsequent weakening of the confederacy caused Tecumseh to side with the British in the War of 1812 with the hopes that the combined efforts of the British and Indians could defeat the Americans.

Tecumseh died on October 5, 1813 in the Battle of the Thames near present-day Chatham, Ontario. His death caused the collapse of the confederacy and signalled the end of Indian resistance to white settlement in the Northwest Territory.

TEST, JOHN, (1771-1849) - a U.S. Representative from Indiana; born in Salem, N.J., November 12, 1771; moved with his parents to Philadelphia, Pa., and attended the common schools; moved to Fayette County, Pa., and operated Fayette Chance Furnace for several years; moved to Cincinnati, Ohio, and then to Brookville, Franklin County, Ind., and operated a grist mill; studied law; was admitted to the bar and began practice in Brookville, Ind.; held several local offices; judge of the third district circuit 1816-1819; elected to the Eighteenth and Nineteenth Congresses (March 4, 1823-March 3, 1827); unsuccessful candidate for reelection in 1826 to the Twentieth Congress; elected to the Twenty-first Congress (March 4, 1829-March 3, 1831); presiding judge of the Indiana circuit court; moved to Mobile, Ala., and resumed the practice of law; died near Cambridge City, Wayne County, Ind., October 9, 1849; interment in Cambridge City, Ind.

THOMAS, JESSE BURGESS, (1777-1853) - a Delegate from Indiana Territory and a Senator from Illinois; born in Shepherdstown, Va. (now West Virginia) in 1777; studied law in Mason County, Ky., where he also served as county clerk until 1803; moved to Lawrenceburg, Indiana Territory in 1803 and practiced law; appointed deputy attorney general of Indiana Territory in 1805; member, Territorial house of representatives 1805-1808, and served as speaker 1805-1808; elected as a Delegate from Indiana Territory to the Tenth Congress to fill the vacancy caused by the resignation of Benjamin Parke and served from October 22, 1808, to March 3, 1809; moved to Kaskaskia in 1809, then to Cahokia, and later to Edwardsville, Ill.; upon the organization of Illinois Territory was appointed judge of the United States court for the northwestern judicial district 1809-1818; delegate to the State constitutional convention in 1818 and served as president of that body; upon the admission of Illinois as a State into the Union in 1818 was elected as a Republican to the United States Senate; reelected in 1823, and served from December 3, 1818, to March 3, 1829; declined to be a candidate for reelection in 1829; chairman, Committee on Public Lands (Sixteenth and Seventeenth Congresses); moved to Mount Vernon, Ohio, in 1829; committed suicide in Mount Vernon, Ohio, May 3, 1853; interment in Mound View Cemetery.

TIPTON, JOHN, (1786-1839) - a U.S. Senator from Indiana; born near Sevierville, Sevier County, Tenn., August 14, 1786; received a limited schooling; moved to Harrison County, Ind., in 1807 and engaged in agricultural pursuits; served with the" ""Yellow Jackets" in the Tippecanoe campaign and subsequently attained the rank of brigadier general of militia; sheriff of Harrison County, Ind., 1816-1819; member, State house of representatives 1819-1823; one of the commissioners to select a site for a new capital for Indiana in 1820; commissioner to determine the boundary line between Indiana and Illinois 1821; appointed United States Indian agent for the Pottawatamie and Miami tribes 1823; laid out the city of Logansport, Ind., in 1828; elected as a Democrat to the United States Senate on December 9, 1831, to fill the vacancy caused by the death of James Noble; reelected in 1832 and served from January 3, 1832, to March 3, 1839; due to poor health declined to be a candidate for reelection in 1838; chairman, Committee on Roads and Canals (Twenty-fifth Congress), Committee

on Indian Affairs (Twenty- fifth Congress); died in Logansport, Cass County, Ind., on April 5, 1839; interment in
Mount Hope Cemetery.

TOWNSEND, M. CLIFFORD, (1884-1954) - governor of
Indiana (1937-1941), was born in Blackford County, Indi-
ana on August 11, 1884, the son of David and Lydia
(Glancy) Townsend. While young, he lived on a farm and
received his education at the common schools. He attended
Marion College and graduated in 1907. In the years that
followed, he worked as a teacher and a farmer. From 1909
to 1919, he was superintendent of Blackford County
Schools, and from 1925 to 1929 was superintendent of
Grant County Schools. At the start of the Great Depres-
sion, Townsend became director of the Indiana Farm
Bureau.

During the years he worked in education, Townsend was
also active in Democratic politics. In 1923, he was a member of the State House of Representatives, and in 1928 he
ran for U.S. Congress, but was defeated. He was nominated by the Democrats for lieutenant governor in 1932,
and won, running on a ticket with Paul McNutt. While
Townsend was lieutenant governor, the Legislature voted to
make his office full-time, and he was accordingly given responsibilities to act as commissioner of agriculture in addition to his regular duties. Townsend ran for governor in
1936 and won over his Republican rival, Raymond E.
Springer by nearly 200,000 votes.

In 1937, during his administration, severe flooding occurred in Indiana and Townsend set up a relief program to
help the disaster victims. His term was also marked by the
creation of a pension fund for firefighters, establishment of
the Division of Labor, and passage of legislation requiring
an exam before the issuance of drivers' licenses.

Townsend left office at the beginning of World War II
and became director of the Office of Agricultural War Relations. From 1942 to 1943, he served as an administrator
for the Agricultural Conservation and Adjustment Administration, and later in 1943 he was named director of the
Food Production Administration. In 1946, after the war,
Townsend ran for U.S. Senate, but was defeated. He died

in Hartford City, Indiana on November 11, 1954. Townsend was married in 1910 to Nora Harris. They had three children.

TRACEWELL, ROBERT JOHN, (1852-1922) - a U.S. Representative from Indiana; born near Front Royal, Warren County, Va., May 7, 1852; moved with his parents to Corydon, Harrison County, Ind. in 1854; attended the public schools of Corydon and was graduated from Hanover (Ind.) College in 1874; studied law; was admitted to the bar in 1875 and commenced practice in Corydon, Ind.; elected as a Republican to the Fifty-fourth Congress (March 4, 1895-March 3, 1897); unsuccessful candidate for reelection in 1896 to the Fifty-fifth Congress; appointed by President McKinley as Comptroller of the Treasury and served from March 4, 1897, to June 15, 1914, when he resigned; moved to Evansville, Ind., in 1914 and resumed the practice of law; elected judge of the superior court of Vanderburg County, Ind., in 1918; renominated in 1922, but died in Evansville, Ind., on July 28, 1922, before the election; interment in Cedar Hill Cemetery, Corydon, Harrison County, Ind.

TUCKER, FORREST, (1919-1986) - was born in Plainfield, Indiana on February 2, 1919.

He began working in 1940 as a rugged leading man in such movies as *The Westerner*, *Sands of Iwo Jima*, *Auntie Mame* and *Final Chapter--Walking Tall*.

In 1958, Tucker toured in the stage musical, *The Music Man* and in 1969, served as an associate producer at Chicago's Drury Lane Theatre.

He appeared on television in various series, beginning with *Crunch and Des*, in 1956. His other shows were *Dusty's Trail*, *Ghost Chasers*, *The Rebels* and perhaps his best known series, *F Troop*, which ran from 1966 to 1969.

Tucker was married three times and had two daughters. He died in 1986.

TYNER, JAMES NOBLE, (1826-1904) - a U.S. Representative from Indiana; born in Brookville, Franklin County, Ind., January 17, 1826; pursued an academic course, and was graduated from Brookville Academy in 1844; spent ten years in business; studied law; was admitted to the bar in 1857 and commenced practice in Peru, Ind.; secretary of the State senate 1857-1861; special agent of the Post Office Department 1861-1866; elected as a Republican to the Forty-first Congress to fill the vacancy caused by the resignation of Representative-elect Daniel D. Pratt; reelected to the Forty-second and Fortythird Congresses and served from March 4, 1869, to March 3, 1875; appointed Second Assistant Postmaster General, serving from February 26, 1875, to July 12, 1876, and as Postmaster General from July 12, 1876, to March 3, 1877; appointed First Assistant Postmaster General, and served from March 16, 1877, until his resignation on October 29, 1881; delegate to the International Postal Congress at Paris in 1878 and at Washington in 1897; Assistant Attorney General for the Post Office Department from 1889 to 1893, and again from 1897 to 1903; died in Washington, D.C., December 5, 1904; interment in Oak Hill Cemetery.

U

UPDIKE, RALPH EUGENE, (1894-1953) - a U.S. Representative from Indiana; born in Brookville, Franklin County, Ind., May 27, 1894; attended the public schools of Whitcomb and Brookville, Dodds Army and Navy Academy, Washington, D.C., Columbia University, New York City, and Purdue University, Lafayette, Ind.; during the First World War served overseas as a sergeant with the Seventy-fourth Company, Sixth Regiment, Second Division, United States Marines, 1916-1919; studied law; was admitted to the bar in 1920; was graduated from the law department of Indiana University in 1923 and commenced practice in Indianapolis, Ind.; member of the State house of representatives 1923-1925; special judge of the city of Indianapolis in 1923 and 1924; special judge of the superior court of Marion County in 1925 and 1926; elected as a Republican to the Sixty-ninth and Seventieth Congresses (March 4, 1925-

March 3, 1929); unsuccessful candidate for reelection in 1928 to the Seventy-first Congress; special at torney in the Bureau of Internal Revenue 1929-1933; resumed the practice of law in Indianapolis, Ind., and Washington, D.C., until March 2, 1942, when he was commissioned a captain in the United States Marine Corps Reserve; served overseas in the South Pacific with the First Marine Division, Fleet Marine Force, and was inactivated June 15, 1945; resumed the practice of law in Indianapolis, Ind., and Washington, D.C., until his retirement; died in Arlington, Va., September 16, 1953; interment in Arlington National Cemetery.

UREY, HAROLD CLAYTON, (1893-   ) - scientist, was born in Walkerton, Indiana on April 29, 1893.

He entered Montana State University in 1914, where he majored in zoology and minored in chemistry. He received his B.S. degree in 1917.

From 1918 to 1919, during World War I, he was a research chemist at the Barrett Chemical Company, where he helped manufacture war material.

From 1919 to 1921, he taught chemistry at Montana State University. He then continued his schooling at the University of California in Berkeley, where his major was chemistry, and his minor was physics and he was awarded a Ph.D. degree in 1923.

After two years of study at the Institute for Theoretical Physics at the University of Copenhagen in Denmark, Urey returned to the United States in 1924. He became an associate in chemistry at Johns Hopkins University for five years and then in 1929, he was associate professor of chemistry at Columbia Unviersity for another five years.

In 1931, along with Drs. George M. Murphy and Ferdinand G. Brickwedde, Urey discovered deuterium, otherwise known as heavy hydrogen. The discovery was a major achievement that had a momentous effect on many types of research, including physics, medicine, biology and chemistry. In 1934, Urey was given the Nobel Prize for Chemistry. He was promoted to the position of full professor of chemistry at Columbia University that same year and was also the editor of the *Journal of Chemical Physics*.

Urey's discovery of the heavy hydrogen isotope led to one of history's most famous events--the dropping of the atomic bombs on Japan during World War II. The enormity of the situation was not lost on Urey and other scientists, who began to speak out with great concern about the responsible use of atomic weapons and the consequences for carelessness.

He held the position of distinguished service professor of chemistry at both the Institute for Nuclear Studies at the University of Chicago, from 1945 to 1952 and at Martin A. Ryerson, from 1952 to 1958. In 1958, he became professor-at- large of chemistry at the University of California in La Jolla.

Urey also pursued his other interests, such as the evolution of the earth and the solar system and the chemical connection regarding each. In two reports he prepared for the National Academy of Sciences in 1960, he supported the idea of space exploration in order to possibly understand the origin of the planets.

In 1930, Urey collaborated on a book with Arthur Edward Ruark, entitled *Atoms, Molecules and Quanta*, and also wrote *The Planets* in 1952. A series of lectures he gave in 1952, *The Planets: Their Origin and Development*, were published by the Yale University Press and he had articles published in numerous periodicals including the *Christian Century*, *Scientific American* and *The Saturday Review*.

Along with the Nobel Prize, Urey was also awarded the Willard Gibbs Medal of the American Chemical Society, the Medal for Merit and the Cordoza award, among others.

In looking back at his controversial place in history, Urey once said, "Above all, I regret that scientific experiments-- some of them mine--should have produced such a terrible weapon as the hydrogen bomb. Regret, with all my soul, but not guilt."

In 1926, Urey married Frieda Daum and they had four children.

V

VAN NUYS, FREDERICK, (1874-1944) - a U.S. Senator from Indiana; born in Falmouth, Rush County, Ind., April 16, 1874; attended the public schools; graduated from Earlham College, Richmond, Ind., in 1898 and from the Indiana Law School at Indianapolis, Ind., in 1900; was admitted to the bar in 1900 and commenced practice in Shelbyville, Ind., moving shortly afterward to Anderson, Ind.; prosecuting attorney of Madison County, Ind., 1906-1910; member, State senate 1913-1916, serving as president pro tempore in 1915; moved to Indianapolis, Ind., in 1916 and continued the practice of law; United States attorney, district of Indiana 1920-1922; elected as a Democrat to the United States Senate in 1932; reelected in 1938, and served from March 4, 1933, until his death on a farm near Vienna, Fairfax County, Va., on January 25, 1944; chairman, Committee on Expenditures in Executive Departments (Seventy-sixth Congress), Committee on the Judiciary (Seventy-seventh and Seventy-eighth Congresses); interment in East Maplewood Cemetery, Anderson, Ind.

VESTAL, ALBERT HENRY, (1875-1932) - a U.S. Representative from Indiana; born on a farm near Frankton, Madison County, Ind., January 18, 1875; attended the common schools; worked in steel mills and factories; attended the Indiana State Normal School at Terre Haute; taught school for several years; was graduated from the law department of the Valparaiso (Ind.) University in 1896; was admitted to the bar the same year and commenced practice in Anderson, Ind.; prosecuting attorney of the fiftieth judicial circuit 1900-1906; unsuccessful candidate for the Republican nomination for Congress in 1908; unsuccessful candidate for election in 1914 to the Sixty-fourth Congress; elected as a Republican to the Sixtyfifth and to the seven succeeding Congresses and served from March 4, 1917, until his death; chairman, Committee on Coinage, Weights, and Measures (Sixty- sixth through Sixty-eighth Congresses), Committee on Patents (Sixty-ninth through Seventy-first Congresses); majority whip (Sixtyeighth through Seventy-first Congresses); died in Washing ton, D.C., April 1, 1932; interment in East Maplewood Cemetery, Anderson, Ind.

VISCLOSKY, PETER, (1949-   ) - a U.S. Representative from Indiana; born in Gary, Ind., August 13, 1949; B.S., Indiana University, Gary, 1970; J.D., University of Notre Dame Law School, 1973; LL.M., Georgetown University Law Center, Washing ton, D.C., 1982; admitted to the Indiana State bar in 1974 and practiced law 1974-1976; staff, United States House of Representatives, Committee on Appropriations, 1977-1980, and Committee on the Budget, 1980-1982; practiced law in Merrillville, Ind., 1983-1984; elected as a Democrat to the Ninety-ninth and One Hundredth Congresses (January 3, 1985- January 3, 1989); is a resident of Merrillville, Ind.

VON ZELL, HARRY, (1906-   ) - radio announcer, actor, was born in Indianapolis, Indiana on July 11, 1906.

His family eventually moved to the West Coast and von Zell went to the University of California at Los Angeles, where he was involved in music and drama. He tried jobs as a bank messenger and a payroll clerk, but really had a yearning to do something in entertainment.

On a visit to a rehearsal for a radio program, some friends decided to jokingly announce that von Zell would be singing in the program. He followed through on their joke and ended up getting offers from smaller stations.

In 1926, KMIC in Inglewood, California hired him as a singer- announcer. He moved on to KMTR as a sports announcer and then went to San Diego's KGB as their program director.

Bandleader Paul Whiteman began a series of shows on radio and chose von Zell from 250 candidates to read the commercials. When the series ended in May of 1930, he went to New York and became a CBS staff announcer. Von Zell decided he wanted to branch out into comedy and was soon doing small character parts with Fred Allen and Colonel Stoopnagle. In little over a year, he began to work with the who's who in radio, including Will Rogers, Phil Baker, Ed Wynn and Eddy Duchin. He was a familiar voice on such shows as *Vick's Open House*, *We The People* and

The Aldrich Family. He also announced more serious programs, such as *The March of Time* and *Newspaper of the Air.* He worked with Eddie Cantor on the *Time To Smile* program and also announced the radio version of *Truth or Consequences* for a short time.

Beginning in 1945, von Zell worked in numerous films, such as *Uncle Harry, You're In the Navy Now* and *Boy, Did I Get a Wrong Number!*

In 1925, he married Minerva McGarvey and they had one son.

VONNEGUT, KURT, JR., (1922 -   ) - is a novelist and playwright whose works are popular among U.S. college students. His novels seem inherently a criticism of society, although he denies that they contain any great truths.

Vonnegut was born in Indianapolis on November 11, 1922 and graduated from Shortridge High School. His studies at Cornell University (1940-42) were interrupted by the outbreak of World War II. Vonnegut served in the U.S. Army, was captured by the Germans, and survived the bombing of Dresden, Germany, in February 1945.

While studying at the University of Chicago (1945-47), Vonnegut worked as a newsman and corporation publicist. He began his career as a freelance writer in 1950. Recognition of his works came in the 1960s, and he has since held positions with the University of Iowa (1965-67) and Harvard University (1970).

Vonnegut's novels include *Player Piano* (1952), *Sirens of Titan* (1959), *Mother Night* (1961), *Cat's Cradle* (1963), *God Bless You, Mr. Rosewater* (1965), *Slaughterhouse Five, or The Children's Crusade* (1969), and *Breakfast of Champions* (1973). He has also written *Welcome to the Monkey House* (1968), a collection of short stories, and *Happy Birthday, Wanda June* (1970), a play. He received the literature award of the National Institute of Arts and Letters in 1970.

The popularity of Vonnegut's books among college students in the 1960s surprised the author. He believes that perhaps they shared his concept of the importance of our planet. Vonnegut claims that he became a writer because he kept out of the clutches of English teachers. His "crazy ideas about socialism and pacifism," however, were acquired in the public schools of his native Indianapolis.

Slaughterhouse Five is the result of his presence as a prisoner-of-war in Dresden during the Allied firebombing that killed 135,000. Bits and pieces of that experience are seen by critics in his earlier works, as well.

VOORHEES, DANIEL WOLSEY, (1827-1897) - (father of Charles Stewart Voorhees), a U.S. Representative and a Senator from Indiana; born in Liberty Township, Butler County, Ohio, September 26, 1827; moved with his parents to Indiana in early childhood; attended the common schools of Veedersburg, Ind.; graduated from Indiana Asbury (now De Pauw) University at Greencastle in 1849; studied law; was admitted to the bar in 1851 and commenced practice in Covington, Ind.; moved to Terre Haute and continued the practice of law; unsuccessful candidate for election in 1856 to the Thirty-fifth Congress; United States district attorney for Indiana 1858-1861; elected as a Democrat to the Thirty-seventh and Thirtyeighth Congresses (March 4, 1861-March 3, 1865); presented credentials as a Member-elect to the Thirty-ninth Congress and served from March 4, 1865, to February 23, 1866, when he was succeeded by Henry D. Washburn, who contested the election; elected to the Forty-first and Forty-second Congresses (March 4, 1869-March 3, 1873); unsuccessful candidate for reelection in 1872 to the Forty-third Congress; appointed and subsequently elected as a Democrat to the United States Senate to fill the vacancy caused by the death of Oliver H.P.T. Morton; reelected in 1885 and again in 1891, and served from November 6, 1877, to March 3, 1897; unsuccessful candidate for reelection; chairman, Committee on the Library (Forty-sixth Congress), Committee on Finance (Fiftythird Congress); died in Washington, D.C., April 10, 1897; interment in Highland Lawn Cemetery, Terre Haute, Ind.

W

WAKEFIELD, DAN, (1932-   ) - author, was born in Indianapolis, Indiana on May 21, 1932.

Wakefield went to Indiana University for a year and then to Columbia University, where he received his B.A. degree in 1955.

That same year, he began work as a news editor for the *Princeton Packet* in Princeton, New Jersey and later became a research assistant at Columbia University.

From 1956 to 1959, he was a staff writer in New York for *Nation*, and after that job, he became a free-lance writer, and contributed numerous reviews, articles and short stories to such publications as *Esquire*, *Playboy*, *Atlantic* and *Commentary*.

He has written both fiction: *Going All The Way*; *Starting Over* and non-fiction: *Island In The City: The World of Spanish Harlem*; *Revolt in the South*; *Between The Lines*; *Supernation at Peace and War*.

Wakefield was awarded a Neiman fellowship at Harvard University in 1963. In 1968, he won the short story prize from the National Council of the Arts, and a National Book Award Nomination in 1970, for *Going All The Way*.

In 1960, he married Mary Avery and they had one son.

WALLACE, DAVID, (1799-1859) - governor of Indiana (1837-1840), was born on April 4, 1799 in Mifflin County, Pennsylvania, the son of Andrew and Eleanor (Jones) Wallace. His family moved to Ohio in 1807 and Wallace attended school in Troy. In 1817, he entered West Point and studied for four years, graduating in 1821 with the rank of second lieutenant. He taught at West Point for a year, then returned to Brookville, Indiana where his family was living. In Brookville, he studied law and was admitted to the bar. He also served in the 7th Regiment, Indiana Militia where in 1827, he rose to the rank of colonel.

Wallace ran for state representative, was elected to the Indiana House, and served from 1828 to 1831. Campaigning on a ticket with Noah Noble, in 1831 and again in

1834, he was elected lieutenant governor. In 1837, he ran for the governorship and won over his opponent, John Dumont, by nearly 10,000 votes. Wallace's administration was marked by an economic collapse in the State's internal improvement program, and the removal of the Potawatomi Indians onto reservations.

In 1840, at the close of his term, Wallace began a law practice in Indianapolis. He ran for U.S. Congress in 1841 and served a single term in Washington, then returned to Indianapolis. He was a member of the Indiana Constitutional Convention in 1850 and was a judge in Marion County from 1856 to 1859. Wallace died in Indianapolis on September 4, 1859. He was married twice: to Esther French Text in 1824, with whom he had four sons; and after her death to Zeralda Sanders in 1836, with whom he had two daughters and a son.

WALLACE, LEWIS, (1837 - 1905) - was a Civil War military leader and author of popular novels including *Ben Hur: A Tale of the Christ.*

Wallace was born in Brookville, Indiana on April 10, 1837. He preferred adventure to study and as a result received a minimum of formal education. His father's election to the Indiana governorship in 1837 necessitated a move to Indianapolis, where Wallace studied law in his father's law office. Upon the outbreak of the Mexican War in 1846, Wallace organized an army of volunteers. He returned to Indianapolis after the war and was admitted to the bar in 1849. He then established a law practice and served two terms (1850 and 1852) as the prosecuting attorney of Covington, Indiana. In 1853, Wallace moved to Crawfordsville and three years later was elected to the Indiana Senate, where he advocated a change in divorce laws and the popular election of U.S. senators.

The onset of the Civil War brought Wallace the appointment of adjutant general of the state militia and, soon afterwards, of colonel of a volunteer regiment. He played a decisive role in the fighting of Harper's Ferry and Romney. His part in the capture of Fort Donelson led to his promotion to major-general on March 21, 1862. The following year, he prevented the capture of Cincinnati and was awarded the command of the Middle Division and the 8th

Army Corps in Baltimore, Maryland. Commanding 4,800 men, he helped defend Washington, D.C., against a force of 28,000 men under General Jubal A. Early in July 1864. Before leaving the army in November 1865, Wallace served on the court martial panels that tried men implicated in the assassination of President Abraham Lincoln and that tried Henry Wirz, commander of the Confederate prison camp at Andersonville, Georgia.

In 1866 Wallace spent several months in Mexico assisting Benito Juarez in his fight against Maximilian and the French. He returned to Crawfordsville, where he established a law practice and ran an unsuccessful campaign for a Republican seat in the U.S. Congress. In 1878 Wallace assumed the governorship of New Mexico, and held the post until President Garfield appointed him to a four-year term as minister to Turkey in 1881.

Wallace is best known for his novels, the most famous of which, *Ben Hur*, was published in 1880. Other works include *The Fair God* (1873), *The Life of Benjamin Harrison* (1888), *The Boyhood of Christ* (1888), and *The Prince of India* (1893). Wallace died in Crawfordsville on Feb. 14, 1905. *Lew Wallace: An Autobiography* (1906) was completed posthumously by his wife.

WALSH, JOHN RICHARD, (1913-1975) - a U.S. Representative from Indiana; born in Martinsville, Morgan County, Ind., May 22, 1913; attended the public schools; was graduated from Indiana University Law School in 1934; was admitted to the bar July 27, 1934, and engaged in the practice of law in Martinsville, Ind., until 1941; Morgan County attorney in 1935 and 1936; deputy attorney general of Indiana in 1941; served in the United States Army with the Thirty-fifth Infantry Division from May 18, 1942, until discharged as a technical sergeant June 15, 1943; in 1943 continued the practice of law in Anderson, Ind.; chief deputy prosecuting attorney of Madison County, Ind., in 1945 and 1946; probate commissioner for Madison County Circuit Court in 1948; elected as a Democrat to the Eighty-first Congress (January 3, 1949-January 3, 1951); unsuccessful candidate for reelection in 1950 and for election in 1954 to the Eighty-fourth Congress; resumed the practice of law in Anderson and continued in practice until his death; member of board of directors and secretary- treasurer, State Security Life Insurance Co., Anderson, Ind., 1953-1958; secretary of state of Indiana from December 1, 1958, to November 30, 1960; delegate, Democratic National Convention, 1960; county attorney of Madison County, 1964-1965; was a resident of Anderson, Ind., until his death there on January 23, 1975; interment in Greenlawn Cemetery, Martinsville, Ind.

WAMPLER, FRED, (1909-   ) - a U.S. Representative from Indiana; born in Carriers Mills, Saline County, Ill., October 15, 1909; moved with parents to Terre Haute, Ind., in 1911 and attended the public schools; graduated from Indiana State Teachers College in 1931 and in 1940; high school athletic director in Bluffton, Ohio, 1931-1933, and football coach in Terre Haute, Ind., 1937-1958; athletic director, Washington Court House, Ohio, in 1936 and 1937; served from January 1944 as a gunnery officer in the United States Navy, with service in the Pacific Theater until discharged as a lieutenant in 1946; served as commanding officer, Naval Reserve, activating training center at Terre Haute, Ind., 1946-1949; sports director for a radio station in Terre Haute, Ind., 1947-1949; during the Korean conflict was recalled to active duty as executive officer aboard troop transport and served from January 1950 to March 1954; promoted to commander, United States Naval Reserve, May 11, 1960; elected as a Democrat to the Eighty-sixth Congress (January 3, 1959-January 3, 1961); unsuccessful candidate for reelection in 1960 to the Eighty-seventh Congress; appointed to the Indiana- Illinois Wabash Valley Interstate Commission on March 13, 1961, and served until his resignation May 26, 1962; unsuccessful candidate in 1962 for election to the Eightyeighth Congress; Regional Coordinator, Department of the Interior, 1963-1970; funding coordinator for state-federal programs, Ohio department of natural resources and transportation, 1971-1976; is a resident of Terrace Park, Ohio.

WARD, MARY JANE, (1905-   ) - author, was born in Fairmount, Indiana on August 27, 1905.

She attended Northwestern University for two years and then went to the Lyceum of Arts Conservatory for a year.

Ward held a variety of jobs such as writing mail order advertising, saleswoman, designing and decorating glass novelties and teaching art at a summer camp.

In her youth, she'd had a talent for music and thought of it as a career choice. But after her 1928 marriage to Edward Quayle, a statistician, whose first love was painting, she decided on writing as a way to earn money. She sold a few short stories, but then quit to write a novel that was never published. She and her husband lived at near-poverty level and she worked at jobs such as reviewing books and concerts for the Evanston (Illinois) *News-Index*.

Her second novel, *The Tree Has Roots*, got published in 1937 as did her third novel, *The Wax Apple*, a year later. Her books, while attaining a modicum of success, did not bring overwhelming financial reward.

In 1939, the couple decided to move to Greenwich Village in New York in hopes of changing their luck, but neither one of them were able to sell their work and in 1941, Ward suffered a nervous breakdown.

While claiming that her next book, *The Snake Pit* was not autobiographical, her nine month stay in a mental hospital after her breakdown was the catalyst for the novel. It was published in 1946, and drew praise from both critics and doctors as being authentic and convincing. It was a dual selection of the Book-Of-The-Month Club for April of 1946 and was translated into sixteen languages. The book was eventually made into a movie and won the Screen Writers Guild Award in 1948. A year later, Ward received an Achievement Award from the Women's National Press Club, "for outstanding accomplishment in Mental Health."

The Quayles bought a dairy farm in 1946, and Mary Jane continued to write books, including *The Professor's Umbrella*, in 1948, *A Little Night Music*, in 1951, *It's Different For A Woman*, in 1952 and *The Other Caroline*, in 1970. Her work was described by a *Saturday Review* writer as having, "sensitive and compassionate insight into feminine psychology."

WARD, THOMAS BAYLESS, (1839-1892) - a U.S. Representative from Indiana; born in Marysville, Union County, Ohio, April 27, 1835; moved with his parents to La Fayette,

Ind., in May 1836; attended Wabash College, Crawfordsville, Ind., and was graduated from Miami University, Oxford, Ohio, in June 1855; clerk of the city of La Fayette in 1855 and 1856; studied law; was admitted to the bar in 1857 and commenced the practice of his profession in La Fayette, Ind.; city attorney in 1859 and 1860; mayor of La Fayette 1861-1865; judge of the superior court of Tippecanoe County, Ind., 1875-1880; elected as a Democrat to the Forty- eighth and Forty-ninth Congresses (March 4, 1883-March 3, 1887); was not a candidate for renomination in 1886 to the Fiftieth Congress; resumed the practice of his profession in La Fayette, Tippecanoe County, Ind., where he died January 1, 1892; interment in Springvale Cemetery.

WAUGH, DANIEL WEBSTER, (1842-1921) - a U.S. Representative from Indiana; born near Bluffton, Wells County, Ind., March 7, 1842; attended the country schools and the high school in Bluffton; enlisted in the Union Army in 1861 in Company A, Thirtyfourth Regiment, Indiana Volunteer Infantry, and served until honorably discharged in September 1864; taught school; engaged in agricultural pursuits; studied law; was admitted to the bar in 1866; settled in Tipton, Ind., in 1867 and practiced; judge of the thirty-sixth judicial circuit 1884-1890; elected as a Republican to the Fifty-second and Fiftythird Congresses (March 4, 1891-March 3, 1895); declined to be a candidate for renomination in 1894; resumed the practice of law; died in Tipton, Ind., March 14, 1921; interment in the mausoleum adjoining Green Lawn Cemetery.

WAYNE, ANTHONY, (b. January 1, 1745 - d. December 15, 1796) was an American Revolutionary War general whose victory at the Battle of Fallen Timbers ended Indian resistance to white settlement in the Ohio Valley.

Wayne was born on the family farm of Waynesborough on January 1, 1745 near present-day Paoli, Pennsylvania, and attended an academy in Philadelphia (1761-63). His training as a land surveyor helped him secure a position in a surveying expedition of Nova Scotia in 1765. He returned to Pennsylvania in 1766 and was eventually elected to several public offices. During the pre- Revolutionary War period, he was aided in the formulation of formal protest resolutions against the British and the organization of a regional army.

On January 3, 1776, Wayne was commissioned colonel of the 4th Pennsylvania Battalion of the Continental Army. His regiment was sent to assist General Benedict Arnold in his retreat from Canada. Wayne then assumed command of Fort Ticonderoga and remained there until February 1777, when he was promoted to brigadier general and ordered to join George Washington's army at Morristown, New Jersey. His participation in the Battle of Brandywine (September 1777) was followed by a dramatic defeat at Paoli, for which he was charged and later cleared of negligence. He resumed his military duties in the battles of Germantown (October 1777) and Monmouth (June 1778).

In 1779, the army was reorganized and Wayne was put in charge of a light infantry brigade. Leading these troops, he captured Stony Point (July 16, 1779), the northernmost British fort on the Hudson River, and prevented Benedict Arnold from turning West Point over to the British (September 1780). Another notable victory came the next year with the defeat of Cornwallis in Green Spring, Virginia. After the British surrender at Yorktown, Virginia, in October 1781, Wayne was assigned to aid General Nathanael Green in disarming the British, Loyalists, and Creek Indians in Georgia. A defeat by Wayne of the Indians in May 1782 resulted in successful treaty negotiations with the Creek and Cherokee.

Wayne retired from the army in 1783 and embarked upon a political career. He held a series of offices including one in the Pennsylvania Council of Censors (1783) and another in the Pennsylvania General Assembly (1784-85). In 1785 he moved to Georgia, where he made an unsuccessful attempt to farm a rice planation given to him by the state for his military service. From 1791 to 1792 he served in the Georgia House of Representatives, but was forced to vacate his seat because of charges of election irregularities.

The unsuccessful campaigns of General Joseph Harmar and General Arthur St. Clair against the Indians of the Northwest Territory brought about another reorganization of the army in 1792. Wayne was commissioned commander-in-chief of the forces and during the next two years he pro-

duced a well-trained force of 1,000 men. His march from
Pennsylvania to the Northwest Territory was marked by the
establishment of Forts Washington, Greenville, and Defi-
ance, which were used to train the soldiers in the basics of
Indian warfare.

The inevitable clash between "Mad Anthony" and the Indians came on August 20, 1794, when Wayne attacked and
defeated the Indian forces at the Battle of Fallen Timbers,
near the present-day city of Toledo, Ohio. Wayne's victory,
combined with the Jay Treaty with England which withdrew
British support from the Indians, made the defeated tribes
more willing to negotiate peace. The result was the 1795
Treaty of Greenville, by which the Indians ceded land in
the present states of Ohio, Indiana, Illinois, and Michigan
to the U.S. government. In August 1796, Wayne took command of the British fort in Detroit. He died Dec. 15, 1796
at Presque Isle (now Erie), Pennsylvania, during the with-
drawl of his troops form the fort.

WEBB, CLIFTON, (ne Webb Parmelee Hollenbeck),
(1894-1966) singer, dancer, actor, was born in Indianapolis,
Indiana on November 19, 1894.

His family moved to New York when he was three and
at the age of seven, by mere luck of being at the right place
at the right time, he began his acting career with the Chidl-
ren's Theatre. After appearing in a few plays, he resumed
his education, graduating from grammar ,chool at thirteen.
At his mother's urging, he began to study singing and art.
He discovered a love for opera, and at sixteen, he made his
debut as Laertes in *Mignon* with the Boston Opera Company. He also had roles in *La Boheme*, *Madame Butterfly*
and *Hansel and Gretel*.

His career went in a different direction when he got a
part in a musical comedy, *The Purple Road*, where he not
only sang, but danced. He soon made a name for himself
as a ballroom dancer, and appeared in many Broadway hits
where he sang popular songs such as "I Guess I'll Have To
Change My Plan," "Easter Parade," "Alone Together," and
"I've Got A Crush On You." The critics were ebullient in
their praise for his many talents, and that also carried over
when he began doing straight theatrical roles, such as *Meet
The Wife*. He made a brief foray into Hollywood in the

1920's and made some films like *Polly With A Past* and *The Heart of A Siren*. His second trip to Hollywood was a more successful venture. In 1944, he made the film classic, *Laura* with Gene Tierney, for which he received his first Oscar nomination for Best Supporting Actor. He got the nomination two more times, for Best Supporting Actor in *The Razor's Edge*, in 1946 and for Best Actor in *Sitting Pretty*, in 1948. The latter was the first of three in his "Mr. Belvedere" series. His other noteworthy movies included, *Cheaper By The Dozen*, *Titanic* and *Three Coins In The Fountain*.

Clifton Webb died of a heart attack on October 13, 1966.

WEBER, DICK, (1929-) - Professional bowler, was born in Indianapolis, Indiana on December 2, 1929.

Weber graduated from Indianapolis Tech in 1948.

Since his father managed a bowling alley, Weber started bowling as a young boy and eventually became good enough to enter tournaments.

Soon after graduating high school, he got married and worked two jobs in order to support his family. In the small amount of spare time he had, he continued his bowling practice.

In 1954, his game was good enough for him to be invited to join the Budweiser Brewing Company's professional bowling team, where his beginning salary was $10,000 a year, plus prize winnings. He and his teammate, Ray Bluth won numerous doubles championships in the Bowling Proprietors Association of America tournaments, as well as the ABC contests.

In 1959, the First Professional Bowlers Association tour was established and Weber was able to make good money by winning several of their tournaments, along with receiving compensation
for televised games and endorsements. He also continued to bowl in the ABC and BPAA matches and in 1963, he made approximately $100,000.

In 1965, Weber had a 211 average in 960 games and was average leader in the ABC tournament for two years in a row. Also that same year, he became the first bowler to achieve three perfect "300" games in one tournament. A year later, he won seventeen of the PBA tournaments and for the second year, was runner up in the Firestone Tournament of Champions.

He hit a two year slump from 1966 to 1968, during which he had switched from his forte, a sharp hook, to a straight ball. He went back to his original style and he was back on track.

Aside from tournaments, Weber increased his income by investments such as instructional pamphlets for which he received royalties, and co-ownership in a bowling alley, and by conducting clinics and exhibitions for which he was paid by the American Machine and Foundry Company. He was also an adviser and an official for the PBA. He has been inducted into both the St. Louis and Missouri Sports Hall of Fame, as well as the American Bowling Congress Hall of Fame.

He married Juanita Dirk in 1948 and they had four children.

WELSH, MATTHEW E., (1912-   ) - governor of Indiana (1961- 65), was born in Detroit, Michigan on September 15, 1912, the son of Matthew and Inez (Empson) Welsh. The family lived in Michigan until young Matthew was 12 years old, when they moved to Vincennes, Indiana. He was a good student and after graduation in 1930 attended the University of Pennsylvania. Following college, Welsh enrolled at the University of Chicago Law School, and received his J.D. degree three years later.

Now a lawyer, he returned to Vincennes, and began a successful practice. As World War II approached, Welsh ran as a Democrat for a seat in the Indiana House of Representatives, and was elected. His term ended in 1943 and he joined the Navy with the rank of lieutenant. Upon demobilization in 1946, he resumed his law practice. In 1950 Welsh became the United States attorney for the Southern District of Indiana. Four years later the people of his district elected him to the State Senate.

Welsh ran for but lost the Democratic nomination for governor in 1956, but achieved that goal in 1960. He went on to defeat his Republican opponent by a 22,000 vote margin. Once in office he quickly responded to a pressing need for more state revenue by enacting a 2% sales tax. Heeding the growing Civil Rights movement, the Governor created the Indiana Fair Employment Commission and set up youth training centers. After his term ended Welsh rejoined his law firm. Seven years later, he ran for governor again, but was handily defeated by the Republican candidate. Matthew Welsh married Virginia Homann in 1937, and had two children.

WEST, JESSAMYN, (1907-   ) - novelist, was born in Indiana, but lived in California from the time she was six. She attended Whittier College, a small Quaker institution and then traveled to England for a short time to study there. Upon her return, she enrolled at the University of California.

Her first book, *The Friendly Persuasion*, published in 1945, was written during her years of bedrest due to her condition, tuberculosis of the lungs. In 1948, she published her second book, *Mirror For The Sky*, which was an opera script for a musical drama on the life of J.J. Audubon.

West's other books include, *The Witch Diggers*, *Cress Delahanty*, *Love, Death and the Ladies' Drill Team*, which was a collection of short stories and *South of the Angels*.

In 1956, she wrote the movie screenplay for *The Friendly Persuasion* and then a year later she wrote of her Hollywood experiences regarding the filming of that script, in the book, *To See The Dream*. Her other screenplays were *The Big Country*, *Lucy Crown* and *Stolen Hours*.

West also contributed numerous articles to magazines, including *Good Housekeeping*, *Redbook*, *New Yorker* and *Reader's Digest* and also taught at writers' conferences at colleges such as the University of Notre Dame, the University of Colorado, the University of Utah and Stanford University.

She married H.M. McPherson, also a Quaker, who had been a classmate at Whittier College.

WHITCOMB, EDGAR D., (1917-   ) - governor of Indiana (1969-1973), was born in Hayden, Indiana on November 6, 1917, the son of John and Louise (Doud) Whitcomb. He attended local schools, and enrolled at the University of

Indiana after high school graduation. Unfortunately, lack of funds forced him to drop out and go to work. He joined the Army Air Force in 1940, and after training as a navigator for bombers, was posted to the Philippines in October 1941. The Japanese took Whitcomb prisoner at the fall of Corregidor on May 7, 1942. After several thwarted attempts, he escaped the Philippines, and returned to the United States in December, 1943. Thereafter, he flew transport missions in Europe before returning to the Philippines in May 1945.

Coming home following these heroic exertions, he enrolled at the University of Indiana, and attained his L.L.B. degree in 1950. Two years later at the age of 35 he was admitted to the bar. In 1951 Whitcomb was elected to the Indiana State Senate, and held that office until being appointed assistant U.S. attorney for the Southern District of Indiana in 1955. He continued his law practice until 1966 when he became Indiana Secretary of State.

As the country debated the War in Vietnam in 1968, Whitcomb ran for governor on the Republican ticket, and was elected. His administration held the line on taxes, and appointed a Economy Task Force to reduce waste and duplication in government. The "pocket veto" was declared unconstitutional during his administration. Once out of office, Whitcomb became a director of the Mid-America World Trade Association in Indianapolis. He was married to Patricia Dolfuss in 1951, and had five children.

WHITCOMB, JAMES, (1795-1852) - governor of Indiana (1843- 1848), was born on December 1, 1795 in Windsor, Vermont, the son of John and Lydia (Parameter) Whitcomb. He attended Transylvania University, then studied law and was admitted to the Kentucky bar in 1822. In 1824, he moved to Indiana and practiced law in Bloomington. Six years later he was elected to the Indiana Senate where he served for two terms.

President Andrew Jackson appointed Whitcomb commissioner of the General Land Office in October, 1836. President Van Buren reappointed him for a subsequent term and he remained at that post until 1841. He returned to Indiana and practiced law in Terre Haute until 1843 when he won the Democratic nomination for governor. He was elected to office later that year.

As governor, Whitcomb worked to alleviate debts accrued by the internal improvements program and approached the State Bank for loans to bolster state finances. With help from these loans, in 1846, the State raised five regiments of infantry for the war with Mexico. Also during Whitcomb's term, the Indiana Asylum for the Education of the Deaf and the Indiana Hospital for the Insane were established.

Whitcomb resigned as governor in 1848 after the Legislature elected him to the U.S. Senate. His term as senator, however, was interrupted by poor health. He died in New York on October 4, 1852. James Whitcomb was married to Ann Renick Hurst and had one daughter.

WHITE, MICHAEL DOHERTY, (1827-1917) - a U.S. Representative from Indiana; born in Clark County, Ohio, September 8, 1827; moved with his parents to Tippecanoe County, Ind., in 1829; pursued classical studies; moved to Crawfordsville, Crawfordsville County, Ind., in 1848; attended the county seminary and Wabash College, Crawfordsville; clerked in a store for one year; studied law; was admitted to the bar in 1854 and commenced the practice of his profession in Crawfordsville; law partner of Gen. Lew Wallace; prosecuting attorney of Montgomery and Boone Counties 1854-1856; member of the State senate 1860-1864; elected as a Republican to the Fortyfifth Congress (March 4, 1877-March 3, 1879); was not a candidate for renomination in 1878; continued the practice of law in Crawfordsville, Ind., until 1911, and died there on February 6, 1917; interment in the Masonic Cemetery.

WICK, WILLIAM WATSON, (1796-1868) - a U.S. Representative from Indiana; born in Canonsburg, Washington County, Pa., February 23, 1796; moved with his parents to Western Reserve in 1800; completed preparatory studies; moved to Cincinnati, Ohio, in 1816; taught school; studied medicine until 1818 and then law; was admitted to the bar in Franklin, Johnson County, Ind., in 1819 and commenced practice in Connersville, Fayette County, Ind., in 1820; clerk of the State house of representatives 1820; assistant clerk of the State senate 1821; president judge of the fifth judicial State circuit 1822-1825; secretary of state 1825-1829; prosecuting attorney of the flfth judicial circuit 1S29-1831; again president judge 1834- 1837; elected as a Democrat to the Twenty-sixth Congress (March 4, 1839-March 3, 1841); unsuccessful candidate for reelection in 1840 to the Twenty- seventh Congress; resumed the practice of law in Indianapolis; elected to the Twentyninth and Thirtieth Congresses (March 4, 1845-March 3, 1849); was not a candidate for renomination; president judge for a third time, serving from 1850 to 1853; postmaster of Indianapolis, Ind., from April 9, 1853, to April 6, 1857; adjutant general in the State militia; moved to Franklin, Ind., in 1857, where he continued the practice of law, and died there May 19, 1868; interment in Greenlawn Cemetery.

WILLARD, ASHBEL P., (1820-1860) - governor of Indiana (1857-1860), was born in Oneida County, New York on October 31, 1820, the son of Erastus and Sarah (Parsons) Willard. He graduated from Hamilton College in 1842, subsequently studied law and was admitted to the bar. Over the new few years he lived in various parts of the country: Michigan, Texas, and Kentucky. He settled in New Albany, Indiana in 1845 and worked as an attorney. Five years later, he was elected to the Indiana House of Representatives and served for one term. He ran for lieutenant governor in 1852 as a Democrat and won by a margin of more than 15,000 votes.

Willard was elected governor of Indiana four years later. During his term, Willard often found himself at odds with the State Legislature. He was critical of the Legislature for focusing on national issues rather than attending to state problems, and for failing to make sufficient appropriations for government expenses. Indiana faced such a financial crises that while the Legislature was adjourned Willard was forced to take out a loan to pay the interest on the state debt.

While governor, Willard's brother-in-law, John E. Cook was arrested and eventually tried and put to death for his part in the famous raid on Harper's Ferry. Although Willard's attempts to help Cook were unsuccessful, Willard's efforts in the matter brought him increased constituent approval at home. Willard left Indiana in failing health and went to St. Paul, Minnesota where he died on October 3, 1860, while still governor. He was married in 1847 to Caroline Cook and had three children.

WILLIAMS, JAMES D., (1808-1880) - governor of Indiana (1877-1880), was born on January 16, 1808 in Pickaway County, Ohio, the son of George Williams. He grew up on farms and was educated in the common schools of the area. About 1831, he moved to the Wheatland region and bought a farm of his own. He entered state politics as a Democrat and served numerous terms in the Indiana House of Representatives: 1843-44, 1847-48, 1851-52, 1857, and 1869. He was elected several times to the State Senate and filled that office from 1859 to 1865, in 1871, and in 1875. During this period, Williams was also a member of the Indiana State Board of Agriculture.

Williams was nominated for governor by the Democrats in 1872, but lost to Oliver P. Morton in the general election. In 1874, he was elected to the U.S. Congress and served until 1876 when he was elected governor of Indiana. Sworn in as governor in January, 1877, Williams' term was marred by labor disputes: a railroad strike that paralyzed much of the Midwest, and worker unrest in Indianapolis. Construction of the Indiana State House began in 1878 during Williams' administration.

James Williams died on November 20, 1880 while still governor. Throughout his political life he was know by the nickname, "Blue Jeans" because he wore blue jeans in nearly all except the hottest months of the year. He was married in 1831 to Nancy Huffman and had four children.

WILLIAMS, WILLIAM, (1821-1896) - a U.S. Representative born near Carlisle, Cumberland County, Pa., May 11, 1821; attended the common schools and received a very limited education; studied law; was admitted to the bar in 1845 and commenced practice in Warsaw, Kosciusko County, Ind.; treasurer of Kosciusko County in 1852; resigned the office of treasurer in order to become a candidate for Lieutenant Governor; unsuccessful candidate for Lieutenant Governor in 1853; managed the Bank of Warsaw for several years; director of the Fort Wayne and Chicago

Railway 1854-1856; director of the Michigan City prison 1859-1862; served in the Union Army as commandant of Camp Allen, Fort Wayne, Ind., in 1862 and as paymaster of Volunteers, with headquarters at Louisville, Ky., until the close of the war; elected as a Republican to the Fortieth and to the three succeeding Congresses (March 4, 1867-March 3, 1875); chairman, Committee on Expenditures in the Department of War (Fortieth through Forty- third Congresses); was not a candidate for renomination in 1874; resumed the practice of law in Warsaw, Ind.; appointed by President Arthur as Charge d'Affaires to Paraguay and Uruguay April 12, 1882, and served until February 14, 1885, when he resigned; returned to Warsaw, Ind., in 1885 and retired from active business pursuits; died in Warsaw April 22, 1896; interment in Oakwood Cemetery.

WILLIS, RAYMOND EUGENE, (1875-1956) - a U.S. Senator from Indiana; born in Waterloo, De Kalb County, Ind., August 11, 1875; attended the public schools and graduated from Wabash College, Crawfordsville, Ind., in 1896; learned the printer's trade in Waterloo, Ind.; moved to Angola, Ind., and engaged in the newspaper publishing business in 1898; postmaster of Angola 1910- 1914; during the First World War served as chairman of Steuben County Council of Defense 1917-1918; member, State house of representatives 1919-1921; unsuccessful candidate for election to the United States Senate in 1938; elected as a Republican to the United States Senate in 1940, and served from January 3, 1941, to January 3, 1947; was not a candidate for renomination in 1946; resumed the publishing business as president of the Steuben Printing Co.; trustee of Tri-State College at Angola; died in Angola, Ind., March 21, 1956; interment in Circle Hill Cemetery.

WILLKIE, WENDELL LEWIS, (1892-1944) - lawyer, business administrator, Presidential candidate, was born in Elwood, Indiana on February 18, 1892.

Willkie went to Culver Military Academy and then attended the University of Indiana in 1909, where he received a B.A. degree in 1913 and an L.L.B degree in 1916.

He came from a fascinating, non-conformist type of family, very much ahead of their time. His mother, along with raising her six children, taught school and practiced law, having been the first woman ever admitted to the Indiana Bar. His grandmother was a Presbyterian minister and his father woke his family up in the mornings by loudly reciting quotations from classic novels.

Throughout his school years, Willkie made money by harvesting grain and being a "barker" for a tent hotel during South Dakota's land boom.

After graduating from college, he joined his parents' law firm until 1917, when he enlisted in the Army after the start of World War I. After the service, he worked in the legal department of the Firestone Company and then at the law firm of Mather, Nesbitt and Willkie in Akron, Ohio. In 1929, he was asked to fill the attorney's positon at Commonwealth and Southern, a large utility holding company. Willke then became president of the company in 1933. His company went head-to-head with President Franklin D. Roosevelt's New Deal policies of which Willkie became an outspoken critic. Eventually the Tennessee Valley Authority, a New Deal agency, paid Commonwealth and Southern over 78 million dollars for its Tennessee properties. The Republican party, taking note of Willkie's victory, convinced him to run on their ticket for President and he won the Republican Presidential nomination in June of 1940. His campaigning methods were different than most in that he was bluntly honest.

He had no trouble publicly agreeing with President Roosevelt about certain policies, but basically opposed his decisions regarding private enterprise and the tax structure of the New Deal. Although he received over 22,000,000 votes, he lost the race and eventually went back to private law practice.

In 1942, he was asked by President Roosevelt to tour Europe and Asia as a special emissary. The next year, he published a book on his experiences overseas, entitled, *One World*.

He married Edith Wilk in 1918 and they had one son.

Wendell Willkie died on October 8, 1944. Two biographies were written about him after his death: *Willkie*, in 1952 and *One Life*, in 1957.

WILSON, JAMES, (1825-1867) - (father of John Lockwood Wilson), a Representative from Indiana; born in Crawfordsville, Montgomery County, Ind., April 9, 1825; was graduated from Wabash College, Crawfordsville, Ind., in 1842; studied law; was admitted to the bar in 1848 and commenced practice in Crawfordsville, Ind.; served in the Mexican War from June 17, 1846, to June 16, 1847; during the Civil War was appointed captain of Volunteers November 26, 1862, and honorably discharged December 6, 1865, as brevet lieutenant colonel; elected as a Republican to the Thirty- fifth and Thirty-sixth Congresses (March 4, 1857-March 3, 1861); Minister to Venezuela from 1866 until his death in Caracas, Venezuela, August 8, 1867; interment in Oak Hill Cemetery, Crawfordsville, Ind.

WILSON, JEREMIAH MORROW, (1828-1901) - a U.S. Representative from Indiana; born near Lebanon, Warren County, Ohio, November 25, 1828; completed preparatory studies; studied law; was admitted to the bar and practiced; moved to Indiana and settled in Connersville and continued the practice of law; judge of the court of common pleas 1860-1865; elected judge of the circuit court in October 1865 and served until his election to Congress; elected as a Republican to the Fortysecond and Forty- third Congresses (March 4, 1871-March 3, 1875); was not a candidate for reelection in 1874; resumed the practice of his profession in Washington, D.C., where he died September 24, 1901; interment in Rock Creek Cemetery.

WILSON, JOHN LOCKWOOD, (1850-1912) - (son of James Wilson ana (1825-1867), a U.S. Representative and a Senator from Washington; born in Crawfordsville, Montgomery County, Ind., August 7, 1850; attended the common schools; messenger during the Civil War; graduated from Wabash College, Crawfordsville, Ind., in 1874; studied law; was admitted to the bar in 1878 and commenced practice in Crawfordsville; member, State house of representatives 1880; appointed by President Chester Arthur as receiver of public moneys at Spokane Falls and Colfax, Washington Territory 1882-1887; upon the admission of Washington as a State into the Union was elected as a Republican to the Fifty-first Congress; reelected to the Fifty-second and Fifty-third Congresses and served from November 20, 1889, to February 18, 1895, when he resigned to become Senator; elected as a Republican to the United States Senate on February 1, 1895, to fill the vacancy in the term commencing March 4, 1893, but did not assume his senatorial duties until February 19, 1895; served until March 3, 1899; was an unsuccessful candidate for reelection in 1898; chairman, Committee on Indian Depredations (Fifty-fourth and Fifty-fifth Congresses); published the Seattle Post- Intelligencer, Seattle, Wash.; died in Washington, D.C., on November 6, 1912; interment in Oak Hill Cemetery.

WILSON, WILLIAM EDWARD, (1870-1948) - a U.S. Representative from Indiana; born in Mount Vernon, Posey County, Ind., March 9, 1870; attended the public schools and the Evansville Commercial College, with which he was associated as teacher, principal, and owner from 1888 to 1904; retired from school work and engaged in the insurance business at Evansville, Ind.; deputy auditor of Vanderburg County, Ind., 1910-1912; clerk of the circuit court of Vanderburg County 1912-1920; unsuccessful candidate for election in 1920 to the Sixtyseventh Congress; elected as a Democrat to the Sixty-eighth Congress (March 4, 1923-March 3, 1925); unsuccessful candidate for reelection in 1924 to the Sixty-ninth Congress; engaged in banking and was later employed by the Chrysler Corp.; died in Evansville, Ind., September 29, 1948; interment in Oak Hill Cemetery.

WISE, ROBERT, (1914-   ) - director, film editor, was born in Winchester, Indiana on September 10, 1914.

He attended Franklin College for a time and then had to quit for financial reasons. His brother was employed at RKO Studios and Wise was hired there as an assistant editor in 1933. Six years later, he was promoted to the position of film editor. In the early 1940's, he edited some major feature films that included *Citizen Kane* and *The Magnificent Ambersons.*

In 1944, Wise was handed his first directing job on *Curse of the Cat People*, after the original director didn't finish the film on time. His first directorial attempt was so impressive that he was assigned to direct other RKO features.

In 1959, he became an independent producer/director for the Mirisch Corporation and four years later, worked in the same capacity for various major studios.

Robert Wise has directed a number of distinguished movies in his career, including: *The Body Snatchers*, in 1945; *The Day the Earth Stood Still*, in 1951; *Somebody Up There Likes Me*, in 1956 and *I Want To Live*, in 1958.

He co-directed the legendary musical, *West Side Story*, for which he and his directing partner, Jerome Robbins, received the Academy Award in 1961. In 1965, he received a Director's Guild of America Award, as well as a second Best Direction Oscar for the highly successful musical, *The Sound of Music*.

Wise also directed, *The Sand Pebbles*, in 1968, *Audrey Rose*, in 1977 and *Star Trek: The Motion Picture*, in 1979.

In addition to serving as predident of the Motion Picture Arts and Sciences from 1984-1987, following the terms as vice- president and first vice-president, Wise sits on the board of trustees of the American Film Institute and chairs its Center for advanced film Studies.

WOLFE, SIMEON KALFIUS, (1824-1888) - a U.S. Representative from Indiana; born near Georgetown, Floyd County, Ind., February 14, 1824; attended Floyd County schools, and was graduated from the law department of the University of Indiana at Bloomington in 1850; was admitted to the bar in 1851 and commenced practice in Corydon, Harrison County, Ind.; edited and published the Corydon Democrat from 1857 to 1865; member of the State senate 1860-1864; delegate to the Democratic National Conventions at Charleston and Baltimore in 1860; moved to New Albany in 1870 and continued the practice of law; elected as a Democrat to the Forty-third Congress (March 4, 1873-March 3, 1875); was not a candidate for renomination in 1874; resumed the practice of law; judge of the Floyd and Clark circuit court 1880-1884; died in New Albany, Floyd County, Ind., November 18, 1888; interment in Fairview Cemetery.

WOOD, THOMAS JEFFERSON, (1844-1908) - a U.S. Representative from Indiana; born in Athens County, Ohio, September 30, 1844; moved with his parents to Vigo County, Ind., in 1853; attended the common schools; taught school two years; studied law in Terre Haute, Ind., and was graduated from the law department of the University of Michigan at Ann Arbor in 1867; moved to Crown Point, Lake County, Ind., in November 1867 and practiced law; corporation treasurer 1870-1872; prosecuting attorney of Lake County 1872-1876; member of the State senate 1878-1882; elected as a Democrat to the Forty-eighth Congress (March 4, 1883-March 3, 1885); unsuccessful candidate for reelection; resumed the practice of law; died in Crown Point, Ind., October 13, 1908; interment in Maplewood Cemetery.

WOOD, WILLIAM ROBERT, (1861-1933) - a U.S. Representative from Indiana; born in Oxford, Benton County, Ind., on January 5, 1861; attended the public schools of Oxford and was graduated from the law department of the University of Michigan at, Ann Arbor in 1882; was admitted to the bar the same year and commenced practice in LaFayette, Tippecanoe County; prosecuting attorney of Tippecanoe County 1890-1894; member of the State senate 1896-1914, and served as president pro tempore 1899-1907; Republican floor leader of the State senate for four sessions; delegate to the Republican National Conventions in 1912, 1916, 1920, and 1924; chairman of the Republican National congressional committee 1920-1933; elected as a Republican to the Sixty-fourth and to the eight succeeding Congresses (March 4, 1915-March 3, 1933); chairman, Committee on Appropriations (Seventy-first Congress); unsuccessful candidate for reelection in 1932 to the Seventy-third Congress; died while York City March 7, 1933; interment in tery, LaFayette, Ind.

WOODEN, JOHN, (1910-   ) - basketball player, coach was born in Martinsville, Indiana on October 14, 1910.

Basketball was a natural for the tall, athletic Wooden, and after he helped his high school team win the state title in 1927, he went on to Purdue University and made All-American for three years straight. As the captain of his team, during his last two years at Purdue, he led them to two Big Ten titles as well as the National Collegiate championship for 1932. He also won the Player of the Year Award.

He began his coaching career at a high school in Kentucky and then went into the Navy for three years. After his discharge, he was the athletic director of Indiana State for two years. In 1948, he got the position of head coach at UCLA and spurred the Bruins on to numerous victories and record-breaking statistics.

The UCLA Bruins were the NCAA champions in 1964 and 1965. Then beginning in 1967, they continued to win the NCAA title straight through until 1973, when during that year, they set a new record of 61 consecutive game wins. Because of his illustrious career, he was inducted into the Basketball Hall of Fame. Wooden's last game before retirement was that in which UCLA won its tenth NCAA title.

Wooden married in 1932 and had two children. In 1964, he was named California's Father of the Year, and in 1969, he had a street named after him in his home town of Martinsville.

WORLEY, JO ANNE, (1937-   ) - actress, singer, was born in Lowell, Indiana on September 6, 1937.

She attended Midwestern University from 1955 to 1957 and Los Angeles City College from 1957 to 1958.

Beginning in 1958, Worley studied theatre at the Pasadena Playhouse and also studied voice and drama. Her first professional stage role was as the "Talking Lady" in the revue, *Laff Capades of 1959.* She then toured with the *Billy Barnes Revue* until 1961.

During the 1960's she appeared in stock plays such as *Gentlemen Prefer Blondes, Naughty Marietta* and *The Student Prince.* She was also the understudy for Kaye Ballard in *Carnival!* and Carol Channing in *Hello Dolly!.*

In 1968, she appeared as a regular on Rowan and Martin's Laugh-In which ran through 1970. She was also a regular on the *Las Vegas Show* series in 1966 and made guest appearances on the *Dobie Gillis* show and *This is Tom Jones.* She did one of her few serious roles in the television movie, *The Feminist and the Fuzz.*

She continues to play the dinner theatre circuit, sometimes with her husband, Roger Perry, who she married in 1975.

WRIGHT, JOSEPH A., (1810-1867) - governor of Indiana (1849- 1857), was born on April 17, 1810 in Washington, Pennsylvania, the son of John and Rachel (Seaman) Wright. While he was still a child, his family moved to Bloomington, Indiana. Wright received his education at Indiana Seminary, studied law, and passed the bar in 1829. He practiced his profession in Rockville until 1833 when he was elected to the Indiana House of Representatives. In 1836, he was reelected. He served a term in the State Senate, and then in the U.S. Congress from 1843 to 1845.

The Democrats nominated Wright for governor of Indiana in 1849 and he was elected, becoming (due to changes in the State constitution) the first Indiana governor chosen for a four year term. During his administration the State formally adopted the new constitution. Strides were made in education: the first State Board of Education was established, and Indiana cities began to collect taxes for educational purposes. In 1851, Indiana had its first State Fair, and in 1852 a State Board of Agriculture was formed, with Wright as its president.

Governor Wright left office in 1857 and went to Prussia as U.S. minister until 1862, at which time he returned to Washington for an appointment to the U.S. Senate. He served for one year. In 1863 he was named commissioner of the Hamburg Exposition. Two years later, he went back to Prussia as U.S. minister and remained at that post until his death on March 11, 1867. Joseph Wright was married three times and was the father of four children.

WRIGHT, WILBUR, (1867 - 1912) -was an engineer and inventor who, together with his younger brother Orville, built the world's first successful powered airplane.

Wright, born in Millville, Indiana on April 16, 1867, was the third of five surviving children of Milton Wright, a bishop of the United Brethren in Christ church. As young boys, Wilbur and Orville (b. August 19, 1871, in Dayton, Ohio) earned money by selling homecrafted mechanical toys. They also published the *West Side News*, a weekly newspaper edited by Wilbur and printed on a press of Orville's design. About 1892 they opened the Wright Cycle Company where they sold, repaired, and later manufactured bicycles.

The written works and subsequent death in 1896 of the German aeronaut, Gustav Lilienthal, inspired the brothers to begin experimenting in the area of aeronautics. In 1899, Wilbur built and tested the first product of their efforts - a biplane kite with a wing spread of five feet and three-axis control. The results of this and similar experiments made it possible for Wilbur and Orville to construct a much-improved glider, which they tested in September 1900 at Kill Devil Hills near Kitty Hawk, North Carolina. In 1902 and 1903, they made nearly 1,000 manned glider flights at Kitty Hawk. This eventually led to the development of a glider with a complete system of control, improved wing design, and greater stability. In 1903, a four- cylinder, twelve horsepower motor was mounted on one such glider and tested at Kitty Hawk by Wilbur and Orville on December 17 of that year. The world's first powered flight was made by Orville, who remained in flight for 12 seconds. The fourth and final flight was made by Wilbur, who remained in flight for 59 seconds and covered 852 feet. An improved model was flown on October 5, 1905, at Huffman Field in Dayton, covering a total of 24 miles, and on May 22, 1906, Wilbur and Orville received a patent for the world's first airplane.

European governments were the first to show interest in the Wright's invention. Consequently, Wilbur spent part of 1908 and 1909 making demonstration flights in England, France, and Italy.

The U.S. Army awarded them a contract for the world's first military plane in 1909, and The Wright Company was organized to commercially manufacture the Wright airplane. The brothers were occupied in improving their planes and training pilots to fly them when Wilbur contracted typhoid fever and died in Dayton on
May 30, 1912.

Y

YNUM, WILLIAM DALLAS, (1846-1927) - a U. S. Representative from Indiana; born near Newberry, Greene County, Indiana, June 26, 1846; attended the country schools, and was graduated from the University of Indiana at Bloomington in 1869; studied law; was admitted to the bar in 1872 and commenced practice in Washington, Indiana; served as the first city clerk; city attorney of Washington, Indiana, 1871-1875; mayor of Washington, Indiana, 1875-1879; presidential elector on the Democratic ticket of Tilden and Hendricks in 1876; moved from Daviess County to Indianapolis in 1880; member of the State house of representatives 1881-1885, and served as speaker in 1885; elected as a Democrat to the Forty-ninth and to the four succeeding Congresses (March 4, 1885-March 3, 1895); unsuccessful candidate for reelection in 1894 to the Fifty-fourth Congress; served for some time as whip of the Democratic minority; was active in the organization of the National (Gold-Standard) Democratic Party in 1896, and was chairman of its national committee 1896-1898; settled in Washington, D.C.; appointed by President McKinley in 1900 a member of the commission to codify the United States criminal laws and served until 1906; member of the board of trustees of the Indiana State School for the Blind 1917-1927; retired from the practice of law; died in Indianapolis, Indiana, October 21, 1927.

Z

ZION, ROGER HERSCHEL, (1921-   ) - a U.S. Representative from Indiana; born in Escanaba, Delta County, Mich., September 17, 1921; attended public schools in Evansville, Ind., and Milwaukee, Wis.; B.A., University of Wisconsin, Madison, Wis., 1943; attended Harvard Graduate

School of Business Administra tion, 1944-1945; served in the United States Navy, 1943- 1946, in the Asiatic-Pacific area and was discharged a lieutenant; became associated with Mead, Johnson & Co., eventually becoming director of training and professional relations, 1946-1965; elected as a Republican to the Ninetieth and to the three succeeding Congresses (January 3, 1967-January 3, 1975); unsuccessful candidate for reelection in 1974 to the Ninety-fourth Congress; president, Resources Development Inc., Washington, D.C.; is a resident of Washington, D.C.

*   *   *